THE SEX LIVES
of Famous Lesbians

THE SEX LIVES
of Famous Lesbians

Nigel Cawthorne

PRION

First published in Great Britain in 2005 by

Prion
an imprint of the
Carlton Publishing Group
20 Mortimer Street
London W1T 3JW

Typeset by e-type
Printed in Great Britain by Mackays

The publishers would like to thank the following sources for their kind
permission to reproduce the pictures in this book. The page numbers for
each of the photographs are listed below, giving the page on which they
appear in the plate section and any location indicator (t-top, b-bottom, l-
left, r-right):

Corbis Images: Bettmann: 1tl, 5, 7; /E. O. Hoppe: 2br; /Hulton-Deutsch
Collection: 2tl; /Mimmo Jodice: 1br. **Getty Images:** Fox Photos: 3;
/Frank Driggs Collection: 4; /John Kobal Foundation: 8.

Contents

Introduction

I t has to be said that, down the ages, lesbianism has never been taken very seriously. Men thought it would go away if they ignored it. True, under Jewish law, the theoretical punishment for an act of lesbianism is flogging. The usual forfeit, however, is shunning, and that is not nearly so exciting.

In the eyes of the Catholic Church, sex between women was both a sin *and* a crime – and yet there are no lesbian circles to be found in Dante's *Inferno* or *Purgatorio*. Sex between women has largely gone unpunished in the Christian world over the centuries, even though the official punishments – the threats, anyway – were terribly severe. They included beating, flogging, banishment to the galleys, the loss of a limb – one limb per encounter – and burning at the stake. The worst punishments were reserved for those who "introduced instruments into the belly of another", though in medieval London women who dressed as men were often paraded through the streets and publicly shamed.

While many thousands of men were tried and condemned to death for homosexual acts over the centuries, just a mere handful of women suffered that fate. One Italian girl was hanged in 1580 for having had a lesbian affair, and two Spanish nuns were burned at the stake for "using material instruments" for sexual purposes. German law records only two trials for lesbian offences – one in 1477 and the other in 1721 – and Switzerland only one, in 1568.

Details of the "crime" were not usually read aloud in case women, with their notoriously weak natures, might get ideas and experiment with their girlfriends. It was thought that a single active "fricative" could turn the whole community of women into lesbians. The 16th-century French courtier and scandalmonger, Abbé Brantome, believed that the fashion had been brought to the French court by an Italian "lady of quality". The good ladies of France had been at it for some time, however. As far back as the 12th century, Etienne de Fougère wrote of French society: "The ladies there have discovered a sport/ Where two little sows make a single one ... / The one stretches back and the other squirms/ The one acts the cock and the other the hen ..."

In Europe, even as late as the 19th century, most legal authorities assumed that the physiology of women prevented real sexual relations between them. It was thought that feminine acts seemed best ignored. However, men in some circles considered that it was perfectly acceptable for their wives to seek satisfaction through the "company" of other women.

At the turn of the 19th century, when lesbianism was all the rage in Paris, the French writer Sylvain Bonmariage* said: "I maintain that two women joined in a fondness for the embrace of Gomorrah cannot be compared to a pair of normal lovers. Their union is episodic, temporary, passing and, in most cases, need not necessarily exclude the man's participation." Wishful thinking perhaps, but you don't see Guy Ritchie getting upset when Madonna snogs Britney on global television. I bet he could not wait to get her home afterwards.

Men only got serious about lesbians – and seriously worried – when their cage was rattled by the feminist movement, led by a series of prominent lesbians. Mary Wollstonecraft, author of *A Vindication of the Rights of Women* in 1792, had a passionate affair with the delightfully named Fanny Blood. American suffragist pioneer and temperance campaigner, Susan B. Anthony, also supped at the well of Sappho, along with Elizabeth Cady Stanton and Amelia Bloomer – another terrific name. In the Women's Liberation movement of the 1960s and '70s, Kate Millett and Rita Mae Brown – leaders of America's National Organisation of Women – were militant about their lesbianism.

Lesbians have come up in other books in my *Sex Lives...* series. You will find Queen Anne* and Queen Mary* – of

William* and Mary fame – in *Sex Lives of the Kings and Queens of England*. Similarly, Greta Garbo* and Marlene Dietrich* get the full treatment in *Sex Lives of the Hollywood Goddesses*. They are having another bite of the cherry, so to speak, here in the chapter on their mutual lover, Hollywood screenwriter Mercedes de Acosta*. And I am holding back a full exposition of the sex life of Queen Christina of Sweden – known in her day as the "Queen of Sodom" – in the hope that I write *Sex Lives of the Crowned Heads of Europe*. If you want me to write that book, or if you have any other ideas for new titles you want to see in my *Sex Lives* … series, email them to me via my website at www.nigel-cawthorne.com and I will see what we can do. And, as there are more lesbians than I could possibly cover in one book, don't hesitate to contact me if you want *The Sex Lives of Famous Lesbians 2, 3, 4, 5 …*

By now, you will have noticed the annoying little asterisks that are dotted throughout the text above. This is part of a new feature that I trust we have now perfected in the *Sex Lives…* series. It is the "daisy chain". The asterisk indicates that the figure mentioned appears in another of the *Sex Lives…* books, or in another chapter of this book. At the back of this volume you will find the "Daisy Chain" section that lists, in alphabetical order, all the people starred, giving details of all the other *Sex Lives…* books that they have appeared in. Back in the 1960s, Truman Capote* developed a game called "International Daisy Chain". The idea was to link any two prominent figures via an interlocking chain of lovers. The player who comes up with the least lovers wins (unlike in real life). This list is designed to help you play the game at home.

Capote* used to say that the Hollywood screenwriter Mercedes de Acosta* was the best card you could hold, claiming: "You could get to anyone – from Pope John XXIII* to John F. Kennedy* – in one move."

As luck would have it, there's a chapter on Mercedes de Acosta* right here in *The Sex Lives of Famous Lesbians*. Read it and you will find out how right he was.

As well as being a turn-on, like the other books in the *Sex Lives…* series, *The Sex Lives of Famous Lesbians* is a mixture of the tragic, the excessive, the absurd and the downright comic. These books, I hope, give a genuine insight into the character of the people who have shaped our history and culture, and, perhaps, they might even shed a little light on the human condition.

So now here you have it. All the lesbians you can eat …

1 Sappho of Lesbos

Well, we all know who started it – Sappho of Lesbos, she's the girl. She was born around 612 BC on the island of Lesbos, just off the Turkish coast, possibly in the city of Eressos or maybe Mytilene, and was probably banished for a while to Sicily, along with the other aristocrats on the island, for plotting against the tyrant Pittacus of Mytilene. She was married to a wealthy merchant from the island of Andros, called Cercolas, and had at least one daughter, called Cleis. Interestingly, Andros means the city of men while Cercolas derives from *kerkos*, the Greek for penis. She married a bit of a prick, then. Even so, she was not well satisfied by her husband and took two male poets as her lovers. Then she leapt to her death from the White Rock of Leucas out of love for the handsome ferryman Phaon. This is the same rock that Aphrodite, the goddess of love, was supposed to have leapt from on account of her love for the beautiful Adonis. So Sappho hardly sounds dykie at all.

However, it is also known that she ran a school for girls that taught poetry, music, singing and dance. In Sparta, they had already developed an all-girl version of pederasty, where a woman teacher took on a young girl as her pupil in exchange for sexual favours – a practice that goes on in girls' schools to this very day. The Greek writer Plutarch writes: "In Sparta, even honest married women fell in love with young girls" – possibly because their men were always off fighting and Sparta's fighting men were expected to get it on with one another to build their *esprit de corps*.

Ancient Greeks took their gymnastics seriously and did it, as the word implies, nude – gymn, or rather *gymo* or *gymos*, which in Greek means naked. In Sparta, the boys and girls did gymnastics together, which must have been fun. In the rest of Greece, the sexes were segregated. Anyway in Sappho's gym classes, she would have had the delightful sight of several handfuls of naked young women doing handstands and, no doubt, she would have been able to take her pick.

Sappho was famous at the time for her poetry, much of which concerns her relationships with other women – although her brother Charaxus was also the subject of some of her poems. At the time, women from good families would form informal associations that were given to relaxation and pleasure. Men would not be allowed and a lot of drinking and a certain amount of nudity and intimacy would occur. Sappho's work dealt with the passions and jealousies that flourished in this heated atmosphere and women would come from all over Greece to attend her readings.

What we know of her sexuality comes from the fragments of her poetry that are extant. She famously wrote a "Hymn to Aphrodite", although this may be from a longer piece written for a wedding. Even so, it was traditional at wedding ceremonies to have nude girl dancers, which must have distracted the best man – not to mention Sappho herself. She also writes of flower petals, shady bowers, luscious fruits and opening rosebuds, all of which may be sexual images. However, there is only one direct reference to physical love in her poems. It occurs when she is bidding farewell to a female friend and remembering the pleasures that they shared. The fragment reads:

> For many wreaths of violets
> Of roses and of crocuses
> … you wove around yourself by my side …
> and on a bed, soft and tender
> … you satisfied your desire …

She also wrote paeans of praise to the beauty of her pupils. Of Gyrinna and Mnasidika, she writes:

> Though delicately soft Gyrinna be
> Yet Mnasidika more fair than she

To the beloved Gongyla, she says:

> I bid you hither come, and God you bless
> Sweet Gongyla, put on your milk-white dress.
>   Oh God, what desire in your beauty lies.

Shouldn't that be "take off your milk-white dress"? She seems to have got a good deal further with another woman called Atthis. She writes:

> Love's palsy yet again my limbs doth wring
>   That bitter-sweet resistless creeping thing.
> Atthis, all thought of me you now do hate,
>   And hover ever at Andromeda's gate.

That is undeniably Sapphic. Andromeda was the beautiful daughter of King Cepheus and it is not hard to imagine where her gate might be. She does not hover there long, however, as she goes on to say:

> Love again hath fluttered my heart, as a squall
> That down from the hills on the oaks doth fall.

How was it for you? She's soon at it again, though.

> Your lovely laugh: that sight does make
> The heart within my bosom shake.
> When I but glance at you, no word
> From my dumb lips is heard,
> My tongue is tied, a subtle flame
> Leaps in the moment o'er frame,
> Sweat dews my brow, quick tremors pass
>   Through every limb, more wan than grass
> I blanch, and frenzied, near to death,
>   I gasp away, lost for breath.

Are we talking multiple orgasms here or what? Sadly, the beautiful Atthis leaves and moves to Lydia, on the mainland of Anatolia – now in Turkey – where, according to Sappho: "Among the women of Lydia she shines, as the moon surpasses the stars in brightness when it rises over the sea." And she misses her, writing: "And often longing will fill your heart, when you think of the sweet voice of Atthis."

It is not only her heart that is empty, it's also her bed. She moans:

> The moon and Pleiades have set, midnight is nigh,
> The time is passing, passing, yet alone I lie.

The Pleiades, as well as being a prominent cluster of stars whose setting marks the end of summer, were the seven daughters of Atlas. So maybe Sappho had some company earlier.

The earliest reference to girl-on-girl action on Lesbos comes from a disputed fragment of poetry, thought to be by sixth century BC poet Anacreon, which talks of a tribade, or a female homosexual, from the island. Lesbos was also famed for its nude beauty contests, which must have beaten the pants off Miss World. At the time, though, the island of Lesbos did not have any gay connotations. In fact, in Classical Greek, the verb "to lesbianise" means to perform fellatio on a fella. I can hear you gagging. Lesbos did, however, have a bit of a reputation, like Corinth, for its free-and-easy sexual ways. This was a time when most women possessed an *olisbos*, or a leather dildo. As Greeks did not make any hard-and-fast distinction between heterosexual behaviour and homosexual behaviour, it is more than likely that the girls got it on.

However, along came Christianity and with it a determination to put a stop to this sort of thing. The first-century Greek Christian scholar, Tatian, denounced Sappho as a "nymphomaniac fornicator who even writes poems about her own debauchery".

It is the second-century Greek writer Lucian, however, who gives the island of Lesbos its enduring reputation.

"They do say that there are women ... in Lesbos, of masculine appearance, who refuse to have sex with men but to be with women as if they were men themselves," he wrote.

In his *Dialogues of Prostitutes*, he describes a hot lesbian scene. Leaina, a guitar player, tells her friend Klonarion what happened in the house of Megilla, a rich prostitute from Lesbos, where Megilla and her female friend Demonassa the Corinthian had asked her to play.

> After a while they got drunk and Megilla said to me: "It's time for bed, Leaina, and since it's late, stay here and sleep with us. We'll put you in the middle." ... At the beginning they kissed me like men, not only on the lips but inside the mouth too, and rubbed my breasts. Demonassa even bit me between her kisses ... After a while, Megilla, flushed, pulled off the wig she was wearing – which did not show at all – and appeared close-cropped, like an athlete. I got scared, but she said: "Have you seen, Leaina, such a beautiful boy before?"
>
> "But, Megilla, I don't see a boy here," I said.
>
> "Don't call me Megilla," she said. "I am Megillos and I have married Demonassa, who is my wife."
>
> "So, Megillos, you are a man and you have been hiding it? But do you have what men have to do to Demonassa what men do?"
>
> "No, Leaina, I don't have it, and I don't need it. I can do the job in a much better way, as you will find out."
>
> "Are you a hermaphrodite then? One of those who has both?" I asked ...
>
> "No, Leaina," she replied. "I was born like any woman, but my character and desires are like a man's ... Come closer and you will see."
>
> And I let her, dear Klonarion ... But don't ask me to tell you more as it is so obscene that, by Aphrodite, I can't go on ...

Boo. Just when it was getting interesting. This, though, is typical of the classical attitude to female sexuality. In both Ancient Greece and Rome, the central icon of art was the male nude, shown in all its glory – genitals, pubes and all. In contrast, the female nude is always shown in the pudic pose – the pose of shame – with one arm covering the breast and the other hand over the pubic area.

Now next time you are in a museum, if you peep down under the lower hand – discreetly now – you will see that the pubic area is a featureless mound. No pubic hair, no cleft, nothing. These things were not shown as female sexuality was considered wild, dangerous and untamable. All this was changed in the Renaissance by Leonardo da Vinci*, who was the first to show openly exposed breasts, female pubic hair, the lot and who, in the process, made the female nude the central icon of Western art. Thanks, Leonardo, you're a pal.

Whichever way you read her sexuality, Sappho was rated as a great poet in the ancient world. Plato named her the tenth Muse and she influenced the Latin poets Catullus and Ovid. However, it was Maximus of Tyre, a pagan philosopher in the second century, who drew the parallel between her relationship with her female pupils and the pederastic relationships between the philosopher Socrates and his beautiful boys.

"What then is the passion of the Lesbian songstress but the love-technique of Socrates?" he writes. "For both of them seem to me to have the same idea of love, the former the love of girls, the latter of youths."

Some lit crit.

He then went on to list Socrates' catamites and compared them to Sappho's own baby belles.

Many of Sappho's poems survived until the Middle Ages, when most were lost or destroyed. As time went by, references to her by other writers were hardly very flattering. Marie Antoinette, for example, was accused of being "at the head of a set of monsters called by each other sapphists, who boast her as a example". Her name had become code among women who liked other women. Then, in the 19th century, *Les Chansons de Bilitis* – "The Songs of Bilitis" – a collection of erotic Sapphic love poems, was published by Pierre Louÿs*, who claimed that he had translated it from a manuscript written by one of Sappho's contemporaries on Lesbos whose name, he said, was Bilitis.

"This little book of ancient love is respectfully dedicated to the young women of a future society," wrote Louÿs in the preface.

It was discovered to be a hoax. Louÿs had made the whole thing up. By then, though, Lesbos had become firmly fixed as the home of Sapphic love and, in 1890, the word "lesbian" entered the language. Despite being unmasked, Louÿs' hoax was far more successful than he could have hoped and young women of a future society took his words to heart. In 1955, the first major American organisation for lesbians was founded in San Francisco. It called itself the "Daughters of Bilitis".

2 Les Beaux Arts

The French animal painter Rosa Bonheur was born in 1822, the daughter of an artist and socialist who preached the then-radical doctrine of sexual equality. Living above a public baths in Paris, Rosa became obsessed with the butcher's shop opposite and was often found stroking its shop sign – the carved figure of a boar.

Despite her father's oft-expressed feminist views, it was Rosa's mother who bore the brunt of their poverty. She worked herself to death. Before she died she managed to put pen to paper and wrote: "I don't know what Rosalie will be, but I have the conviction that she will be no ordinary woman."

And no ordinary woman was she. Rosalie went to boarding school but was expelled after an incident in the headmistress's rose-garden. At the age of 14, she took on the burdens of being a housewife, as mother to her younger siblings and went to work in her father's studio. Then she enrolled at the Louvre to study painting and sculpting. There – because of her masculine dress – she was know as "the Little Hussar". By 16 years of age, she was spending most nights in the slaughterhouse studying carcasses.

"You must know what is going on under the skin," she said. "Otherwise your animals will look like a rat rather than a tiger."

And it was not just the dead ones that she was interested in. The family apartment began to fill up with animals, including a sheep and numerous birds. When she was 19 years old, the family moved to a bigger place, along with a goat and a collection of chickens, rabbits, ducks, finches and quails – all adding to her burdens as a housewife.

The following year, her father remarried and added a vivacious young widow to the menagerie. By this time, Rosa was having a relationship with Nathalie Micas, the daughter of the woman who had sold animals' skins to Rosa's mother, and she became a regular guest in the Micas household.

In 1849, she received a government commission to paint *Ploughing in the Nivernais* for the salon. In the painting, she said she intended to "celebrate with my brush the art of tracing the furrows from which comes the bread that nourishes all humanity". Hmmm. To prepare for this, she read the radical cross-dresser Lucie Dudevant's studies of peasant life. Dudevant wrote novels under the name Georges Sand*.

When Rosa was asked whether she thought Sand was "immoral", she said: "I don't think so. I venerate Madame Sand and have only one reproach to make against her. She was too womanly, too kind and dropped the treasures of her noble heart and the pearls of her soul on the dung-heap, where cocks found the pearls and swallowed them without being able to digest them."

So Georges Sand was heterosexual? You have a problem with that, Rosa? Oh, you do.

Following the death of her father, Rosa took over his position as head of the government's School of Drawing for Young Girls. She also moved in with Nathalie Micas. While Rosa's family disapproved, Nathalie's were happy with the match and, when the Micas *père* lay dying, he summoned the couple to his deathbed to give his blessing to the union and urged them to stay together.

Asked publicly about their relationship, Rosa said: "My private life's nobody's concern."

Sorry we asked, Rosa.

On other occasions she was more forthcoming, once remarking: "I have only God to thank for the protection He has always granted me by giving me a guardian angel in my friend."

Rosa's goddaughter, Rosa Mathieu, said: "Nathalie Micas literally worshipped Rosa Bonheur."

On her knees, I trust.

And a close friend wrote: "Nathalie made herself small, ungrudgingly, so that Rosa could become much greater."

I think I am getting the picture here.

Nathalie also painted – kitsch pictures of kittens playing with balls of wool and the like – in stark contrast to the muscular realism of Rosa's paintings, giving them the classic butch-*femme* split at work as well as play. However, in an uncharacteristically butch moment, Nathalie invented a revolutionary new brake for express trains, perhaps inspired by the relentless pounding Rosa was giving her.

At home, Rosa wore men's clothes to paint. She also wore men's clothes when she was out – for practical purposes, she insisted – when mixing in the all-male world of the slaughterhouse and the horse market. She passed effortlessly as a man and obtained a special permit – *une permission de travestissement* – that allowed her to wear male clothes, except at "spectacles, balls or other public meeting places". These permits, which had to be renewed every six months, were given "for reasons of health" and were countersigned by her doctor.

During the Franco-Prussian War, she seized the opportunity to don an army uniform and train with the men. Of course, she always insisted that she did this not for fun, but to facilitate her work. This was not entirely true. When painter Paul Chardin visited her studio, he found her dismounting from a horse in a "frock-coat, loose grey trousers with understraps, boots with spurs, and a queer hat … A masculine costume that was really grotesque".

Wearing breeches on a sketching trip near Nice in later life, she was amused to see how puzzled people were by her appearance.

"They wonder which sex I belong to," she told her sister. "The ladies especially lose themselves in conjectures about 'the little old man who looks so lively'. The men seem to conclude: 'Oh, he is some aged singer from St Peter's in Rome who has turned to painting in his declining years to console himself for some misfortune.' And shake their beards triumphantly."

Her first biographer, Eugène de Mirecourt, recorded that she once turned up at the opera in drag. In addition he said: "She also rides every morning on a broomstick, flying off up the chimney like a witch, especially going out on a Saturday night, which is the hobgoblins' frightful hour of orgies."

On the few formal occasions that she could be persuaded to dress as a woman, it caused almost as much trouble. She was once arrested in the street by a policeman who suspected her of being a man in drag. Outraged, she hit him so hard that he was convinced it was true. How her true sex was established is not recorded, but, rest assured, it was the policeman who would have received a dressing down the next day in court.

Nathalie was the one who liked dressing up. Claiming Spanish descent, she dressed in red and black, with hats sporting ostentatious plumes.

"Sometimes I think Nathalie would have made a fine wife for one of the court jesters of the olden times," said Rosa.

She had little time for men. An androphobe, when she had trouble with dealers, she would tell them to go home to their mothers and "mend stockings or make *petit point*". When a man saw her out riding with a male friend and remarked the friend's wife should be worried, she said: "If you only knew how little I cared for your sex, you wouldn't get such queer ideas into your head. The fact is, by way of males, I only like the bulls I paint."

It was clear that no man could compete. Nor should any wife worry. The son of the sculptor David d'Angers remembered seeing her on horseback and said: "She was in masculine dress. Her trousers had bootstraps, the last pair of the kind I remember seeing. Her cap was the queerest part of the odd get-up. It reminds me of those sometimes worn by the lady bicyclists of the present day. She was naturally short, and the cut of her jacket made her look still shorter in the saddle. The ensemble of the costume was not happy."

But then he was a man. What do they know?

On a visit to Scotland, she toned it down. A local said: "Her dress was a compromise between that of a woman and a man; she wore her hair in a brown curly crop and she rode horseback astride, to the horror of kirk-going folk ..."

Astride a horse! Well, she was a well-known lover of animals.

"To be loved by wild animals, you must love them," she once said.

Marriage was an entirely bad thing in her eyes, condemning a woman to the life of a "subaltern".

Her sister Juliette's conventional life horrified her. "She has too much of the motherly instinct for my taste," Rosa said. "I am afraid she will get more happiness out of having children than from an artistic career."

De Mirecourt said: "Having made up her mind not to contract marriage, Rosa Bonheur pitilessly turns away all suitors for her hand."

And she had offers. It is said that English master animal painter and confirmed bachelor Sir Edwin Landseer offered to become "Sir Edwin Bonheur". However, it seems that this proposal was a ruse by the Press to accompany Rosa's visit to England, as, when asked, she said: "I was never asked in marriage except on one occasion by an apothecary at whose shop I used to stuff my pockets with a provision of cocoa. We got tired of one another. The courtship lasted a week. An apothecary's cannula" – a small tube for insertion into a body cavity, according to *Webster's* – "did not command high respect."

I suspect that he would not even have commanded her respect if he had been a fireman, a roustabout or Monsieur Eiffel himself.

Rosa was only happy in a marriage where she was the man and commanding officer. Her paintings brought in enough money to head a household that comprised Nathalie, the Micas *mère*, the Micas children and a ménage of horses, donkeys, dogs, sheep, goats, monkeys, lapwings, hoopoes and the odd otter. It was a *ménage à nombreux*.

And she was publicly honoured. One day in 1864, the Empress Eugénie* dropped by unannounced to award her the Grand Cross of the Legion of Honour, only to find that Nathalie was taking a bath in the studio while Rosa worked. It was a good job that Nathalie had not been receiving the award. There would have been nowhere to pin it. Rosa Bonheur was the first woman to receive the Grand Cross of the Legion of Honour and Eugénie said that she "wished that the last act of my regency be dedicated to showing that in my eyes genius has no sex". In that case, it was a good job that it was not Rosa who was taking the bath.

Invited to Fontainebleau by Eugénie, she requested special permission not to wear *décolletage*, which was *de rigueur* at the time, and turned up in a velvet jacket buttoned to the neck while all the other ladies had their tits out.

Rosa and Nathalie had been together for 47 years when Nathalie died in June 1889. Nathalie, she said, was a woman "who I had loved more and more as we advanced in life ... Her loss broke my heart and it was a long time before I found any relief in my work."

She did find relief, though. Later that year Anna Klumpte turned up. After a visit from Buffalo Bill Cody, John Arbuckle, the president of the Royal Horse Association, dropped by bringing the young American painter Anna Klumpte as an interpreter. She quickly filled the hole left in Rosa's life.

One of Rosa's masculine traits, frequently commented on at the time, was her lifelong love of smoking – at a time when women did not indulge. One visitor to her studio said: "Even when she was as old as 75, I have seen her sitting up on the side of the table in a negligée position just like a young man, with a smoking cigarette in her hand. Her pretty foot would then slip conspicuously from under her trousers, which did not seem to displease her; for the truth is she was proud of her small feet and hands."

After ten years together, Rosa died of pneumonia, presumably exacerbated by smoking, leaving Anna her sole heir. Rosa was buried next to Nathalie in Père Lachaise Cemetery. Anna was also to write Rosa's "official" biography – that is, the one without the juicy bits.

"No man could write my biography," said Rosa.

True, we would all be wanting to know what went on under the sheets.

When Anna died, in 1945, she too was buried in Père Lachaise, next to Rosa and Nathalie. It was a *"mort-age à trois"*.

The three women's tomb bears the inscription: *"L'amitié, c'est l'affection divine,"* meaning, "Friendship is heavenly affection" – although *"amitié particulière"* is a euphemism for a lesbian relationship.

3 L'Amazone

The leading lesbian of her day, American poet Natalie Barney was known in Paris as *l'Amazone* after the Symbolist author Rémy Gourmont immortalised her in *Lettres à l'Amazone*. The Nobel Prize-winning Catholic writer François Mauriac called her "the Pope of Lesbos". She also set up the Académie des Femmes as a counterpart to the all-male Académie Française. She was one of nature's gynocrats.

Born in Dayton, Ohio, Natalie was the daughter of railroad magnate Albert Clifford Barney and whiskey heiress Alice Pike Barney, who was an accomplished artist and portrait painter. Mrs Barney was a natural bohemian. After her husband died, she took a series of lovers from among her male models, eventually marrying one of them. One of her admirers was Henry Morgan Stanley, who famously located Dr Livingstone on the shores of Lake Tanganyika in 1872. He named a stretch of the Congo River after her, calling it Lady Alice Rapids.

Natalie's older sister, Laura, followed in her mother's artistic footsteps. She sculpted a recumbent nude in concrete and put it on the lawn of the family home in Washington, DC. The Press claimed, falsely, that the nude was Natalie, but such was the stir that the police came and covered it with a tarpaulin.

Natalie herself had first begun to feel sexual stirrings at the age of ten. At first she would listen outside her mother's bedroom, but soon found that what she overheard was not to her taste. Instead, she turned her attention to her cousin, a dazzling blonde, who sometimes travelled with them on their Continental jaunts. Each night, her cousin would take the photograph of a young man out of her suitcase and smother it with kisses. Natalie would watch with a mixture of passion and jealousy. Then the two girls would get into bed together and snuggle up. Natalie's pretty cousin might marry the man in the photograph one day, but for now, at least, she was hers.

Natalie and her sister Laura were sent to the select boarding school Les Ruches – "The Beehives" – in Fontainebleau. The school later became notorious thanks to *Olivia*, the scandalous autobiography of Dorothy Strachey – sister of Lytton* – which lovingly describes her lesbian relationships there. Natalie could only have regretted not being in Dorothy's year. Her own recollections were of girls playing hockey rather than making love. However, it was at Les Ruches that she learned to love her own sex. She developed a crush on one of the older girls in the heated atmosphere of the school and called her "my little husband". This is presumably before "My Little Pony" was invented. That would have been entirely different. Though the crush was innocent enough, Natalie began writing poetry, celebrating the beauty of the other girl in a very – well – Greek kind of way.

There were other manifestations of the sexual heat that the school generated. During Natalie's stay, two older American girls caused a scandal by courting the attentions of two French cavalry officers. One night, one of the other girls mysteriously had all of her hair cut off.

When it was time for Natalie and Laura to leave Les Ruches and return to the United States, they begged their parents to engage their favourite schoolmistress as a governess. A German woman, she was all too eager to take up the position as her dearest friend was another schoolmistress who now lived in Washington.

Back in the United States, the mystery surrounding the pupil's missing hair was solved. One night the German governess came down the stairs in her nightdress. It was plain that she was sleepwalking. Wielding a pair of scissors, she proceeded to cut up the straw hats belonging to Mr Barney and a visiting friend that were hanging in the hall. Plainly she had to go and while arrangements were made for her to leave, a dog collar would be fastened around her ankle at night and she was chained to the bed to prevent any further sleepwalking.

Her replacement was a young Austrian girl who had fallen in love with a young nobleman, but who had been spurned by his family. As the girl tearfully related the tale, Natalie whispered sweet nothings in her ear and clutched the emotional young woman to her budding bosom. Soon the young woman was all smiles and had forgotten about her young nobleman. Natalie had stumbled on a salve that balmed a broken heart. She showed a similar knack in soothing the female models that posed for her mother, by gently caressing their body parts.

Out riding in Washington, she met Victoria Leiter – the future wife of Lord Curzon*, who became viceroy of India – and developed a mad crush on her. Victoria's beauty had a similar effect on Natalie's friend, Evalina – Eva – Palmer*. A pre-Raphaelite beauty, Eva initiated Natalie into the full-blown rites of sapphism and Natalie kept a lock of her hair – upper or lower, we don't know – into old age. They attended school together in New York, lived together in Paris and, for a period of 12 to 15 years, spent their summers together in Maine, living out a sapphist dream. A limited edition of Natalie Barney's *Album Secret* was published in Paris in 1894. This reproduces photographs of Natalie, Eva and friends cavorting naked in the field in Maine and skinny-dipping in Duck Brook and Bar Harbor. It has to be said that they are beautiful girls and that the photographs leave nothing to the imagination. The introduction said that they "metamorphosed the undergrowth of Duck Brook and the shores of Maine into the beaches of Lesbos". The *Album* also contains love letters and poems between the three girls, some of which are inflammatory. In the British Library, it is confided to the "Closed Case" where the library's magnificent collection of pornography is stored. It has to be perused in a special area where librarians can keep an eye on the reader and the book must not be left unattended on the desk. In future, I think that it would be a wise precaution if the library hosed down readers who had been handling "Closed Case" material.

The girls had a completely open relationship. Travelling to Paris that summer, Natalie seems to have had a shipboard romance with Leonora Howland, a married woman. Despite the presence of a chaperone, there are indications that Natalie misbehaved.

She went to Paris again in 1897, this time with her family. The Washington newspapers mention that the party included her fiancé William Morrow. No further reference is made to him. Natalie persuaded her parents to let her stay on in Paris when they returned to Washington. She was soon having a torrid affair with a married woman. This saved her life. One night she was with her lover when she should have been attending a charity bazaar where a fire broke out, killing numerous society women. When Natalie saw the sky reddened by the flames, she said it was glowing to celebrate her new love. However, the fire also brought with it the glare of publicity. The reason why she had not been burnt to a frazzle came to light and she was ordered home. For her family this turned out to be a mistake, as Natalie immediately performed in the Washington production of Victorien Sardou's risqué play *L'Etrangère*, delivering a passionate monologue about the prostitution of Mary Magdalene, and the family found itself on the verge of social ostracism.

Back in Paris the following year, Natalie went out riding in the Bois de Boulogne where she took pleasure in "exchanging long looks and half-smiles in passing" with other women. One day, she was out riding with a suitor when they came upon a line of open carriages, each carrying the most ravishing-looking women. Natalie was immediately smitten by a slim, androgynous creature who to her seemed more dazzling than the rest. Her companion pointed out that this was no great lady but the famous courtesan Liane de Pougy*. Knowing little of the world of the *grandes horizontales*, Natalie was even more intrigued. She began sending Liane flowers and begging for a rendezvous.

Liane was amused by Natalie's forwardness and decided to play a trick on her. She invited the young American to her house where, in a darkened boudoir, an elderly friend was reclining on the chaise-longue. Liane herself hid behind a screen.

Natalie arrived, dressed in the costume of a Florentine page-boy carrying armfuls of flowers. She knelt before the chaise-longue in humble supplication, but then heard twitters from behind the screen and realised that she had been duped. All was not lost, however. Liane then appeared from behind the screen in a white dress that was so sheer it was transparent. She was quite taken with the young American girl and decided to go for a ride in the Bois de Boulogne with her. First, though, she had to get dressed. Natalie watched in awe as Liane performed her toilette and changed her clothes. In her own literary autobiography *Souvenirs indiscrets*, she drew a veil over what happened next. Liane was not so discreet, however. An accomplished writer herself, she recorded the scene in her novel *Idylle saphique*. It created a sensation when it was published in 1901.

The courtesan in the novel is called Annhine de Lys and she is approached by a blonde American girl dressed as a Florentine page whose name is Emily Florence Temple – or Flossie for short, which is one of the pet names that Liane gave Natalie in real life. Colette* also used the name Flossie for a character based on Natalie Barney. In Liane's novel, Flossie first sees Annhine on the stage at the Folies Bergères, where Liane herself performed. She, of course, resists Flossie's blandishments. However, although she is only 20, Flossie is an accomplished seductress. Natalie was also an accomplished seductress by this time, particularly with otherwise straight women like Liane.

The morning after they meet, Flossie turns up at Annhine's home and is ushered into her bedroom, where she finds Annhine wearing a sheer, lacy nightgown sprawled seductively across an ornate bed that had once belonged to Madame de Pompadour, the mistress of Louis XV. The action then moves to Annhine's Louis XV-style bathroom, where Annhine removes the nightgown. Flossie throws herself to her knees and, in a passionate delirium, begins kissing and caressing Annhine's ankles, shins, knees, legs, thighs ... To escape her embraces, Annhine leaps into a perfumed bath. She then lets Flossie join her in the fragrant water – but only if she promises to behave. Afterwards, the two women take turns massaging each other, which turns into erotic love play ... And this is where Liane draws a veil. It is a technique she used to get the reader – and, presumably, Natalie – to come back for more. Natalie also wrote a fictionalised account of their affair. In it all the veils were off, but her publisher was too shocked to print it.

That evening, in *Idylle saphique*, Flossie lies at the feet of Annhine in her box at the theatre where Sarah Bernhardt* was playing the lead in *Hamlet* – the Bernhardt production was playing at the time Natalie and Liane were having an affair. Flossie also had a docile fiancé called Will – William Morrow, perhaps – a millionaire who she intends to marry so she can use his money to lavish on Annhine.

Flossie says she likes women because they are pretty, delicate, fragile things. She particularly liked the little flower, with its exquisite petals, that they have for a soul. She says that she was first aware of this at the age of eight when she watched her pretty cousin kiss the photograph of a man. In the novel, just as in life, her sexual initiation comes with a flaming red-haired girl called Eva.

In the book, Annhine is confronted by Flossie's former lover at a masked ball. She was a married woman named Jane, who stabs herself and expires at Annhine's feet. The courtesan then flees. She travels around the Iberian peninsula, having affairs with men which, after experiencing the delights of sapphic love with Flossie, are generally unsatisfactory. Returning to Paris, she resumes her affair with Flossie, contracts tuberculosis – as all good romantic heroines, especially courtesans, did back then – and dies while being nursed by Flossie, who was dressed as a nun.

In real life it was Liane who became the nun – but only after she had become a princess by marrying the Romanian Prince George Ghika and entering the highest realms of society. When her prince ran off with a younger woman, she consoled herself with a series of lesbian lovers. The couple were eventually reconciled. Then, when the prince died, Liane entered a convent under the apt name of Sister Mary Magdalene of the Repentance.

In real life, Liane's affair ended when Natalie's father caught her reading a passionate love letter from Liane and packed her off back to the United States. At this time she was also enjoying the attentions of male suitors and she got engaged no less than three times. One of her fiancés was Lord Alfred Douglas*, who she had met when he was on a foxhunting trip to the US. Natalie's father did not want the family's name to be mixed up with the Oscar Wilde* scandal, however, and broke it off. The courting of Douglas, who was exclusively gay, may have been a ploy to stop her father pressuring her into marriage, and even in stuffy Washington society she continued to write hot letters and passionate poems to any woman she fancied.

As she became more independent, Natalie spent as much time as she could in Paris. Under the Napoleonic Code, there was no law against homosexuality of either variety and Parisian life was untainted by the Puritanism of the English-speaking world. As a result, she could love whoever she liked. She began writing poetry in French, which was passionate, promiscuous and lesbian – and often directed toward a woman she aimed to seduce, or toward those who had already succumbed. These women are identified by their initials. In her first volume of verse, *Quelques Portraits-Sonnets de femmes*, published in 1900 when she was 24, the initials of some two dozen lovers appear. It is possible that two of them are Sarah Bernhardt* and Princess Troubetzkoy.

An American who had married into European royalty, Princess Troubetzkoy and her husband had been regular summer guests of the Barneys in Washington. She wrote poetry under her maiden name, Amélie Rives, along with controversial plays and books. When *Portraits* came out, one critic called Natalie the "new Amélie Rives". Another newspaper was blunter, headlining its review "Sappho Sings In Washington".

When Natalie's father read *Portraits*, he went to the printers, bought every single copy of the book and destroyed them, along with the plates. Fortunately, Natalie had a cache, which she gave out to friends. Some still survive to this day.

One of the poems – an erotic evocation of the bare-breasted goddess of the hunt (yes, *hunt*) Diana – is addressed to P.M.T. No, not pre-menstrual tension. P.M.T. were the initials of a young English girl named Pauline M. Tarn, who would later write poetry in French under the name Renée Vivien.

"Would Renée Vivien have found her way without me?" Natalie wrote in her memoir *Souvenirs indiscrets*. Natalie helped Renée find her way by introducing her to Sappho – both the poetry and the practice. Renée soon began to produce exquisitely crafted lesbian love poetry.

Around this time, Natalie also became acquainted with the French writer Pierre Louÿs*. She had already come across his novel *Aphrodite*, which described the life of a courtesan in ancient Alexandria and which had caused a sensation when it was published in Paris in 1896. Banned in the United States, Natalie got her hands on a copy and read it while sunbathing on one of her Sapphic summers in Maine. When she read *Les Chansons de Bilitis*, she sought him out and showed him the manuscript of the book she had written about her affair with Liane de Pougy. He offered to help her revise it for publication, but she turned down his generous offer as she was too busy writing Sapphic poetry set in Ancient Greece along the lines of *Les Chansons de Bilitis*, much of which seems to have been directed toward Renée Vivien.

Despite Natalie's claim to have helped her find her way, Pauline Tarn was no stranger to lesbian love when she met Natalie. At the age of 13, she had developed a deep passion for an American girl in Paris called Violet Shilleto. They lived together for three years until her parents brought her back to England where she was required as a debutante to be presented at court. Coming out – in the old-fashioned sense of the word – was not Pauline's thing, however. When she came of age, she escaped the marriage proposals and the stuffiness of English society and headed back to Paris, where she renewed her liaison with Violet Shilleto.

The Shilletos had been neighbours of the Barneys back in Ohio and Natalie had bumped into Violet one day in the Bois de Boulogne. When Violet heard that Natalie was now a poet, she proposed introducing her to Pauline and it was arranged that the girls should go to the theatre together. Just before they left for the show, a letter from Portugal arrived for Natalie from Liane de Pougy lamenting their lost love. Natalie was so preoccupied that Pauline made little impression on her, though she did note that the English girl was very pretty. Liane's letter had stirred up such passions in Natalie that she could concentrate neither on the play nor on the conversation afterward. However, Pauline then recited some of her poetry and Natalie forgot all about Liane. Pauline's poetry was so full of a morbid yearning for death that Natalie decided there and then that it was her job to incite a new desire for life in this talented girl.

The pretty, feminine, young Pauline was very much to Natalie's taste. Liane de Pougy said: "We loved long hair, pretty breasts, simper, charm and grace, not boyishness."

Natalie particularly abhorred female transvestites, both on political and aesthetic grounds. If men were so pathetic, why impersonate them? "Why try to resemble our enemies?" she said.

Natalie took Pauline ice-skating on their first date. Watching Pauline's slender figure gliding over the ice, Natalie was distracted by a number of professional beauties she had last seen in the company of Liane. This time, for once, it was Pauline who made the pace. One night soon after, she invited Natalie to her room, which was filled with white lilies – a flower she dedicated to Natalie. She had transformed her room into a chapel of love and the two supplicants knelt before one another all night – one at a time, I trust.

These devotions became a regular occurrence. After each assignation, Pauline bombarded Natalie with flowers. While Natalie was happy simply gratifying her senses, for Pauline, their love existed on a higher plane; it had moved into the realm of the imagination. When they moved in together, Pauline covered Natalie with exotic jewellery – anklets, bracelets, Lalique rings and a weird comb for her hair that was shaped like a dragon spewing pearls. Natalie was being put on a pedestal and Pauline was worshipping her from below.

It had the desired effect. The subject of Pauline's poetry turned from death to love. When she started to publish her poetry, she deliberately chose the pseudonym "Vivien" to symbolise her return to life. In fact, her first volume was published under the name "R. Vivien" and it was assumed that the author was a man addressing the poems to his mistress. When it was discovered that the poet was a woman, the book became an instant sensation. Fans sought her out. Jealous of her privacy, Renée got her old chaperone – a large woman with a huge wart on her beaky nose – to pose as the author. The fame went to the old lady's head and she married Renée's Classics teacher, a tall, bony, dishevelled man. Natalie thought that this was wonderful – such a hideous match would surely put all young women off heterosexual love.

Natalie and Renée loved dressing up and were photographed in costume, frequently swapping roles. Natalie wrote a poem to Renée, as Hamlet addressing Ophelia. Renée wrote a poem to Natalie, as Sappho* addressing her Atthis*. Natalie adopted the role with some relish and proposed that they form a Sapphic circle under her tutelage. It is not known how seriously Natalie took this. She had a lively sense of humour and was often self-deprecating. In spite of the high-flown intellectual terms the circle was dressed up in, it might easily have been an easy way to find new lovers.

The first recruit was to be the young English poet Olive Custance. Natalie wrote to her in London, extending an invitation. Olive responded enthusiastically in verse:

> For I would dance to make you smile and sing
> Of those who with some sweet mad sin have played,
> And how Love walks with delicate feet afraid
> Twixt maid and maid.

Olive turned up in Paris in 1901. Beautiful, young and fresh, she immediately provoked a fit of jealousy in Renée. Natalie referred Renée to the work of Sappho, which indicates that she and Atthis frequently took other lovers, but still remained true to one another in their hearts. That old trick. If they were to have a proper Sapphic circle along the lines of ancient Lesbos, all those who shared their interest must be welcome. Fate then made her point for her. Renée received a telegram from Violet Shilleto. She was in Nice, where she had been struck down by a mysterious ailment. She was dying and wanted Renée to be at her bedside. Renée left immediately, leaving Natalie in Paris with Olive.

The next day, Natalie popped around to Olive's for tea. Unfortunately, her mother and a handsome young man called Freddy, the Viscount of Canterbury, were there. After tea, Natalie invited Olive over to her place "to discuss poetry". Freddy asked if he could come too, but Natalie said no. They were going "to discuss poetry" and he would find himself left out.

Freddy quickly developed a crush on Natalie, which restricted the two women's opportunities "to discuss poetry". Eventually, Freddy and Olive's mum were persuaded to head back to England, allowing the two lovers to head off to Venice. Unfortunately, they both came down with malaria on the trip.

It also transpired that Olive had decided to do the decent thing and get married. She, too, set her cap at the unfeasibly popular marriage prospect Lord Alfred Douglas*, though both her family and his were against the match. Naturally, this only served to inflame her passion. Natalie then came up with a novel solution. She would defy her father and marry Lord Alfred Douglas and the three of them would live in a *ménage à trois* – or a *ménage à quatre* once Renée got back. I really can't see Oscar Wilde's* Bosie going for this arrangement. The thought of being hitched to one woman would have turned his stomach but with two, or possibly three, of them in tow, he would have lost the will to live. Bosie and the boys really hated women. (See *Sex Lives of the Famous Gays*.)

When Violet died in Nice, Renée returned to Paris. Inconsolable, she locked herself in a room and started to write poem after poem about death again. In one, she shows herself adoring Natalie as a beautiful corpse. This was all too much for Natalie, who announced that she was off back to the United States for the summer. Renée suddenly recovered her senses and said that she would come along as well.

Arriving in Bar Harbor on board the yacht *Sappho*, Renée was soon wriggling her naked arse in the grass of Maine. They would plunge nude into the cool, clear water and took turns to photograph each other naked in a series of erotic poses – sometimes alone, sometimes with the two of them together.

Judging by the photographs of Renée in *Album Secret*, that summer was indeed a Sapphic idyll. But it could not last. That autumn they moved to Bryn Mawr College, Pennsylvania, to attend the classes of the feminist intellectual Professor Mary Gwynn. While Natalie sat at Professor Gwynn's feet and recited poems to her, Renée would mope around the graveyard, absorbed once more by thoughts of death.

That winter, they parted again. Natalie was to spend the festivities with her family in Washington, while Renée was to return to Paris, where she moved into an apartment in the house where the late Violet Shilleto had lived with her sister Mary. Natalie turned up there in the spring of 1902, but Renée was out, so she waited in the courtyard outside. When Renée arrived and saw Natalie waiting, she told her chauffeur to drive on.

Natalie then went up to see Mary Shilleto to find out what was going on and, through the window, saw Renée walking with the sexually rapacious Dutch Baroness Hélène van Zuylen de Nievelt, née Rothschild. It was plain from their body language that the two of them were on intimate terms.

Natalie was convinced that the baroness was the *éminence grise* behind their break-up. However, although Renée's first volume of poetry had been dedicated to "N———", the rest of her books were to be dedicated to "H.L.C.B." These were the jumbled initials of her new lover, Helen Betty Louise Caroline. They collaborated on a number of books of poetry and prose under the name Paule Riversdale.

Natalie tried to win Renée back, by writing poetry to her in a Sapphic metre and appearing in front of her house mounted magnificently on horseback. One night, Natalie and the opera singer Emma Calvé disguised themselves as street singers and serenaded Renée. She fell for the ruse and opened the window. Natalie lobbed in a bunch of flowers and a love sonnet, begging Renée to see her. The bouquet and the poem were returned the next day with a curt note asking her to desist.

Eva Palmer was then sent to Renée's apartment as a go-between. She was eagerly invited in, but Renée still refused to see Natalie. Instead she put the make on Eva and invited her to the opera. This played into Natalie's hands and she turned up in

Eva's place. It worked. The two of them sat through Robert Schumann's* *Manfred* clasped in each other's embrace. They arranged to meet again the following day, but Renée stood Natalie up. When Natalie phoned, Renée explained that they could not relive the past. It was over. However, when news came that Natalie's father was gravely ill in Monte Carlo, Renée offered her help, being well versed in tending to the dying on the Côte d'Azur. Natalie told her, petulantly: "I need no one."

Natalie inherited the estate when her father died. She moved into an apartment with Eva directly across the street from Renée's and began having numerous affairs.

It was said that she could make 18 dates in a single night. She left behind her a trail of broken hearts and broken marriages, but denied being a Don Juan.

"Man tears woman apart without decoding her," she said. Her own desire, she claimed, was never mechanical or anonymous, like a man's – never purely physical – but focused on the being of the beloved in her entirety. She was not entirely altruistic, though.

"I never act except according to my pleasure," said Natalie.

She did not forget about Renée, though, despite all of the fun. In 1904, when she heard that Renée was going to the Wagner* festival in Bayreuth, she and Eva headed off in hot pursuit. It was not difficult to spot her among the crowds, and Renée did not attempt to evade them. Indeed, Eva swapped seats every night with Renée, so that she and Natalie could sit together holding hands, lost in Wagnerian rapture. Natalie plied her with prose poems commemorating their love. Renée was soon ensnared. She agreed to meet Natalie in Vienna. From there they travelled to Lesbos.

As they steamed into port at Mytilene at dawn, full of romantic thoughts, the mood was broken by a coarse French song that someone had slipped on the phonograph. There were to be more disappointments. The language the inhabitants of the island spoke was not the classical Greek of the Aeolic dialect that Sappho had used. There were no good-looking women about and the only attractive Lesbians they saw were blokes!

Nevertheless, they leased two adjoining villas in an orchard and had an idyllic time. Renée began work on a translation of Sappho and pledged that she would remain on Lesbos and await her love whenever Natalie went away. But Natalie said she had no reason to go away. Then Renée received a letter from Baroness van Zuylen de Nievelt saying that she was on her way to the island to get her. This put the fear of God into them and, rather than defile their spiritual home with a terrible scene, they decided that it would be best if the two of them returned to Paris where Renée would tell the baroness that she now intended to live with Natalie. When they arrived back in France, however, Renée did not have the willpower to defy the powerful baroness. She continued to write heart-breaking letters to Natalie, eventually begging her to hand over the lease to her villa on Lesbos so that Renée could live there with the baroness.

The letters continued for the next five years and they even met up occasionally. Natalie attended soirées at Renée's flat where Colette* danced. She even turned up on one occasion with a new conquest, an actress with golden eyes. The baroness, now no longer jealous, also attended. She was curious to meet Natalie, although she conspicuously dressed up for the occasion.

Natalie eventually moved away, finding a place in Rue Jacob on the Left Bank, which became her *"Temple l'Amitié"* – that is, her Temple of Love. According to Colette*, Renée slowly started to waste away. Three days before she died, Renée converted to Catholicism, so that she could be with Violet Shilleto in heaven.

When Natalie heard that Renée was gravely ill, she rushed to her door with a bunch of violets, only to be turned away with the news: "Mademoiselle has just died."

At the time, it was reported that morbid old Renée's last words were: "This is the best moment of my life."

Another source, however, said that she died with "Lorély ..." on her lips. Lorély was the priestess of a Sapphic cult that had recently been revived – that is to say, invented. It was also the name of Renée's poetic transposition of Natalie.

Renée Vivien's biographer, André Germain, added the words: "... She was my only love."

For her part, Natalie preferred the first version, saying matter-of-factly: "Her life was one long suicide."

While Renée lay dying, Natalie was already consoling herself with another woman who, ironically, Renée had introduced to their circle. Her name was Lucie Delarue-Mardrus*. She was a poet, a great beauty and the wife of the Orientalist Dr Joseph-Charles-Victor Mardrus, who translated the *Arabian Nights* into French. An impulsive man, he had proposed to Lucie after hearing her reading a poem and married her just two weeks later.

Two years later, her reading had a similar effect on Renée, who sent her a volume of her own poetry with a dedication hailing Lucie as "the greatest poetess of our time". Reading Renée's work reminded Lucie of the poems she had written when she was young and she had developed a crush on an older girl.

When Renée came to call, Lucie was immediately struck by her "heavy, delicate eyelids with their long, black eyelashes". She invited the couple to dinner. Accepting, they found themselves served a meagre meal – Renée was a vegetarian as well as a vagitarian – in a dim, airless room.

There were treats in store, however.

"After dinner we suddenly saw an amazing slim creature appear from behind the draperies, an authentic heroine out of Dante Gabriel Rossetti*," Lucie recalled. "Her dark purple, velvet, medieval dress revealed her somewhat angular, archaic body. Two huge plaits of red hair were wrapped around her head like a laurel wreath. Her face was like an Italian primitive with blue eyes ... I didn't have eyes enough to gaze on this girl from another age, who was as beautiful as a poem."

This was Evalina Palmer, who invited them to accompany her to the theatre the next day. There Lucie met Natalie Barney and was attracted by "her delicate complexion, her very feminine form, her fairytale blonde hair, her Parisian elegance" and her ability to create a very false impression by "blushing like a shy novice".

Natalie invited the Mardruses to dinner, then made herself a regular guest at their suburban villa. Natalie and Lucie were spending nights out together. They would go riding during the day with Natalie dressed in a conventional woman's riding habit and Lucie dressed as a cowboy, complete with a ten-gallon hat.

At the Mardruses' summer home in Normandy, they would spend time frolicking in the hayfields. Natalie called Lucie "Princess *Amande*" because her body was as pale and as smooth as an almond. Eva would sometimes join what Natalie called their "harem". It was Maine without the Box Brownie.

Naturally Dr Mardrus wanted to join in too. He even suggested that Natalie bear him a child, so that Lucie's strength could be saved for her literary efforts. Lucie was all for this, but Natalie declined. However, Natalie had some genuine affection for Dr Mardrus. He was the only man she addressed as *tu*. She did not mind it when he called her "Blondie" and she referred to him as Dr "Jesus Christ" Mardrus so regularly that some people thought it was his real name.

It is clear that Natalie introduced Lucie into lesbian love from her love poems *Nos Secrètes Amours* published posthumously at Natalie's expense. These poems are positively panting with passion – or should I say pantless with passion – as the "harem" chomped the grass in Normandy as well as on outings down by the Seine.

Lucie got emotionally involved with Natalie as time passed and began fulminating against the "blonde bitch", Eva, when Natalie was flagrantly unfaithful. In 1906, Lucie wrote the play *Sapho désespére* to express her despair and even appeared on stage in it. By this time, Dr Mardrus had finished translating the 16 volumes of the *Arabian Nights* and took his wife away. Later, the two-year affair between Natalie and Lucie turned into friendship that lasted nearly 30 years. It ended in 1930, when Lucie published the novel *L'Ange et les Pervers* (*The Angel and the Perverts*), which placed Natalie in a world of hermaphrodites and homosexuals of all sorts and condemns her as "perverse, dissolute, selfish, unjust, obstinate, sometimes avaricious, often play-acting, most of the time irritating … in short, a monster". Now tell us what you really think.

38

To sugar the pill, Lucie also said of Natalie: "You are a true rebel and always prepared to lead others in rebellion. And deep down inside you are a decent person."

However, in the novel, Natalie is portrayed playing cat and mouse with pretty women she did not even really want. Renée, Eva and Natalie were rich, spoilt and promiscuous.

"You make 25 rendezvous all over Paris for the same hour," said the then-divorced Lucie. "You invent little situations, you play childish games with love. At bottom, you are a bunch of schoolgirls – dangerous schoolgirls at that – for in the midst of all this there is a man who loved his wife and who has lost her, a woman who was leading a peaceful life and who is now launched on adventures that lead her astray."

Besides, Lucie said, Natalie "would probably not exist but for the literary pose she adopts".

Somewhat understandably, *L'Ange et les Pervers* does not rate a mention in the chapter Natalie devotes to Lucie Delarue-Mardrus in her memoirs.

Natalie would often write performance pieces to entertain her lovers. These usually had an audience of two, as Natalie was particularly fond of threesomes. Sometimes, though, she would put on bigger pieces, which often featured acts of "pagan love" performed by courtesans who had been hired for the occasion.

Colette* recalled a production of a piece by Pierre Louÿs* in Natalie's garden at her country house in Neuilly, starring Evalina Palmer in a scanty Greek tunic. Then, from behind a screen of foliage, a naked Mata Hari appeared riding a horse. She was, Colette said, "a dancer who did not dance much". Colette had seen her perform before.

"The only pleasant certainties on which her drawing-room audience could count were a slender waist below breasts that she prudently kept hidden, a fine, supple moving back, muscular loins, long thighs and slim knees," Colette said. "It should be said that the finale of her dance, the moment when Mata Hari, freed of her last girdle, fell forward modestly upon her belly, carried the male – and a good proportion of the female – spectators to the extreme limit of decent attention."

Natalie often employed Mata Hari to perform erotic Javanese dances for small, exclusively female audiences. After Mata Hari was tried as a German spy during the First World War and shot, Natalie sought out the French officer who had been in charge of the firing squad to find out how she had faced her death, disbelieving the lurid accounts in the newspapers.

On the whole though, Colette said, she preferred the nude Mata Hari to the clothed one, as with her clothes on she could be rather pretentious. But then they were in the same business. Colette was also seen dancing naked in Natalie's garden for the entertainment of her guests – male and female. She even appeared nude in a pagan ritual performed as a memorial to Renée Vivien.

Natalie's theatricals persuaded Eva to adopt the scanty Greek chiton full time. This caused a sensation when she arrived in New York in 1907 on her way to marry a real Greek poet, Angelos Sikelianos, Isadora Duncan's* brother-in-law, at Bar Harbor. By that time Natalie was busying herself with the actress Henriette Rogers and Colette – even though she disapproved of the fact that Colette would sometimes submit to sex with men. Natalie was a dedicated heterophobe.

She also entertained in the garden at rue Jacob. Among those attending were Jean Cocteau*, André Gide*, Gabriele D'Annunzio*, Max Jacob*, Marcel Proust*, Gertrude Stein*, Rainer Maria Rilke, Isadora Duncan*, Paul Valéry*, Nobel Prize-winning author Rabindranath Tagore and James Joyce – though it is not recorded how he reacted to the cavorting nudes.

Another literary giant who came into her orbit was the reclusive writer Remy de Gourmont. Desperate to be admired by the foremost intellect of the time, Natalie bewitched the poor old man. Too shy to express his desire for her, he poured all of his emotions into Lettres à l'Amazone. Once this was published all of Paris called Natalie "the Amazon".

Gourmont died in 1915, an event that went almost unnoticed because of the First World War. His Letters to the Amazon first appeared in English in 1931 at the height of the

Depression. By then the pre-war world of Gourmont seemed remote and this may go some way to explain why Natalie Barney is not well known in the English-speaking world.

The writer André Germain also celebrated Natalie in literature as a voracious siren called "Lorély" or "Undine", but it was the name "Amazon" that stuck. Natalie even celebrated America's entry into the First World War with the poem *"D'Une Amazone américaine"* which was printed in the *New York Herald*. She also published her pacifist tracts as *Pensées d'une Amazone* in 1920.

She had been urged to leave France at the beginning of the war, but she stayed on for the love of Elisabeth de Gramont, the Duchesse de Clermont-Tonnerre* – or Lily as Natalie knew her – who was descended by birth and marriage from Henry IV. In 1915, Natalie met the American painter Romaine Brooks*. Born Romaine Goddard, she had been married for about a year to handsome homosexual John Ellington Brooks, who had fled England after the trial of Oscar Wilde*. She actually claimed to have bedded Wilde's lover, Lord Alfred Douglas*. She also had affairs with Gabriele D'Annunzio* and his mistress Ida Rubinstein, who was the model for many of her highly erotic female nudes. And she was the lover of Princess Edmond de Polignac*, who had the uncanny knack of attracting all the pretty women in Paris. However, in Natalie she had found a woman who, according to her biographer, "idealised every aspect of Romaine, as if Romaine were a goddess to be worshipped" – on her knees again presumably. A romantic, Romaine believed that they could have a sacred union "to be one", but Natalie, as usual, had other fish to fry – well, eat at least. That did not stop her from being fiercely jealous. When Romaine was away in Capri, Natalie wrote: "I know that you have not bathed without everyone on that hot island desiring you – that they could follow the glimmer of your perfect form to the ends of the earth."

It was Romaine who sought fidelity, though, and there were numerous rows over Natalie's frequent affairs. Lily, who also believed that it was necessary to have several love affairs going on at the same time, simply looked on and laughed. In the end,

Romaine had little choice but to accept Natalie as she was – and that meant accepting Lily, too. From then on, they began to share their friends.

In 1927, Natalie and Romaine built a house at Beauvallon on the Riviera – really two houses connected by a common dining room – called the Villa Trait d'Union, or the "hyphenated villa", so that they both had their privacy to get on with what, or who, they wanted. They would spend most of the summer there until, late in the season, Natalie would head for Normandy to stay with Lily. From there, she would write love letters, assuring Romaine that she was the one and only.

Natalie also wrote poetry dedicated to Romaine, who responded by supplying two female nudes for Natalie's weird Gothic novel *The One Who is Legion*. She produced portraits of those in Natalie's circle, including Lady Una Troubridge* in men's clothing and Eyre de Lanux as a bare-breasted huntress.

During Natalie's frank, though not intimate, relationship with the art critic Bernard Berenson, he said in shock: "You've had so many ladies ... more than I."

Berenson brought her into the circle of Ezra Pound, T.S. Eliot, Sinclair Lewis and Gertrude Stein*. By the late 1920s, Natalie was seen as *"l'impératrice des lesbiennes"* and Radclyffe Hall* came to call. She portrayed Natalie as Valérie Seymore in *The Well of Loneliness*.

Throughout the 1920s and 1930s, new lovers never stopped coming. Natalie's most intense affair of the period was with Dolly Wilde, the daughter of Oscar Wilde's* elder brother Willie*. They met at a fancy-dress party, where Dolly came dressed as her uncle – it was said that she looked "both important and earnest". Natalie came dressed as *"une femme de lettres"*, which hardly qualifies as fancy dress at all.

Just as Renée had been, Dolly was "half in love with death" and already had a heavy drink-and-drugs habit. What literary talent Dolly possessed was dissipated in a dinner table conversation. They shared a love of Virginia Woolf* and Dolly praised Natalie as "half androgyne and half goddess" in the love letters she published.

Dolly was soon banished by Romaine's jealousy. Natalie

continued to arrange secret assignations with her – though, as always, she had other interests.

"Where are you, darling?" reads one note from Dolly. "In what bed do you lie, and under what sky?"

The whole affair was fraught. On one occasion, determined to finish with her, Natalie bought Dolly a plane ticket to London and sent her to the airport. Dolly thought better of it, however, and returned by taxi to rue Jacob, where she found a tearful Natalie comfort-eating chocolate.

Dolly and Romaine joined forces when Natalie took in the young Chinese lawyer Nadine Hoang*, who had come to Paris in uniform as a representative of the Chinese Communist Party and who had run out of money. Even André Germain was distressed when, taking the uniformed figure of Nadine for a pretty young boy, he found to his horror that he had been attracted to a woman.

Dolly tried slashing her wrists when Natalie took up with an actress. On another occasion, she swallowed a whole bottle of sleeping tablets. At the same time she was heavily into both opium and cocaine. In 1940, she was diagnosed with cancer and headed for Lourdes. The two lovers were finally separated when they had to flee in front of the invading Germans. Dolly died the following year.

In the Second World War, just as in the First World War, Natalie decided to stay in Europe, despite boasting of one-quarter Jewish blood, though she left Paris and sought refuge in Beauvallon, before joining Romaine in Mussolini's* Italy. Staying in a villa outside Florence, she describes Nijinsky's* daughter, who danced there, in such sensual terms that it is not hard to imagine that something went on between them.

At the end of the war, Natalie returned to Paris, but soon many of her old friends were gone. Then, in 1954, both Colette* and Lily died. She still had Romaine, though. She had moved to Nice and Natalie often visited her there.

By this time, Natalie was in her seventies and was confiding in the biographer Renée Lang. After boasting of "a thousand liaisons", she told Renée that she intended to give up love before it gave her up. Then, one day, Natalie was sitting on a bench on the Promenade des Anglais in Nice when 50-something fan Janine Lahovary approached. Once again Natalie said she had been "struck by lightning".

"What shall I do?" she asked Renée.

"As luck has smiled on you once again," said Renée, "why not take advantage of your good fortune?"

Janine had no previous same-sex experience. She was married to an elderly Romanian ex-diplomat, who she had married when she was 17. Over the years, however, through her reading, she had fallen in love with the myth of *l'Amazone*. She offered herself "body and soul" to Natalie. After a whole lifetime of mental foreplay, Janine, to no one's surprise, "erupted like a volcano".

Natalie started to join the Lahovarys at their house in the Swiss village of Grandson on Lake Neuchâtel where they would swim in the summer. Janine's husband grew uneasy at the idea of playing host to his wife's lesbian lover, but Natalie persuaded him that he had better learn to share his wife with her – or face a scandal.

Romaine, who also visited, grew increasingly jealous of the relationship and, when Janine's husband died, she broke off with Natalie, despite Natalie's repeated protestations that she, Romaine, was her one and only love. Like Renée Vivien, she retired to a darkened room and refused to see Natalie when she visited Nice. She died at the age of 96 in 1970.

Natalie died two years later. Her body was laid out in the crypt of the American Cathedral in Paris, where Renée Vivien had wept over the body of Violet Shilleto 70 years before. She was buried in the cemetery at Passy, near Renée.

4 Claudine en ménage

Colette is one of those rare creatures who commuted from heterosexuality to lesbianism and back again so quickly that it makes your head spin. But then, she was largely a creation of her own pen and lived out her life as the heroines of her own novels – the most famous of which was a precocious schoolgirl called Claudine.

Born Gabrielle Sidonie Colette in Burgundy in 1873, her father was a one-legged war hero and an avowed atheist. Her mother had been married before to an alcoholic womaniser who drank himself to death. During her first marriage, Colette's mother had taken other lovers and had a free-and-easy approach to sex. She objected to the practice of corseting unmarried girls to hide their pregnancies and encouraged Colette neither to marry nor procreate.

At her boarding school, Saint-Sauveur, Colette was a tomboy. Already using the single name Colette, she was a permanent headache to the headmistress, who was rumoured to be the mistress of the local mayor. Like most French adolescent girls, Colette developed those passionate friendships the French call *amitiés de pensionnaire*, where growing girls compared their budding breasts and the early sprouting of their pubic hair. Then came the disturbing moment when Colette announced a visit from her "cousin Pauline" – her first period.

It was a troubled time for the young Colette, who took to eating clay and charcoal, drinking mouthwash, sticking pins in her palms and reading dirty books. Her older sister's pregnancy filled her with embarrassment and disgust, and she witnessed the pains of childbirth. The sight of her disabled father passionately kissing her mother's hand filled her with "confusion". She was repelled by the sight of a hired hand embracing the kitchen maid and, when two servants got married, her imagination was tormented with images of what was going on in their bedroom on their wedding night.

At the age of 14, she fell for her mother's friend Adrienne de Saint-Auburn who, like her mother and Colette herself, had some African blood in her. She wore a ring inscribed with the words *"ie brusle ie brusle"* – "I burn I burn". Adrienne teased Colette by recounting a time when she and Colette's mother had exchanged babies and she had suckled at her breast. This filled Colette's mind with the erotic vision of "Adrienne's dark breast with its hard, purple nipple".

The family fell on hard times and had to sell up and move in with Colette's half-brother in Châtillon on the outskirts of Paris, curtailing Colette's education. Colette was 17 and she was hot to trot. Any man would do.

"It has to be said that when a girl puts her hand into some hairy paw or offers her mouth to ravenous and impatient lips, gazing serenely at the huge male shadow cast on the wall by some unknown man," she said, "it is because her sexual curiosity has whispered powerful urgings in her ear."

But the dangers were clear.

"In a few short hours an unscrupulous man can turn an innocent girl into an accomplished libertine who is disgusted by nothing."

It worked. Colette later wrote that: "Disgust is not a female failing."

Colette naturally threw herself in front of the first unscrupulous man who came along. He was 31-year-old Henry Gauthier-Villars, a journalist who worked under several noms de plume, including "The Usherette" and "Willy" – a diminutive of Villars, apparently. The Usherette described Willy this way – "thinning blond hair, baby-faced, a bit conceited; the heavy lips of a sensualist, myopic eyes, still young looking."

The Usherette also reported that Willy had "considerable success with women, and lets it be known" and he was often seen with a "Willa", a female who was not necessarily his wife. Colette described the slightly overweight Willy as "bulging", with "a powerful skull, popping eyes, a stub nose without bone, jowls – everything rounded". Umm, tasty, eh, girls?

She did say that he had a nice, rather dainty mouth and that he was right to hide his weak chin behind a short beard. Willy flattered himself that it made him look like Bertie, Prince of Wales*. Colette said that it made him look Bertie's mother, Queen Victoria*.

In 1889, Willy had had a child by a married woman, who divorced, then died. Recognising the bastard as his own, Willy had come to Châtillon looking for somewhere to farm out the child. He may have known the Colette family and later claimed to have known Colette herself since the age of ten. There is nothing disgustingly paedophilic here, however. It was Colette, as a saucy schoolgirl, who started bombarding Willy with love letters. Willy, who seems to have been genuinely heartbroken following the death of the mother of his child, was flattered and responded with visits and gifts. Colette was bowled over. During a visit to Paris, two glasses of sparkling wine went to her head and she told him in the carriage home: "I will die if I am not your mistress."

How Willy reacted is not recorded in detail, but Colette later said that her life as a woman began "with the help of ... a guilty intoxication, an appalling and impure adolescent élan". She did not think that she was unique in this.

"They are numerous," she wrote, "those barely nubile girls who dream of becoming the plaything, the entertainment, the erotic masterpiece of an older man. It is an ugly desire, which they expiate by fulfilling it."

On the other hand, Colette told her third husband, Maurice Goudeket, that Willy had raped her before they were married.

The Parisian newspapers got wind of the affair. The daily *Gil Blas* said: "There is much talk in Châtillon of the intense flirtation going on between one of the best of the Paris wits and an exquisite blonde known throughout the region for her extraordinary head of hair. Nothing is said about 'marriage'. So we suggest that our beautiful owner of the incredible golden braids follow the advice of Mephistopheles and withhold her kisses until there is the ring on her finger."

Too late. Willy took exception to this piece. He challenged the editor of *Gil Blas* to a duel and wounded him with a sword thrust to the stomach. Colette was upset, on the grounds that it could have been her Willy that was injured – and we wouldn't want that now, would we? Against all expectations, they were married two weeks later. She wore a dress of white muslin and a corsage of red carnations – make what you will of the symbolism.

"What do you want?" she told a friend. "I didn't have a choice: either to stay a spinster or become a schoolteacher."

Champagne sent Colette to sleep at the "wedding breakfast" that evening. By the morning, she said, "a thousand leagues, abysses, discoveries and irreparable metamorphoses seemed to separate me from the night before."

The experience left something to be desired, however.

"Is that all? Don't we start over again?" she wrote later. "Let's not contemplate too long the flattering shadow of Priapus surging on the moon-washed or lamp-lit wall. This shadow will ultimately reveal the shadow of a man, already marked by age; a watery glance, troubled and unreadable; the tremendous gift of tears; the marvellously veiled voice; that strange lightness of an obese body; the hardness of an eiderdown stuffed with stones."

Not good for you then. But worse was to follow. When Colette came downstairs the following morning, her mother was still wearing her black silk party dress as if she was in mourning. She had been up all night while her daughter was – officially at least – losing her virginity. Her face was racked with sorrow. What a downer.

Although, technically at least, Colette had lost her maiden name along with her maidenhead, she retained it and, from now on, became known as Colette Willy. The newly-weds headed off for Paris and the word quickly spread that the couple were married. They moved into Willy's bachelor flat – his "Venusberg" – "as in the *mons veneris*," he said – overlooking the Seine which was full of pornographic German postcards "glorifying women's underclothing with ribbons, garters, stockings and buttocks". Colette soon found that she, too, was required to pose like this.

"So many women want to be corrupted," she said, "so few are chosen."

Even so, he was hardly turning her into the "erotic masterpiece" she craved and, she said, the first six weeks of her marriage to Willy were among the unhappiest of her life – probably because Willy still had numerous women left over from his bachelor life.

They moved into a dismal flat in the rue Jacob, where Colette helped Willy with his correspondence and corrected his galley proofs. She soon began writing in her own right, following him on his journalistic rounds of the cafés, restaurants and theatres at night, where he ogled young models who wanted press coverage and nubile actresses on the make. At grand dinners she had to wear low-cut dresses and she told her mother that she was "embarrassed" to parade her near-naked bosom under the eyes of so many strangers. Willy soon had her posing for pornographic postcards of his own, however, and once when young music critics came round to rue Jacob to persuade them to be less harsh in their criticism of Camille Saint-Saëns*, Willy said: "Colette's taking a bath. Do you want to see her?"

They had been married for just over a year when Colette received an anonymous letter, giving her an address in Montmartre where she might catch her husband with his mistress. She hurried there and, in a small mezzanine hideaway, caught Willy with Charlotte Kinceler, not in bed, but poring over an account book on the kitchen table.

Charlotte was a "little brunette", Colette said, "not pretty, but passionate and graceful". Her sister was a prostitute and Charlotte herself lived on the fringes of the demi-monde. On seeing Colette, she grabbed a pair of scissors.

"Are you looking for me?" said Willy, as he bundled Colette out of the flat.

After this baptism of fire, Colette got used to Willy's mistresses, even making a point of befriending them. She entered into a cordial correspondence with Charlotte, writing: "Is he going to play the pasha, this Willy, in his virginal dressing gown? The pasha with nine cocks? But one's enough, he says, provided it's a good one."

Being a very physical woman, the easiest way for Colette to

cope with Willy's mistresses was to take them as her own lovers. She also took other lovers of her own. Within a year of her marriage, she fell for her piano teacher, Augusta Holmes, a student of César Franck, who had lovers of both sexes and had been a mistress of Richard Wagner*. She had four unacknowledged children by the literary editor of *L'Echo de Paris*, Catulle Mendès, who squandered her fortune and left her. Colette later fell under the spell of another of Mendès' mistresses, a young actress from the Comédie Française named Marguerite Moréno, "who seemed to have stepped out of a Burne-Jones* painting". Marguerite promptly left Mendès telling Willy that the literary editor read poetry to her all night and "can't deliver".

It was a sexy world, but it was a world tinged with tragedy. Dropped by Willy and Colette, Charlotte went into business selling herbs that induced abortions. Then, one afternoon when she was 25, she took a revolver and blew her head off.

Colette came down with an acute case of gonorrhoea, which was epidemic in Paris in the 1890s – though in her novels she gives the Willy character chronic genital herpes for good measure. Other authorities claim that they both had syphilis. At the time, doctors prescribed two years' celibacy for anyone who contracted it. This would explain why Willy became a voyeur and encouraged Colette to have lesbian affairs and why, by 1906, he had become impotent and was increasingly unable to maintain his concentration.

For Colette, the treatment included scalding baths aimed to raise her body temperature to 40°C – 104°F. She was nursed by the Symbolist poet Marcel Schwob, a friend of Oscar Wilde* whose mistress – in the nature of things, a consumptive young prostitute named Louise – had just died. Schwob was translating Daniel Defoe's *Moll Flanders* into French at the time and Colette was particularly delighted by the line where Moll says: "I own I was much wickeder than he."

In her sickbed, Colette was also visited by woman-of-the-world Madame Arman de Caillvart, the model for Madame Verdurin in Marcel Proust's* *À la recherche du temps perdu*, who brought the galley proofs of Anatole France's* latest novel, *Le Lyes rouge*, for her to correct.

No sooner was Colette back on her feet than she was back on her back with Willy, bringing a "notorious model" back for threesomes. However, he did take her to convalesce on Belle-Isle-en-Mer, where she took to wearing a sailor suit. When she and Willy were seen making love on the beach, it was assumed that he had seduced a cabin boy and, from then on, he was known in the area as the "disgusting Parisian". They were joined on the trip by writer Paul Masson who, at the time, was working on the catalogue of the Bibliothèque Nationale. Colette spotted him scribbling titles in a notebook and expressed her amazement that he could work on a catalogue such as this from memory. Masson explained that he was not working from memory, but from imagination. He had spotted that that National Library was light on Italian and Latin titles from the 15th century and was adding titles of his own.

"Until the day when the gaps were filled," he said, "I am making notes of interesting works that should have been written."

"You mean, these books have never been written?" asked Colette, naïvely.

"I can't be expected to do everything," said Masson.

Back in Paris, Colette wore her sailor suit to dinner parties because it showed off her well-formed legs – even though cross-dressing, off the stage, was against the law for women.

To make ends meet, Willy began writing risqué novels and employed a number of ghost writers – slaves or *nègres* as he put it – to generate material under his various pen names. Colette was encouraged to contribute. Her first book, *Claudine in School*, related the adventures of an innocent young girl who attends a school where the headmistress is sleeping with her assistant, the comely Aimée. As part of the research, Willy took Colette back to Saint-Sauveur, where he strolled into the girls' dormitory with a huge bag of sweets and poured them into a basin. This melted the girls' shyness. Then Colette, wearing a blouse of sheer linen, came in and kissed them.

Claudine in School was a huge hit and three more Claudine novels followed, covering the naughty adventures of Colette's libertine ingénue as she grew into womanhood. All four appeared under Willy's name. He certainly edited and shaped them, but how much he contributed to the writing is not known. The series, however, was one of the greatest successes in French literature. They were soon adapted for the stage. Everyone identified Claudine with Colette and postcards of Colette in a schoolgirl's uniform kneeling in front of Willy sketching the putative author circulated.

They were soon rolling in it. Willy rewarded Colette with clothes and jewellery, but he spent most of the money financing his infidelity.

"For what I have spent on free love," he said, "I could have got laid regularly by a professional."

Why Willy was paying for sex no one knows. Wannabe Claudines threw themselves at him and nymphets regularly turned up at their door. One day, Colette came across Willy sitting very close to a young Claudine-lookalike in the living room. As she passed, Colette whispered to her: "Be quick, you poor thing, the next one has been waiting for 15 minutes."

Another time, Willy brought home one of the painter Léandre's promiscuous models, the notorious Fanny Z, who threw her hat on the marriage bed and, through force of habit, opened the front of her dress to display her voluptuous charms. This made Colette's blood boil.

Willy was usually more discreet, though. He took a bachelor's flat where he entertained lesbian couples who wanted to play naughty, Claudine-style schoolgirls to his professor, though he later told a friend that their "mediocre Sapphic performances turned into a deadly bore".

While Willy was entertaining himself elsewhere, he kept Colette locked in her study for four hours a day. The result was a series of bondage scenes where the female protagonist is humiliated, beaten and forced to perform a number of degrading sexual acts. However, the spunky heroine still pulls through for the sake of her second-rate Svengali.

It may well have been Willy's idea to include a strong lesbian streak in the *Claudine* series – it was certainly a key element in the series' success – but it helped pique Colette's interest in the Sapphic arts. When Willy took Georgie Raoul-

Dual, née Urquhart, the daughter of a wealthy Louisiana family, as a lover, Colette seduced her too. Georgie, it seems, got off on "perfidious and unnecessary danger" – organising assignations with Willy and Colette in the same bedroom only an hour apart. On one occasion, Willy even smelt Colette's perfume on her lover and warned Georgie that if Colette found out what they were up to she would shoot her. The whole thing all ended very badly, when Georgie and Colette fell in love with one another. To help her get over it, Willy set Colette up with Natalie Barney*. Colette made the list of Natalie's "half-loves", though in later life they paid more fulsome tribute to each other.

Colette told Natalie: "I often reflect that nothing had come to me from you, great or small, that has not been good."

In response, Natalie wrote *The Colette I Have Known* and a friend told her biographer: "Colette must have been more satisfactory to Natalie than almost anyone else in her life." However, they could not stay together as they were both promiscuous when it came to other women.

According to Colette's fictional account in the Claudine novels, Claudine's husband sets up the lesbian liaison with the fictional Georgie, gets to watch and then joins in. This was, of course, a literary sensation, which Willy exploited by having Colette and Polaire – the young actress who plays Claudine on stage – appear together dressed in identical outfits all over Paris with him. Colette even had to have her long hair cut short to be like Polaire's. Other would-be Claudines were recruited in Willy's usual fashion, to play their understudies.

Polaire claimed that she had never been Willy's mistress and that she had never made love to Colette. Others say that there was something going on between the two women, but that they broke up after Polaire had left Colette alone with her lover, a wealthy playboy, and had come back to find her making love to him.

Colette recalled that, on another occasion, she and Willy were summoned to Polaire's flat because a boyfriend had beaten her up. She remembered being confronted by a young man's bare chest and muscles – instead of Willy's flabby form – and "love in all its youthful brutality" and realised that she was jealous. On the other hand, Colette does not seem to have been so jealous of Polaire when she was the lover of Pierre Louÿs. Generally she was generous with her loves. Around this time, Colette met the painter José Maria Sert. Finding his studio chilly, she suggested that he needed a harem to keep him warm in bed and introduced him to a circle of her girlfriends to provide the heat.

She arranged another special entertainment for Sert. One night after he had had dinner in a private room in a restaurant, a giant cake was carried in by four liveried footmen. Out of the whipped cream leapt two naked women – Colette and Polaire – who kicked the meringue over the guests with their bare feet.

The young Jean Cocteau* spotted Willy, Colette and her bulldog at the skating rink on the Champs-Elysées one evening at five o'clock – the hour when the sons and daughters of the bourgeoisie went home and the *cocottes*, *demicastors* and the *grandes horizontales* came out.

Liane de Pougy* was soon seen gliding by on sterling-silver skates with her hand in a silver fox-fur muff. Meanwhile "a slim, very slim Colette" sat next to Willy, looking like a "little fox dressed in a cyclist's garb, a lock of dark hair tied back at the temple with a red ribbon". Then Polaire turned up and stole the show.

"She dominates fashion, she exasperates women, she excites men," wrote Cocteau.

By now, Willy was encouraging Colette's lesbian affairs, but he advised her not to waste her time on ordinary girls and to concentrate instead on women who he could get column inches in the newspapers out of. He put her in the way of the Spanish dancer *"La Belle Otéro"*, one of his mistresses who would go on to become one of the most famous courtesans of the *belle époque*. A star of the Folies Bergères, she became the mistress of the Kaiser*, the Prince of Wales*, Alphonse XIII, the Grand Duke Nicholas, Gabriele D'Annunzio* and 11-time premier of France, Aristide Briand. She had a staff of 16 and her secretary was the former Spanish consul to Lisbon. Famous for her jewels, she wore three strings of pearls – the first had belonged to the Empress Eugénie*, the second to the Empress of Austria and the third to the courtesan Léonide Leblanc. When the necklace broke one night, spilling the pearls across the stage of the Folies Bergères, the audience demanded that the show be stopped until every one of the pearls had been retrieved. She also had a diamond bolero, made by Cartier, which was kept in the vaults of the Credit Lyonnais. When she wanted to wear it, it was brought to her in an armoured carriage and she was guarded at all times by two gendarmes.

The *New York Truth* said that Otéro "preferred the company of women" who, "like men, want to pay tribute to her beauty". Colette and Otéro were on *"tu"* terms and she would attend intimate dinners with Otéro, either alone or with a small number of women. After they had eaten, Otéro would pick up her castanets and, dressed only in a sheer petticoat, would dance for their pleasure. This was a good move on Willy's part. It both promoted Otéro and introduced Colette to a network of wealthy and aristocratic lesbians.

Gradually Colette became something of a celebrity. She began to exercise regularly – a thing unknown then – after the "little naked creature in her veils", the American dancer Isadora Duncan*, brought the "unfettered experience of the body" to Paris.

Although Colette flaunted their open, "modern" marriage, she still felt that they could be happy if Willy gave up his other lovers. Even though she began to find Willy rather "feminine", Colette did not take male lovers. Instead, she surrounded herself with gay men – though she continued to take female lovers, often middle-class married women, something that Willy encouraged for his own entertainment. He particularly excited when he came home to find Colette wrestling on the floor with the actress Renée Parry, one of Sarah Bernhardt's* troupe, and encouraged the two women to exchange blows. Colette maintained that a little rough-housing made the sex better.

Colette and Renée went out together dressed as father and son and appeared at the Mardi Gras at the notorious Bal Wagram dressed identically – with a young, blue-eyed girl in tow.

In 1904, a newspaper said of Colette: "How disconcerting and strange this woman with the body of a slim urchin, who dresses indifferently as a woman or a boy and looks in either attire an androgyne, a creature of undetermined sex." However, because of her short hair and her indifference to the advances of men, it was assumed that she was entirely lesbian.

With Pierre Louÿs'* *Les Chansons de Bilitis* and Liane de Pougy's* *L'Idylle saphique*, not to mention the Sapphic subculture of the great courtesans as described by Marcel Proust* and Emile Zola, lesbianism was all the rage – especially among respectable married women who found that they could take a woman as a lover without risking pregnancy or venereal disease, even though discretion was vital. The ringmaster of "Paris-Lesbos", or sometimes "Paris-Mytilene", was of course Natalie Barney*, and Colette and Willy attended the famous garden party at Neuilly where Mata Hari* appeared nude on horseback. Initially Colette steered clear of Renée Vivien*, whose decline she put down to "not only too much alcohol but also too much sex". When they later became neighbours, they got a good deal closer.

Through Natalie, Colette met the Baroness Deslandes, the muse of art nouveau who had fallen for a lion tamer at the Neuilly fair. On one occasion, she entered his lions' cage dressed as a Druid priestess and, surrounded by lions, recited a poem specially written for the occasion by naturalist Jean Richepin, who went on to become director of the Académie Française. The baroness was bisexual and, whenever she fell in love with another woman, cross-dressed. There was also the provocative Marquise Casati, a friend of Gabriele D'Annunzio*, who wore bizarre costumes, made up her face with black powder and shared her home, which she had emptied of furniture, with a boa constrictor which she fed two sheep a month. In an armoire, which she opened only for intimate friends, she kept a waxwork of the 17-year-old Baroness Veczéra – who died mysteriously a few days after becoming the mistress of Archduke Rudolph. Later she squandered her massive fortune on a metaphoric quest for art and purity.

Colette also bedded Lucie Delarue-Mardrus*, the Princess de Polignac*, Claude Chauvière, Musidora, Germaine Beaumount, Renée Hamond, Thérèse Robert, Germaine Patat and Annie de Pène and Hélène Picard, who both left their husbands for her.

When Natalie invited Colette to one of Mata Hari's nude performances of erotic Javanese dancing, Willy was fiercely jealous. He wanted to come too, but it was an all-girl do. As it was Natalie Barney said that he laid down what she considered to be "indecent conditions" before he let Colette attend. What they were she would not say, but in *Souvenirs indiscrets*, she records that Colette said: "I'm embarrassed that you had the chance to see the chain I wear."

The affair between Natalie and Colette was then at its height.

"My husband kisses your hand," said Colette. "I kiss all the rest."

Although, for the most part, the two women conducted their affair in privacy, the ageing Willy now needed Colette to act out what they did in front of him at home to get his rocks off. One of the regular alter-Claudines, Colette was now required to make up a threesome with an aspiring actress and student at *Le Conservatoire d'Art Dramatique*. Colette introduced her to the Sapphic arts in her studio while Willy looked on. She had "very clear and beautiful eyes" and "looked like the adolescent King Louis XV". Colette liked her, but Willy grew bored and replaced her with Meg Villars, who had been born to French parents in England. Under Willy's tutelage, she wrote *Les Imprudences de Peggy*, about a bisexual French girl's adventures in an English boarding school.

Although Colette still loved Willy, she was getting no sexual satisfaction from their relationship. So he encouraged her to begin an affair with lesbian transvestite, Sophie-Mathilde-Adèle-Denise de Morny, Marquise de Belboeuf – also known as Missy, Mitzi or Uncle Max. Ten years older than Colette, she was shy and stocky. Colette says she was: "Pale, like Ancient Roman marble ... she had all the ease and good manners of a man, the restrained gestures, the virile pose of a man." She had short-cropped hair and wore men's clothing from the finest tailors in London and Paris.

Missy was the daughter of the first Duke de Morny, the illegitimate son of Hortense de Beauharnais, the daughter of Napoleon's* Joséphine*, who went on to become queen of Holland. An industrialist, dandy and famous womaniser, the duke died when Missy was nearly two, but she spent the rest of her life trying to emulate him. His death sent Missy's mother around the twist. She remarried and, it seems, Missy was sexually molested by her stepfather. At the age of 18, she was married off to the Marquis of Belboeuf, but she was already dressing in men's clothing and did her best to avoid her husband's sexual advances – not wholly successfully, though, as she fell pregnant and had an abortion. Divorced after four years, she kept her husband's name to humiliate him with the scandal that surrounded her lesbian lifestyle, which she flaunted. She had a pair of carriage horses called "Vanilla" and "Garlic". In French, a vanilla pod is known as a *gousse*, as is a clove of garlic. The word *gousse* is also slang for "dyke". She also had a morphine habit and a taste for all-girl orgies.

As Missy was wealthy and was happy to support her materially, Colette seized her chance to leave Willy and moved in with her.

"At least no one can call me a cuckold," said Willy.

Colette took her literary revenge by killing off the Willy character in the Claudine series, but the public had grown a little tired it of anyway. Nevertheless Willy began to call Colette "my widow". Others called her *"la sous-Belboeuf"*.

Willy eventually tried to divorce on the grounds of her desertion. Colette counter-sued on the grounds of adultery, but that was not enough for the French courts. A husband had to install a mistress under the marital roof for his infidelity to qualify. This is what Willy eventually did and he went on to marry Meg Villars.

Although Colette and Missy were both women, they did not characterise their relationship as a lesbian one. Missy considered herself to be a man. She hated seeing two women together in drag and complained that "they don't tuck their bottoms in as they should". She also looked down on Natalie Barney for the money that she had was made in trade and for her Jewish blood.

As far as fidelity was concerned, Colette had jumped out of the frying pan and into the fire. Missy was as much of a womaniser as her father had been. She was always out on the pull and maintained a string of actresses, models, shop girls and young female factory workers. They were housed in a series of *garconnières* – or bachelor flats – each with a "love chamber" that contained a trapeze. The mind boggles. Willy visited one of these establishments one day to find a nude woman sitting on the trapeze in a position that offered a good view of her backside.

Apart from emulating the duke, it is not known what Missy got out of this. She once confided that she "didn't know what pleasure was – that she had renounced the possibility of experiencing pleasure, but that she wanted to give it at all costs".

She was a generous and skilful lover, wanting nothing for herself. Indeed, Colette said that Missy was "shocked by the salacious expectations of women".

"I don't know anything about completeness in love, except my idea of it," she told Colette.

Of Missy, Colette observed that "her very natural platonic tendencies ... resembled more the suppressed excitement, the diffuse emotion of an adolescent, than a woman's explicit need".

So it's horses for courses – or rather, Vanilla and Garlic for courses.

Even though divorce proceedings were under way, Colette and Willy still shared hotels rooms when they travelled, wrote passionate love letters for a number of years and, it seems, continued to be intimate. Even after any intimacy had ceased, they continued to collaborate professionally.

Although Willy and Colette had split, Natalie still asked Willy whether she could "borrow" his wife for an "entertainment" at Neuilly. Colette was to play a shepherd boy who falls for Eva Palmer's* nymphet, before Mata Hari* cut in with the dance of the seven veils. This was Colette's showbiz debut. After that she began to perform in shows in private clubs or in the salons of rich lesbian friends – first in Greek attire, then naked.

She would attend private functions with Missy where half the woman wore dinner suits, smoked cigars and enjoyed the kind of cabarets put on at that time for an audience of wealthy men. They naturally featured a great deal of female nudity. As cross-dressing was illegal, Missy would wear an opera cloak to hide her attire when they went out to cruise the Bois de Boulogne or to visit one of the secret libraries of lesbian erotica. In addition, like a considerate wealthy male lover of that – or any other – era, Missy plied Colette with expensive gifts.

It has to be said that Willy missed Colette terribly, but when a friend said that he was sure he could get her back, Willy lamented that he could not longer afford both Meg and Colette.

However, now that Colette's career in the performing arts was burgeoning, he did write a play for her. It was a drag role. She was to play a gigolo who was introduced to a hooker by a barman. At rehearsals, in front of Missy, Colette gave Willy a flirtatious glance.

"When Madame was married to me, she never looked at me like that," said Willy.

After her stage debut, Colette went on to play a nymphet in *Pan*, where she danced on stage nearly naked. The critics panned the performance. However, it was noticed that her lesbian friends in the audience, led by Missy, "went delirious when she lifted up her skirt". On the night Pan was played by a man. Missy had been up for the part, but had got cold feet, much to everyone's disappointment. The role required her to sing and she told the press, somewhat ambiguously: "I have a frog in my throat."

Missy did pluck up the courage to go on stage at the Moulin Rouge for *Rêve d'Egypt – An Egyptian Dream* – where Colette appeared as a mummy, who wakes up, strips off her wrappings and acts out a love scene. The climax came when she and Missy, using the stage name Yssim, kiss. It was a long, passionate embrace and it was clearly not simulated. It would cause a scandal, but Missy's ex-husband was ready. The audience was packed with the Marquise de Morny's hirelings, who booed and hissed. The show ended with them screaming "Down with dykes" and throwing things. The police had to be called to quell a riot.

"A new artist is born," wrote the satirical magazine *Le Rirer*, "Yssim, a name that ladies pronounce on their knees. We lick our lips over the act, if we may say so ..."

I think we've got the message.

Willy, who was in a box, was taunted with cries of "Cuckold! Cuckold!" Various mistresses – many of whom wanted to marry him – spread rumours about Colette, as much out of hatred for her as out of love for him. In an article in *Frou Frou*, she insisted that he was not a cuckold. She had no male lovers. It was just a vile rumour put about by women who hated her. She also talked of her black blood, which had come to her via the Caribbean. African art was all the rage just then thanks to Henri Matisse* and Pablo Picasso*.

However, Colette was not getting a good press at the time. The avant-garde poet Guillaume Apollinaire* said that she acted like a chambermaid who could do what she liked because she was sleeping with the master of the house, while Sylvain Bonmariage* called her a "voluptuous beast" who smelt like "men in rut" and behaved like "a cat on heat for whom life is a succession of rooftops". I trust Colette crossed him off her Christmas-card list.

Later, when Willy and Colette fell out, Willy satirised her "amphibian" – his word for lesbian – relationship with the Baronne Gousse de Bize – which means "Lumpy Dyke" – with a "high and masculine forehead whose nudity she hid with considerably more care than she concealed her rear end" in his book *Lélie fumeuse d'opium – Lélie the Opium Smoker*. Mind you, another character is an English girl who wears socks but no underwear and who is plainly based on his own main squeeze, Meg.

Without Willy's professional support, Colette began to publish her work in pornographic magazines and was forced to make a living from nude stage work – a thing she did not altogether object to.

"I want to dance naked if the leotard bothers me and spoils my figure," she told her mother.

Even in the melodrama *La Chair – The Flesh* – her dress is ripped open, exposing her left breast. The young Maurice Chevalier* was also on the bill. He said the breast was "well fleshed out" and fell instantly in love with its owner.

"The view of Colette's tit gave even more importance both to the scandal and to the tit," he said. "She had a heavy, full, well-supported breast."

Sylvain Bonmariage* also saw her naked around this time and agreed with Chevalier's assessment. Bonmariage had visited her small apartment near the Bois de Boulogne to find her still in bed.

"She threw the sheets back, jumped forth like a young tiger and rose up naked," he said. He was treated to a view of her "superb bust, her breasts barely fallen". Unfortunately, he was also presented with her "heavy thighs ... boxer's loins and her enormous, flat behind".

Audiences often got to see the whole thing, too. Theatre managers often tended to err on the side of more nudity rather than less. Total nudity was often required for her dance parts, although if there was trouble with the authorities she would be shrouded in a diaphanous veil.

Both Chevalier and Bonmariage – and any amorous theatre managers – were out of luck, however. Colette was not playing.

"I want to retreat to some desire island if I so desire, or frequent women who use their beauty to make a living," she said, "as long as they are gay and full of fantasy, or melancholy and wise like so many *femmes de joie*. I want to write sad books and chaste books where there will be nothing but descriptions of landscapes, flowers, sorrow, pride and the straightforwardness of animals that shun men."

Sex with other women was better than with men, she maintained.

"A woman enjoys the certainty in caressing a body whose secrets she knows and whose preferences are suggested by her own," she said.

This certainly did not apply to Missy who, Colette told a

friend, tried to tame her by using a whip on her huge buttocks.

Nothing seemed to dull Bonmariage's passion for Colette though. Fifty years after the event, he recalled an incident backstage: "After a passionate scene, Colette, who was half-naked, repaired to the wings glistening with sweat. She brought a strange odour with her, a fragrance that I had never noticed anywhere else and which still lingers in my nostrils when I think about it."

Another of Colette's lovers, the actress Thérèse Robert, identified the smell.

"She has the unexpected odour of a man, and that makes her so thrilling," Thérèse said. "The magic of her seductiveness lies in this bizarre fragrance."

Bonmariage thought that her secret lay in the way that she moved, as if she were offering herself.

Colette got Bonmariage ghost-writing work for Willy and installed him as Thérèse's protector, keeping the young woman hot with "passionate and indecent letters that sent Thérèse dreaming and sighing", Bonmariage said. She even joined them on a holiday in Holland.

She was also playing around with men at the time, admitting to Bonmariage one afternoon when she was drunk in the Carlton Bar that she was going to bed with "an incredible variety of actors and flashy South Americans". One of her male lovers was wealthy socialite Willy de Blest-Gana – another Willy – who was said to be the best swordsman in Paris. No, a real swordsman. He presided over all the upper-class duels. He was also a friend of Polaire. At the time, Polaire was having an affair with the 19-year-old son of a Parisian grocer. She organised a special treat for him – an afternoon à trois in a hôtel particulier with Colette. However, the young man turned rather too much of his attention on Colette, who ended up, thanks to Polaire, with two black eyes. To get her own back, Colette asked Blest-Gana to tell his friend, Polaire's protector, the cognac millionaire Jules Porgès, that Polaire was using his money to hire gigolos. When Blest-Gana refused, Colette finished with him.

Colette herself was picking up gigolos at Luna Park, the Watrin terrace or the Café of Sportsmen at Porte-Maillot, whose clientele included many racing car drivers. There she met the 20-year-old millionaire Lucien Fauchon, who would welcome her at the Thé Ceylan in the rue Caumartin with a slap on the *derrière*. Asked why she put up with it, she said: "The kid adores me and I don't feel the slaps through my skirt."

Fauchon complained that Colette was his "most expensive mistress". To which she retorted: "You can never pay too much for pleasure."

On tour with *La Chair*, Colette indulged in heterosexuality once again. Twenty-four-year-old army officer, playboy, heir to a department store fortune and backstage Johnny, Auguste Hériot was plainly impressed with the left breast and wanted to see more of her. He began sending her flowers. He had already been a lover of Polaire and Liane de Pougy*.

"I granted him half-an-hour of conversation – during lunch," Colette said. "He put his motorcar at my disposal, and I profited from it immediately by … going up to my room."

Soon they headed off on an "unmarried honeymoon" to Capri.

In Nice, they were joined in bed by the young beauty Lily de Rême, who became the model for Holly Golightly*. Colette was delighted to be enjoying the nocturnal comforts of two young people who loved her and they were plainly enjoying themselves too.

She made a lightning visit to see Missy at her country house in Rozven, before heading off to North Africa with Hériot and Lily. Colette soon grew tired of Hériot, however, and dumped him. He went to lick his wounds at Rozven, where he made "puppy eyes" at Missy.

"Perhaps he's planning your conversion," said Colette, unkindly.

Meanwhile, she wrote to her mother raving about "the beautiful eyes of the young Jewesses here". The problem was keeping Lily in check. She tried to visit a harem with a male friend in disguise and wanted "to touch everything, including the stunning daughter of the family" they were staying with in

Tunis. She then implored Colette to take her to India, but enough was enough for Colette and she skedaddled back to Missy.

Men got the impression that she was up for grabs again after her dalliance with Hériot. Proust's* friend, the novelist Louis de Robert, tried to get fresh. Colette was "horrified, revolted, filled with pity and a bit overwhelmed". He tried to trap her in a room, as she explained to Missy: "This man with the dead hands, the sickly breath, the fever sores on his mouth, who desires me absolutely, tried to bar my way, sobbing desperately."

He certainly does not seem very appetising.

"You know what a terrible thing physical disgust is?" Colette said. "You know you cannot compromise with it. I contained my fury and when he begged to kiss me" – what? with those fever sores? – "I nearly beat him up."

Too right, girl.

Back flashing her tit on stage in Paris, Colette was approached by Henry Bertrand Léon Robert, Baron de Jouvenel des Ursins who, as well as being an aristocrat, was a journalist on *Le Matin*. Three years younger than Colette, he already had one child by his wife, the beautiful and ambitious Claire Boas, and another by his mistress, the blonde bombshell, Isabelle de Comminges, also known as "The Panther".

One night, after seeing that tit on stage, Jouvenel took her back to his bachelor flat, a Swiss chalet on the western edge of the city. In her fictionalised account, Colette said that he pinned her to the floor: "After two minutes of resistance, I give him to myself like a respite. How sweet the naked mouth is, the full lips ... How sweet it is to lose oneself to the point of thinking, 'Here I am, freed from the care of thinking ... But this mouth belongs to an enemy made savage by a kiss, who knows me weakened, and who spares me nothing.'"

It seems she was very much back in the heterosexual camp again.

Soon she was calling him "Sidi" – Arabic for Pasha – which suited both his athletic physique and his sensual, aristocratic manner.

Later, Colette called one of her cats Sidi and put these thoughts in the tomcat's head: "I am the male of the species. I lead a restless life of all those who love has created for its hard labours ... It is that savage season of love that weans us from all other joys and multiplies, diabolically, in the gardens, our lanky females ... I want all of them without preferring or recognising any one of them. Once she had submitted to my cruel embrace, I no longer hear her sob ... There is no lover inaccessible to me."

That's real lurve.

When Jouvenel told "The Panther" that he was leaving her for Colette, Madame de Comminges threatened to kill Colette and pursued her with a pistol. Missy was also displeased. Then Isabelle turned up at Rozven in hot pursuit, she hit it off with Hériot and made off with him.

"Monsieur Hériot and Madame la Panthère have just embarked on the *Esmerld*" – his yacht – "for a six-week cruise, having shocked Le Havre, their home port, with their drunken orgies. Nice, isn't it?" Colette wrote to a friend.

Colette and Jouvenel holidayed in Lausanne, then returned to Paris where Colette was to appear dancing nude in a new show at the Ba-Ta-Clan Theatre. The troupe teased Colette for neglecting her training and giving up the parallel bars for the bedsprings.

"Who says I am neglecting my gymnastics?" said Colette. "I just have a new method, that's all – the Sidi method. It's excellent. No public classes. Just private classes – damned private."

In accordance with the unwritten code that governed these things, Jouvenel now took over from Missy as Colette's protector. She was soon annoyed by his infidelities, but found that she could not afford to leave him. Then Colette's mother died.

"De Jouvenel tends to my sorrow," wrote Colette, "in a loving and delicate manner."

It was plainly a very loving, but not so delicate manner, as they "accidentally" conceived a child. Colette was rather pleased. The responsibility of a child, she thought, would rescue her from her life of promiscuity.

"Love – so I thought – had already served me ill in monopolising me for 20 years in its exclusive servitude," she wrote. Little did she know it, but she was a lifer.

With a child on the way, Jouvenel concluded his divorce from Claire Boas. He and Colette were married on December 19, 1912, at the climax of a week of gastronomy laid on by his colleagues at Le Matin. They concluded by carousing till dawn.

"If this child isn't the lowest of high-livers, I give up," she said.

Colette, pornographer, nude dancer and notorious lesbian, was now the Baroness de Jouvenel des Ursins. She passed the pregnancy writing another in the series of her autobiographical novels whose heroine was the fictional Renée. The birth was difficult – 30 hours of screaming finished off with chloroform and forceps. She named the child – a daughter – Colette-Renée, after herself and her fictional alter-ego. The child was then handed over to a number of nannies, women friends and, at the age of eight, boarding school.

Determined to get her physical and erotic self back together quickly, Colette went into training and played a lot of tennis. When the First World War started, Jouvenel joined the infantry as a sergeant and was sent to Verdun, while Colette comforted herself with a circle of girlfriends – Marguerite Moréno, the novelist Annie de Pène and the waif Musidora, who had been one of Willy's "infatuated little minors" and had seduced Colette by sending her nude sketches of Claudine. She was to go on to be a movie actress.

Colette eventually smuggled herself into Verdun where she passed the "ultimate test of love" by learning chess, Jouvenel's passion. She endured the terrible bombardment there, knowing that at the front she had no rival for Jouvenel's loves.

"At night," she said, "Sidi returns to his harem" – that is, herself.

In 1915, Colette went to Italy as a war correspondent. Gabriele D'Annunzio* tried his level best to seduce her there and complained that she only resisted him because of her "adoration of a cruel husband". Her marriage to Jouvenel was not going well, though. She would humiliate him in front of everyone, saying things like: "You, at your age, with the kind of life you have led and you don't even know how to fuck."

Natalie Barney* had long had doubts about their marriage, writing: "This handsome, dark-haired man in the prime of his life, vain and intelligent, so attractive to women – who were so attractive to him – how could he be tied down to one woman, even if she was Colette?"

And he wasn't. When he was on leave and they spent two months together at Lake Como, he enjoyed himself with a "very Catholic harem" in the hotel, while Colette amused herself by going out rowing or sunbathing nude. Then the fledgling Italian movie industry began taking an interest in her books. She wrote screenplays and managed to disentangle Musidora from her latest boyfriend – a pimp – to play her alter-ego Renée. Colette stayed on in Rome, while Jouvenel returned to the army in Paris, where he had a staff job. When she returned to Paris, he went back to the front.

They lived increasingly separate lives after the war and she was seen out and about with the writer Francis Carco, who was 13 years her junior and who had once been one of Willy's ghost writers. He was, it was said, a man who "knows how to talk to a woman". They cruised the dives of the Pigalle together. Meanwhile, a plump Meg Villars, who had dumped Willy for a Belgian nobleman, was testing the bedsprings with Jouvenel. Even so, she still managed to find the time to visit Colette and her new lover Germaine Beaumount, the daughter of her former lover Annie de Pène.

Although Jouvenel had taken up with a young woman who would be his mistress for the next ten years, he still grew jealous when Colette wrote *Chéri*, a novel about an older woman who takes a much younger lover. Even so they managed to spend a pleasant Easter together with his former wife and his first son Bertrand. By and large Colette, at least, was happy. She told Francis Carco: "When a woman is earning money, has pretty clothes, a man to fuck her, another begging to fuck her, a third – a superb and smitten gigolo making the same proposal – if this woman is sad and yellow, there's something wrong with her."

Colette, though, was not to be trusted. During the holiday, she made it her business to teach 16-year-old Bertrand de Jouvenel how to swim at Rozven. She wore a tight black bathing suit that left little to the imagination and she was still very fit. One day when he came back from training, "she passed her arm around my waist," he said. "I trembled uncontrollably."

When he went up to bed, she insisted on kissing him – not on the cheek, but on the mouth. He almost dropped the kerosene lamp he was carrying. All she said was: "Hold steady."

Once his mother and father had left, the poor boy found himself at the mercy of three rapacious women – Colette's secretary Hélène Picard, who wrote the scandalous volume of poetry *For a Bad Boy* about her love for Francis Carco, Germaine Beaumount, who was having an affair with a married man she rarely saw, and Colette herself, who was still stuck on Jouvenel but, as he was enamoured elsewhere, only got to sleep with him once every few weeks. It was not enough.

"It is time for you to become a man," she told Bertrand and asked which of the three women he preferred. And when the young man was too shy to pick, Colette chose for him.

As Germaine was the youngest by a good 20 years, Colette decided that she should take Bertrand's virginity. However, when Germaine took him into the bedroom, he was so nervous that she failed to deflower him. He admitted that he had already surrendered emotionally to his stepmother in his head and when he emerged from Germaine's bedroom "depressed and unhappy in the middle of the night" he found Colette waiting for him on the landing. Even so, he later admitted, it took "all of her skills to complete his initiation", but as a tutor she proved "demanding, voracious, expert and rewarding". It was the beginning of a five-year affair. Only at the very end did she tell him that she loved him.

"The pleasures she gave me," he wrote as an old man, "were all those that open a window on the world, which I owe entirely to her."

Both of them revelled in the thrill of incest.

When Bertrand returned to his mother that autumn she found him changed – "corrupted" – and complained to his father. However, neither of them realised what had exactly gone on, or who was the source of the corruption.

Colette still loved her husband passionately and was hurt by his constant infidelities, so she did not feel the slightest guilt about her own misdemeanours. There were other clouds on the horizon, however. Henry de Jouvenel had been elected to the senate and Colette was something of an embarrassment to his budding political career. She was supposed to attend an important political dinner, but was away in the South of France with Francis Carco and sent her regrets at the last minute.

"We were expecting Picasso* and Colette," said another guest, "but Picasso is expecting a baby, and Colette is having a face-lift."

Bernard returned to Rozven the following summer, though now he was working for his father. A strange ménage were also on hand – Henry de Jouvenel's mistress, Germaine Patat, who Colette also seemed to be having a thing with. Then there were Francis Carco and his wife, who were desperately trying to conceive a baby, Willy's ex, Meg Villars, and Bertrand's half-brother, Renaud. Colette, meanwhile, had had something of a reconciliation with his mother, Isabelle de Comminges – she even found accommodation for her nearby.

Despite the distractions, Colette took Bertrand in hand once again and continued his education in the arts of love. Writing to Marguerite Moréno, Colette said of the merry crew at Rozven that summer: "There is also Bernard de Jouvenel, who his mother has consigned to me for his health and happiness. I give him rub downs, force-feed him, buff him in the sand and brown him in the sun."

Despite his mother's suspicions, Colette took Bertrand to Algeria where they saw the dancer Zorah perform, dressed only in her "brown flesh and a silver girdle". They stayed with the Prince and Princess de Polignac*. However, there was a little embarrassment when they arrived at their hotel in Algiers only to find the French president and a large delegation staying there. As the wife and son of a senator, Colette and Bertrand were invited to all the official functions. That must have been nice.

There were other embarrassments back in Paris. At a dinner for prominent politicians, Colette caressed the breasts of the wife of playwright Henry Bernstein. By this time, Henry de Jouvenel had found a new love – the writer Marthe Bibesco, née Lahovary, a Romanian princess who seems to have been related to Natalie Barney's last lover and who had done the rounds of Natalie's literary salons. Men found her irresistible, though she later admitted: "Making love isn't what I do best."

Even so, both Henry and Marthe promised to divorce their respective partners and marry as soon as Marthe's daughter, Valentine, was married off. In the meantime, Henry continued to see Germaine Patat, although he put off any confrontation with Colette.

"From the moment they are smitten, all men are dishonest," Colette wrote to Germaine, as she prepared herself for the inevitable.

Instead, Henry led a political delegation to – of all places – Romania. He then planned to visit Colette for a holiday, but never showed up. His forwarded mail showed that he had left Paris for some unknown destination. Colette wrote to Marguerite Moréno: "Love, amour ... a good anagram for amour: Rouma. All you have to add is the 'nia' and you come up with a woman who is built like a horse and foals two-volume novels. Poor Sidi has no luck at all ... I expect him any moment, from one hour to the next, from one day to the next, one week to the next."

While she was waiting, she comforted herself with Bertrand and shared "intimate little miseries" with Germaine Patat, who had taken over the care of Henry and Colette's daughter, Colette-Renée.

Bertrand celebrated his 20th birthday with his parents – Colette was pointedly not invited. His mother asked Henry to take her son away from Colette and suggested sending him on a political internship to Czechoslovakia where the foreign minister was a personal friend.

When Henry told Colette of this plan, she said that she did not want Bertrand to go away and admitted having an affair with his son. In another version of the story, Henry caught them in bed together. However it happened, Henry stormed out. Bertrand defied his parents' wishes and travelled south to Marseilles to be with Colette, who was protesting her innocence to Germaine. Okay, she may have gone to bed with his son, but Henry had contrived the whole thing to force a separation.

"If one must be punished for loving, for loving too simply and too diversely at the same time, I will be punished," she wrote. "I am someone who has never acted in her own best interests, who has never known a greedy passion except – to cherish."

Oh, cherish me with your greedy passion, baby.

Bertrand caused a scandal by moving into his father and stepmother's flat in boulevard Suchet – divorce proceedings were soon under way. Then, Henry's brother Robert, Bertrand's uncle, died. The beautiful young daughter of a family friend was steered towards Bertrand at the funeral, and he was then pressed into accepting the post in Prague. Desolate, Colette went to Rozven where she consoled herself with her new and adoring secretary, Claude Chauvière, a young woman who had no real skills for the job but who had wanted to become Colette's biographer. She quickly became her lover.

Bertrand returned briefly to Colette, but his family had arranged a marriage to a young heiress who had "been waiting with the patience of a virgin", as Colette put it.

During a revival of *Chéri*, Colette played opposite her old playmate Marguerite Moréno. (Liane de Pougy* told the tale that Marguerite was stuck with another guest in the country one wet week and, when asked what they should do to amuse themselves, Marguerite said simply: "Fornicate.") After the show one night, Colette and Marguerite were invited to dinner with some society friends where they met 35-year-old Maurice Goudeket. As an awkward, guilt-ridden Jewish youth, he had achieved some degree of sexual liberation of his own through the literary work of Colette and had declared, seemingly preposterously at the time, that he would marry her one day. Goudeket was less than impressed with the 52-year-old when he saw her in the flesh. After dinner, in breach of all etiquette,

Colette stretched herself out on the host's sofa "like a big cat" and the fastidious Goudeket noted that she was "a bit too fat".

Goudeket was having an affair with the young and svelte Andrée Bloch-Levalois at the time. They were staying at the Hotel Eden on Cap-d'Ail, when Marguerite and Colette turned up. This seems to have been Marguerite's idea, but Colette went along with it because Bertrand was staying nearby with his fiancée in an adjacent hotel. Colette invited him to lunch. He came alone. She came with Goudeket. The situation was awkward but, as they were leaving the restaurant, Colette took Bertrand aside and invited him to visit her in the Eden that night. He came. In the early hours, she asked him whether he wanted to come back and live with her again. He said he did. Something must have gone wrong in the next few hours of lovemaking, however, as, by dawn, they had agreed that it was impossible.

It seems as though something was already going on between Colette and Goudeket. When he received a telegram recalling him urgently to Paris, he lent Colette both his car and chauffeur. In return, she gave him a book inscribed: "Our relationship stops here. It is all for the best." However, when he failed to get a berth in the night train to Paris, Colette gallantly offered to give him a lift to Paris – in his own car. By the time they had reached Paris, Maurice Goudeket had been christened Monsieur Goodcock.

It was hot that summer in Paris and Colette complained that there was "a satyr behind every leaf". She and Goudeket spent their days apart, but their nights were "orgies of mineral water, oranges, grapefruits and cigarettes".

"The boy is exquisite," she wrote to Marguerite Moréno. "What masculine grace there is in a certain softness, and how one is touched to see the interior fire melt its containing envelope."

He was also "Satan".

Within months, Colette was writing to Marguerite saying: "You know what the kid Maurice is? He's a bastard, a so-and-so, a cool guy with skin of satin."

Moréno's reply was: "Great. What a lovely mess. You've

pulled your finger out of the dyke. [!] You can't know peace, you miserable woman. Give you a servant and you make him a master."

However, Colette and Maurice soon patched it up and went off on a holiday to the Midi together, where they skinny-dipped on deserted beaches and slept out under the stars.

"He is charming and I love him," she wrote to Marguerite. "Wasn't it last winter that you told me I would meet a man who would change my life?"

Goudeket was soon feeling the same and missed her terribly when she went on the road with a series of her plays. She sold her place at Rozven and they moved to St Tropez. They lived a peaceful life there, though Colette could not resist heading off to the Cap-d'Ail for the odd sex party, especially if Goudeket's old love, Andrée Bloch-Levalois, was involved. Always on hand for a bit of lesbian love was her devoted secretary, Claude Chauvière.

She enjoyed an "athletic" sex life with Goudeket. She drank and smoked little, swam and walked a lot and enjoyed toning massages. To keep up with Goodcock, she was also given a transfusion of blood from young women back in Paris. Colette did not deem this to be an unwarranted exploitation of her own sex. In 1928, she published the polemic tract *Why I Am Not a Feminist*.

"I have never had any confidence in women," she wrote. "The eternal feminist having betrayed me from the outset in the guise of my mother."

Feminists, she said, deserved the whip and the harem. Ooh.

The financial shock waves following the Wall Street crash of 1929 left Goudeket bankrupt, but he and Colette could still afford to move into the Claridge hotel on the Champs-Élysées. As they were not married, they lived in adjoining rooms.

Willy and Colette clashed in print over her contribution to the Claudine novels. After hiding out in Monaco to avoid his creditors, he was now living in a 15-franc-a-night hotel room with his new protégée Madeline de Swarte, the future Madame Sylvain Bonmariage*. Willy and Colette met up on one occasion, but did not resume marital relations. She now "has an arse as big as a stagecoach", he told a friend, "which doesn't tempt me to ride."

She cannot have been tempted either. "His ravaged face, with red blotches, his faded blue eyes were pitiful," another friend said. Seemingly suffering from tertiary syphilis, he staggered like a drunk. Nearly blind, he had been hit by cars crossing the street on two occasions and, after the second accident, suffered a stroke. He died in 1931. Leaders of the Académie Française and three thousand mourners followed his coffin to Montparnasse cemetery. Colette was not among them.

She set about writing the screenplay for her first talkie and got her daughter a job as a script girl. Colette-Renée was having problems with her boyfriend, who was away on military service.

"How great is human folly, and young folly above all," wrote Colette. "My beautiful child doesn't understand a thing about what she's squandering."

She should have read some of *maman*'s books which were still full of sexual – particularly what she called "unisex" – love. Or perhaps she should have turned up at one of *maman*'s literary lunches, whose guests included Marguerite Moréno, Lily de Gramont, Winnie de Polignac*, Germaine Beaumount, Marguerite Rachilde, Lucie Delarue-Mardrus*, Marie Laurencin, Gertrude Stein* and Romaine Brooks*, along with the younger generation of American and English lesbian artists and writers who had flocked to France – Radclyffe "John" Hall*, Sylvia Beach, Djuna Barnes, Lady Una Troubridge*, Mina Loy, Noelle Murphy and Janet Flanner. Missy was also in touch, but she had lost her youth, her money and her edge. When she turned up one day at the Claridge to find Colette's suite swarming with women, instead of taking advantage of the situation, she fled, terrified, into the rain.

Goudeket was in Paris when Colette was in St Tropez and she had the young writer Georges Kessel – who was recovering from a car accident caused by his addiction to cocaine – to stay. Instead of sleeping in the annex, where guests were usually put up, he slept in the main house – possibly in her bed as several people thought. Goudeket sent a jealous letter, to which Colette loosed off an angry reply. As if she would do such a thing! However, she blatantly referred to the affair in her fiction. Ironically, Goudeket and Kessel collaborated in editing a magazine called *Confessions*.

St Tropez was now becoming a popular destination for campers, which also brought fresh attractions.

"The women are naked," she wrote to a friend in 1937. She did not entirely approve, however, as their "nudity is not athletic but frivolous".

She also disapproved of the men who wore briefs.

"I find men in briefs make women look bad," she said.

And she did her best to banish them. One hot evening, she got 26-year-old movie heart-throb Jean-Pierre Aumont* to strip naked in her garden so that she could hose him down and water the plants at the same time.

Colette was unconcerned about the rise of Hitler*, noting only that he did not seem "to like fucking, not even men". She continued her extraordinary output of books concerning every aspect of that particular activity. She did not take much notice of Mussolini's* invasion of Abyssinia either, even though her former husband Henry de Jouvenel had moved to have Abyssinia admitted to the League of Nations in 1923 and had then become the French ambassador to Rome.

In 1935, Colette and Goudeket were offered passage on the maiden voyage of the liner *Normandie* from Le Havre to New York. As they were not married, they would not be able to share a cabin. To get around this problem they married. Colette's daughter followed her to the altar, but Colette-Renée's marriage did not survive the honeymoon and she, too, became a lesbian.

Also on board the *Normandie* was Bertrand de Jouvenel, who was travelling to New York to visit his lover, the future war correspondent Martha Gellhorn, the future wife of Ernest Hemingway*. Martha found Colette "a terrible woman".

"She was lying on a chaise-longue like an odalisque," she said, noting that her hair was tinted with henna.

Colette gave the blonde bombshell Gellhorn the once over

and then insisted that she pencil her eyebrows, which were "so blonde as to be non-existent". When Martha complied, Colette said: "My dear, what dreadful thing have you done to your face?"

"She was jealous of me," said Gellhorn. "And Bertrand just adored her all his life. He never understood when he was in the presence of evil."

In New York, Colette went to see a Mae West* film, toured Harlem, went to the Cotton Club and visited the headquarters of Parker Pens – the brand she habitually used.

Back in France, Colette heard that Henry de Jouvenel had died from a heart problem – "No kidding," she said. She delighted in the rumour that Jouvenel had been with a prostitute when he died, much to the horror of her daughter. She also ranted about Willy, who was still getting the credit for her early work.

The Depression was now biting hard and Colette supplemented her income by writing ad copy for Ford, Lucky Strike and Perrier. Meanwhile, she was having an affair with the beauty queen and adventurer Renée Hamon, who she called the "Little Corsair". She asked Colette what had attracted Goudeket to her.

"It's my male virility," she replied. "Sometimes I shock him, and yet I'm the only one he can live with. When he wants to sleep with someone, he chooses a very womanly woman. He likes to surround himself with that kind of woman, but he couldn't live with them."

As Europe moved toward war, Colette was seen dining once more with Georges Kessel, who she called "Smoke". Then she and Goudeket headed off to Fez to cover the murder trial of the famous prostitute Oum-El-Hassen, known professionally as Moulay, who had been recommended for the Legion of Honour for protecting her French clients during the colonial uprisings of 1912 and 1925, but who now admitted to torturing and killing child prostitutes in her brothel.

With the outbreak of the Second World War, Colette found herself sharing an air-raid shelter in the basement of the Palais-

Royal with a sex-crazed concierge. During the Occupation, Colette continued to work and socialise as if nothing had happened. Then came the knock on the door. The Gestapo arrested Goudeket, who was Jewish. He spent six weeks in a detention camp in Compiègne. He seems to have been saved by her prestige, but under the Nazi race laws he was no longer allowed to work. Colette was sometimes taken for a Jew because of her frizzy hair, even though she wrote openly for right-wing magazines. She also hung out with Jean Cocteau* who, as a decadent homosexual, was an obvious target for the Nazis and their collaborators. And still she wrote about sex, publishing *Gigi* – the story of a girl raised by two elderly sisters to become a courtesan – in 1943.

The Second World War consumed many of her former lovers, but following the liberation, Natalie Barney* and Lily de Gramont* returned to Paris to visit her. A younger generation of feminists also paid court. As much as she enjoyed the company of youthful sapphists, though, she always looked forward to a return visit once the girl had been humbled by "the hand, the mouth, the body" of her first man.

In 1948, she was visited by Jean-Paul Sartre* and his lover Simone de Beauvoir – or should that be the other way around? De Beauvoir described Colette as the "only really great woman writer in France".

"She was once the most beautiful woman," she wrote. "She danced in the music halls, slept with a lot of men, wrote pornographic novels … slept with women, too." Now aged 75, "she can tell stories and smile and laugh in such a way nobody would think of looking at a younger, finer woman."

De Beauvoir admitted that she was already in love with Colette through her books. She was to publish *The Second Sex* the year after meeting her.

Colette, at the time, was pumping herself full of male hormones, which made her nipples ache. Meanwhile, *Gigi* was adapted for the stage. In 1958, it was made into a movie starring Leslie Caron* and Maurice Chevalier*.

Colette died in Paris on August 3, 1954 and was the first woman to be given a state funeral by the French Republic.

Toward the end of her life, Colette wrote: "My conviction is that Sapphic love is the only unacceptable one."

Now it may be true that a woman needs a man like a fish needs a bicycle, but I don't think that Colette's acquaintanceship with Willy did her any harm at all.

5 The Belles of Bloomsbury

Okay, so I covered the Bloomsbury Group and its gay denizens E.M. Forster*, Maynard Keynes*, Lytton Strachey* and Duncan Grant* in *Sex Lives of the Famous Gays*, so you probably don't want to hear about the novelists Virginia Woolf* and Vita Sackville-West*. If you've read that, you've had enough of Bloomsbury already. But I lived in Bloomsbury, so I am allowed to be a bit partisan. I have written most of my *Sex Lives …* books in Bloomsbury, in the Round Reading Room of the British Museum, where Marx*, Dickens and Shaw once sat. This book is coming to you from the new British Library just over the border in St Pancras, but as soon as I have finished writing this paragraph I am going to nip over the Euston Road to a pub in deepest Bloomsbury for a mid-afternoon livener. So, if you would like to raise your glasses for Virginia and Vita, please, ladies and gentlemen, bottoms up.

Virginia Woolf's titles always have a slightly Sapphic feel to them – *A Room of One's Own*, *The Voyage Out*, *Night and Day*, *Mrs Dalloway*, *Between Acts*, *The Waves*, *To the Lighthouse* – no, delete that last one. And who can blame her. When she was about six on a family holiday to St Ives, her half-brother Gerald Duckworth, who was about 17 at the time, lifted her up on to the ledge in the hall where they used to stand the dishes and began to explore her undercarriage.

"I can remember the feel of his hand going under my clothes, going firmly and steadily lower and lower," she said. "I remember how I hoped he would stop; how I stiffened and wriggled as his hand approached my private parts. But it did not stop. His hand explored my private parts, too. I remember resenting it, disliking it – what is the word for so dumb and mixed a feeling?"

This incident stayed with Virginia throughout her life. Just two months before she died, at the age of 59, she wrote to the lesbian composer Ethel Smyth: "I still shiver with shame at the memory of my half-brother … exploring my private parts."

From then on Virginia described men as "beings possessed of knives".

Virginia's sister, Vanessa – another leading light of the Bloomsbury Grope, sorry, Group – also suffered at the hands of Gerald's older brother George, though there does not seem to have been one single incident that she could focus on. However, Vanessa admitted to being in love with George, as well as suffering the same shame and disgust as her sister. George and Gerald were the stars of the family, so the two girls had no one to tell except each other. This drove them together to such an extent that they thought they committed "thought incest".

When Virginia was 15, her mother died, leaving her and Vanessa as the only two surviving women in a family of men. This made the onset of puberty particularly difficult. Their burgeoning breasts threatened to make them, once more, the object of male attention. When their periods came, the two girls would retire to bed like invalids to avoid any unwanted attention. However, this paradoxically drew the eyes of the household to their condition. And, once they were alone in their bedroom, they still had to endure the night-time visits of George. When she was in her 40s, Virginia admitted that, for ten years, she had fashioned sanitary towels out of kapok rather than ask a shop girl for them. To do this, Virginia thought, would be to make the terrible admission that "I too am a woman".

George Duckworth continued his erotic interest in the two girls throughout their childhood, particularly after the death of their mother had robbed them of her protection. Vanessa constantly complained about the unwanted embraces of George, who even fondled her in company, but it was Virginia who suffered worst of all. It is not known how far these caresses went, but Virginia claimed that their sainted brother was, in private, her lover and referred to him as "my incestuous brother". She even told her Greek teacher Janet Case about it.

"She has a calm interest in copulation," said Virginia, "and this led us to the revelation of all George's malefactions. To my surprise, she has always had an intense dislike of him; and used to say 'Whew – you nasty creature', when he came in and began fondling me over my Greek. When I got to the bedroom scenes, she dropped her lace and gasped like a benevolent gudgeon. By bedtime she said she was feeling quite sick."

The "bedroom scenes" Virginia related always occurred in the dark as George insisted that she did not turn the light on.

"Sleep had almost come to me," said Virginia, recalling the scene. "The room was dark. The house silent. Then, creaking stealthily, the door opened; treading gingerly, someone entered. 'Who?' I cried. 'Don't be frightened,' George whispered. 'And don't turn on the light, oh beloved. Beloved –' and he flung himself on the bed and took me in his arms."

There is speculation, by several female authors I hasten to add, that these embraces were not as unwelcome as Virginia made them out to be. Now motherless, she craved "pettings" – even Vanessa was asked to provide them. The craving for darkness may well have been her own. She was not happy with her body and had a lifelong aversion to the looking glass.

Later, when Virginia began to suffer from mental problems, Vanessa brought up the matter of George's night-time forays with Virginia's specialist, Dr George Savage, something which must have been difficult for a sensitive young woman to do in that era.

Virginia herself told Dr Savage: "George would fling himself on my bed, cuddling and kissing and otherwise embracing me."

Savage thought the matter serious enough to speak to George Duckworth about it. George seems to have reassured the doctor that he was merely comforting Virginia, as her father, now terminally ill, lay dying three storeys below. As one man of the world to another, George managed to convince Savage that he had been misunderstood and that these innocent girls had got things terribly wrong. All this could be seen as a male conspiracy. On the other hand, in her book *Moments of Being*, Virginia writes a not unsympathetic portrait of George and his kisses. Added to that, Vanessa was happy to go to Paris with George in 1900 and then to Rome in 1902 and seems to have suffered no ill effects. Gerald's assault on the six-year-old Virginia was of another order, but then again it was his firm who published her first novel.

Virginia's father, Sir Leslie Stephen, was a true Victorian who did not believe in educating his daughters, but gave them the run of his extensive library in their house in Kensington. That scarcely compensated for the seven unhappy years they suffered until his death in 1904. George Duckworth married the same year. Gerald found himself some bachelor accommodation and Virginia and Vanessa moved, with their two brothers Thoby and Adrian, into Bloomsbury, which was then cheap and unfashionable. The Bloomsbury district of West London near the British Museum is famously built up around a series of gardened squares, leading to the famous adage about the Bloomsbury Group – they lived in squares and loved in triangles.

By the time they moved, Virginia had already had inklings of her true nature. She had had violent crushes on Madge Vaughn and Violet Dickinson, both 17 years her senior.

In 1906, Thoby died of typhoid and, two days later, Vanessa, who was now becoming a well-known painter, accepted the proposal of art critic Clive Bell. He was that rarest of things – a member of the Bloomsbury Group who was not, in the parlance of the times, a "bugger". During his time at Cambridge, he had managed to stay out of the "Apostles" – the homosexual debating society that proved such a fertile recruiting ground for the KGB when they were putting together the Cambridge spy ring in the 1930s. Instead, he had been initiated into the mysteries of heterosexual love by an older woman at an early age and instantly fell for "Vanessa and her sister – the two people I love best in the world".

Although Vanessa married in a state of shock and grief, Virginia noticed that her vigorous sex life with her new husband did wonders for her health. When Vanessa fell pregnant and had a baby, however, she turned all her attentions to motherhood. This left Clive and Virginia the time to develop an intense flirtation – maybe more.

"[Va]Nessa has all that I should like to have," Virginia told Clive, "and you ... have her."

They made little effort to hide their feelings for one another, so Vanessa sought comfort elsewhere. In the summer of 1911, she began an affair with Roger Fry who, at the time, was following the lead of Eric Gill* and painting "really indecent subjects – I suggest a series of copulations in strange attitudes". Roger's unconditional love made Vanessa feel wonderful.

"It can only do you good sometimes to have someone around you who admires every movement of your body and mind," she said. Especially your body.

And she felt the same about him.

"I can never tell you quite how beautiful and splendid you are," she wrote.

Holidaying together in Turkey, Vanessa managed to lose a ring that Clive had given her. She then suffered a miscarriage in a remote part of the country, and he nursed her through it, probably saving her life in the process.

Now that people were mixing and matching, sexual liberation became the talk of fashionable Bloomsbury circles. The actual moment when the dam burst and the whole edifice of Victorian sexual reserve came crashing down – for the Bloomsburyites at least – was recalled by Virginia in a paper she delivered to the Memoir Club in 1922.

It seems that she and Vanessa were together in the drawing room at 46 Gordon Square. Clive was expected at any moment and Virginia knew that they would begin to argue – "amicably, impersonally at first; soon we should be hurling abuse at each other and pacing up and down the room".

Meanwhile, Vanessa sat silently toying with some sewing, while Virginia prattled away.

Suddenly the door opened and the long and sinister figure of Mr Lytton Strachey* stood on the threshold. He pointed a finger at a stain on Vanessa's white dress.

"Semen?" he said.

Can one really say it? I thought and we all burst out laughing. With that one word all barriers of reticence and reserve went down. A flood of the sacred fluid seemed to overwhelm us. Sex permeated our conversation. The word bugger was never far from our lips. We discussed copulation with the same excitement and openness that we had discussed the nature of good. It is strange to think how reticent, how reserved we had been for so long.

Despite the smutty talk, Virginia felt comfortable around Lytton Strachey and the other gay men in the Bloomsbury Group. There was no danger of them giving her a Duckworth. Even so, ducking was always on her mind. She wrote to Vanessa complaining that she could not write, saying that when she tried "all the devils came out – hairy black ones". I think we know what you're talking about.

Virginia decided that she wanted Lytton Strachey as her husband. Four years her junior, he was, like her, a tortured soul, but he was also an incorrigible homosexual – who even boasted of passing pretty boys around the Apostles at Cambridge. Vanessa also championed the match, as it would end any rivalry between the sisters. If Virginia formed a "bloodless alliance" with Lytton, she would be the intellectual, while Vanessa would be the sexy one.

Despite her own fling with Roger Fry, Vanessa was still concerned about her husband's interest in Virginia. She was also worried that Roger might be showing some interest in that quarter, too.

"You know I don't really mind your going to see Virginia if you like," she wrote to Roger with evident pique, but warned him: "She's really too dangerous."

Vanessa also wrote to her sister, reminding Virginia of her "sapphism" – that is, her often-expressed preference for the company of women. This would make a perfect match for Lytton's "sodomism" Vanessa had said. It brought any rivalry between the two sisters to an end. They would be working opposite sides of the street – Vanessa straight; Virginia bent. And Vanessa had a cunning plan to lure Strachey into the trap.

"I should like Lytton as a brother-in-law better than any one else," she wrote in the summer of 1908, "but the only way I can perceive of bringing that to pass would be if he were to fall in love with Adrian."

So poor baby brother Adrian's arse was to be offered up as a sweetener in the deal.

Lytton did indeed propose to Virginia the following February, but immediately retracted "in terror lest she should kiss me", or so he told fellow Apostle and Bloomsburyite Leonard Woolf.

The following day, Virginia told Strachey, petulantly, that she did not love him anyway. It was not true and Lytton did not believe her. Fifteen years later, she wrote in her diary: "Oh, I was right to be in love with him 12 or 15 years ago. It is an exquisite symphony, his nature, when all the violins get playing as they did the other night; so deep, so fantastic."

Vanessa continued to push for a marriage between Virginia and Strachey, though her husband had now resumed his relationship with Mrs Raven-Hill, the woman who had first introduced him to the pleasures of sex and was his mistress up until the time of his marriage. She had even given Vanessa insider information on contraception and advanced sexual etiquette. Despite her helpful advice, Vanessa referred to Mrs Raven-Hill in her correspondence with Clive as "your whore". Meanwhile she happily continued her own affair with Roger Fry.

"Oh Roger, it was delicious today in spite of the sordid surrounding, like a little water when one was very thirsty," she wrote after a hard day in the studio. "I have always had a taste for lovemaking in the midst of quite ordinary things, as it turns them into something else. Not that it wouldn't be divine to do it in Asia Minor, too."

At this time Lytton was in full flight from Virginia and, to save himself, began urging Leonard Woolf to come on to Virginia.

"You have the immense advantage of physical desire," wrote Strachey.

This is not entirely true. Leonard, Clive and Lytton had all fancied Virginia's brother, Thoby, at Cambridge, but Leonard and Clive had transferred their affections to Vanessa.

Nevertheless, Leonard had remained a virgin – heterosexually – until the age of 25 when he was in the colonial service in Ceylon (now Sri Lanka) and had been offered the services of a mixed-race prostitute, which he accepted.

Strachey and others thought that Woolf was a highly sexed man, but Leonard himself said "the pleasure of it is, of course, grossly exaggerated". For him, riding a horse at a gallop was "better as a pleasure than copulation". I guess it all depends on the mare.

Maybe he had just spent too long in the Apostles. In 1907, he wrote to Strachey: "Most women naked when alive are extraordinarily ugly, but dead they are repulsive."

When a friend offered him a second crack at straight sex in Jaffna, Leonard said: "I went to the room and saw a half-naked woman sitting on a bed. But I was too utterly bored to feel even the mildest disgust, which was my only feeling (if there was any). I just sat down on a chair dumb with dejection and finally, without doing or saying anything, gave her all the money I had on me and fled."

On self-examination, Leonard did not even think that a bit of S&M would do the trick. He did write a love poem to a Tamil girl, but it was full of self-loathing. However, when he got to grips with Virginia, he seems to have thought that this vast experience of the universe of passion qualified him to boast of being "lustful". It turned Virginia off immediately.

"I feel angry sometimes at the strength of your desire," wrote Virginia, recoiling. "As I told you brutally the other day, I feel no physical attraction in you. There are moments – when you kissed me the other day was one – when I feel no more than a rock."

A rock? No, that's my …

Despite her lack of response, Clive grew jealous – though Virginia's response to Leonard's advances hardly gave him cause. At Christmas 1911, however, Leonard moved into the house Virginia shared with her brother Adrian, Duncan Grant* and Maynard Keynes* in Brunswick Square and in January he proposed. This got Virginia into bed – unfortunately alone, with "a touch of my usual disease", but, after a short period in a nursing home, she consented to marry Leonard – "a penniless Jew", she told her friends. Well, give the boy a big build-up.

Despite the casual anti-Semitism of her class, Vanessa was delighted; Clive was less so.

"I know I'm not unworthily jealous, I know I am not cold. But I'm dreadfully puzzled," he wrote. "You know, whatever happens, I shall always cheat myself into believing that I appreciate and love you better than your husband does."

Clive consoled himself with a series of other mistresses. Virginia believed that he never forgave her.

"Now all is second best," he told her accusingly.

As the wedding approached, Vanessa's attitude started to become more ambivalent, too. Maybe she was worried about losing her sister and their "thought incest". She interrupted the wedding service and wrote to Virginia on her honeymoon, saying: "I have given up all belief I ever had in your affection."

Virginia's reply was the equally catty: "You have the children and the fame that by rights belongs to me." And presumably the husband, too.

Vanessa also stirred the brew with honeymoon letters to Leonard.

"You sound so happy," she said. "I long to hear more details, but I suppose I must wait for them till I see you."

Nosy.

In another letter she enquired directly about their sex life, strangely referring to Virginia as a man and calling her Billy.

"Billy may well be an apt pupil considering that he's been so much used as a brooding ape. Ask him if he feels more attracted by the male than the female figure. Does he like manly strength and hardness?" – Hardness! – "Also, do tell me how you find him compared with others you have had."

If that was not a joyful enough missive to get on your honeymoon, Vanessa wrote to Virginia again, asking: "Are you really a promising pupil? I believe that I am very bad at it. Perhaps Leonard would like to give me a few lessons, but, of course, some people don't need to be so skilful."

Despite this poison, the honeymoon in Somerset, then France, Spain and Italy, seems to have been a success.

"We talked incessantly for seven weeks" – talked! – "and became chronically nomadic and monogamic," Virginia told one girl friend. With another she was positively blithe.

"Why do you think people make such a fuss about marriage and copulation?" she said. "Why do some of our friends change upon losing chastity? Possibly my great age makes it less of a catastrophe." She was 30. "But certainly I find the climax immensely exaggerated."

After four months and no big O, they consulted Little Miss Sex – Vanessa – herself, and, ever the discreet one, she relayed the gist of the conversation to Clive: "The Woolves ... are evidently both a little exercised in their minds on the subject of the Goat's [Virginia's] coldness. I think that I perhaps annoyed her, but may have consoled him by saying that I thought she never had understood or sympathised with sexual passion in men." This consoled him? "Apparently she still gets no pleasure at all from the act, which I think is curious. They were very anxious to know when I first had an orgasm. I couldn't remember. Do you? But no doubt I'd sympathise with such things if I didn't have them from the time I was two."

While that was Vanessa's side of the story, the writer Gerald Brenan told a very different tale.

"Leonard told me that when on their honeymoon he had tried to make love to her, she had got into such a violent state of excitement that he had to stop, knowing as he did that these states were a prelude to her attacks of madness. So Leonard ... had to give up all idea of ever having any sort of sexual satisfaction. He told me he was ready to do this 'because she was a genius'."

After Virginia Woolf's death in 1941, Leonard was asked whether he had ever had any sexual relationships outside their marriage. He said he had not because he was sure that Virginia would have found out, and that the discovery would have killed her. And he could not have discreetly visited prostitutes. After his experiences in Ceylon, he had found that he was too fastidious for that sort of thing.

However, the marriage was not entirely sexless. Virginia confided to her diary that Leonard sometimes kept "cheerful illusions going merrily till bedtimes, when some antics ended the day" – without specifying what these "antics" were. And, on one occasion, she wrote to Vanessa: "We were kept awake till four this morning by mice in our bedroom. At last Leonard started to make his bed, and a mouse sprang out from his blankets, whereupon he had a wet dream – you can't think what his sheets were like in the morning."

The mouse was presumably a little furry animal looking for its hole. And the state of the sheets would not have bothered Virginia at all. To her "dung is merely dung, death death and semen semen", said Leonard.

However, Virginia showed no compassion toward her husband's sexual frustration. In fact, she never had much time at all for Leonard and looked down on him because he was Jewish. Leonard, however, was to continue to love and support Virginia for the rest of her life.

Now that her husband was safe from the clutches of her sister, Vanessa dumped Roger Fry and replaced him with the painter Duncan Grant*, even though Grant was having a gay affair with David "Bunny" Garnett. What Vanessa wanted, though, Vanessa got.

"I copulate on Saturday with her with great satisfaction to myself physically," Grant wrote in his diary. "It is a convenient way the females [provide] of letting off one's spunk and [making one] comfortable. Also the pleasure it gives is reassuring. You don't get this dumb misunderstanding body of a person who isn't a bugger. That's one for you, Bunny."

Vanessa wanted another baby and Duncan gave her one, thereby cementing – or should that be sementing – the Bloomsbury Group a little closer together. As Roger Fry wrote: "Hers really is an almost ideal family, based as it is on adultery and mutual forbearance with Clive, the deceived husband, and me, the abandoned lover. It really is a triumph of reasonableness over the conventions."

Not everyone was so reasonable though. As a teenager, Angelica Bell discovered that her father was not Clive Bell but Duncan Grant. For revenge she decided to marry Bunny Garnett, her father's lover who had been present at her birth.

Her parents, unsurprisingly, were not best pleased. However, Angelica and Bunny were married for 30 years and had four daughters.

It was Virginia, though, who really wanted Vanessa. Pushing 50, she fessed up to her sister: "With you I am deeply, passionately, unrequitedly in love ... and thank goodness your beauty is ruined, for my incestuous feeling may be cooled – yet it has survived half a century of indifference."

On another occasion, Virginia wrote to her sister more in sorrow than in anger: "You will never succumb to the charms of any of your sex. What an arid garden the world must be for you! What avenues of stone pavements and iron railings! Greatly though I respect the male mind ... I cannot see that they have a glowworm's worth of charm about them. The scenery of the world takes no lustre from their presence. They add, of course, immensely to its dignity and safety, but when it comes to a little excitement – (I see that you will attribute all this to your own charms in which I dare say you are not far wrong)."

Virginia, of course, was to get her share of excitement from Vita Sackville-Race – sorry, West – the wife of Harold Nicolson, a diplomat and homosexual. She was an accomplished poet and author as well as being a beautiful, exotic and outspoken lesbian. They first met at dinner at Clive's in 1922. In her diary the following day, Virginia wrote: "She makes me feel virgin, shy and schoolgirlish."

Vita's own introduction to sex had occurred when she was 11 years old. A local farmer's son, called Jackie, "told me a great many things he oughtn't have told me," she said. One day by the ghillie's hut he said: "Miss Vita, Miss Vita, Vita, Vita, I love you" and put his hand on her thigh.

"But because of his inborn respect and his sense of class, he didn't rape me," she said. He masturbated instead. In case this was not a graphic enough demonstration of the facts of life, he made her take hold of a dog's penis and work it back and forth until "the dog reached the point where it came and squirted its semen all over my shoes". After this charming introduction to male sexuality, Harold Nicolson's obsession with young aristocrats' nether regions must have seemed positively wholesome.

The following year, Vita got to know Violet Keppel, the daughter of Mrs Alice Keppel*, the mistress of Edward VII*. Indeed, it is thought that Violet might even have been the king's daughter. The two little girls had a lot in common and became firm friends. However, it was an older girl at school called Rosamund Grosvenor who took Vita's fancy at that time. Travelling to Italy, Vita and Rosamund slept together and they were still in the throes of a full-blown affair when Vita and Harold got engaged. Naturally, she blamed Harold for this mix-up.

"You were older than I, and far better informed," she wrote later. "I was very young, and very innocent. I knew nothing about homosexuality. I didn't even know that such a thing existed – either between men or between women. You should have told me. You should have warned me. You should have told me about yourself, and have warned me that the same sort of thing was likely to happen to myself. It would have saved us a lot of trouble and misunderstanding."

This is disingenuous. Although she attracted a number of male admirers on her travels, Vita was late for her first date with Harold because she had been with Rosamund. Not that it mattered. Harold had been posted home with the clap at the time. It did not bother Vita much either.

"Men did not attract me in what is called 'that way'," she said. "Women did. Rosamund did ... Oh, I dare say I realised vaguely that I had no business to sleep with Rosamund, and I should certainly never have allowed anyone to find out, but my sense of guilt went no further than that."

Of course, Harold did not mind. It was rather convenient for him to have a wife who had her own interests and allowed him to pursue his own path. Besides, she was rich and he wasn't.

For Vita, there was no conflict between being "engaged to Harold and at the same time being so much in love with Rosamund". Harold was merely a "playmate".

"Our relationship was so fresh, so intellectual, so unphysical, that I never thought of him in that aspect at all," she said.

"Some men seem born to be lovers, others to be husbands; he belonged to the latter category." Meanwhile, with Rosamund: "It was passion that used to make my head swim, even in the daytime."

The three of them "played about" together. Vita and Rosamund took off to Italy once more. Vita claimed that she and Rosamund never actually made love, but on one occasion, when they had been parted, Rosamund wrote: "My sweet darling ... I do miss you darling one and I want to feel your soft, cool face coming out of that mass of pussy fur like it did last night."

However, Violet was always there on the sidelines and Rosamund became jealous. Not without good reason. One evening Vita went out for a walk with Violet.

"She is mad," wrote Vita. "She kissed me as she usually does not, and told me she loved me. Rose does not know that I went out with Violet this evening."

Vita then went to stay at the Keppels' in Ravello. Meanwhile Rosamund had got rather half-heartedly engaged to a guards officer.

"Oh my sweet, you do know, don't you, that nothing can ever make me love you less whatever happens," wrote Vita. "I really think you have taken all my love already as there seems very little left and I am so cold and heartless."

It was then that she decided "to marry Harold and get it over with".

"But I continued my liaisons with Rosamund," she said. In the meantime she amused herself by lunching at the Ritz with the rapacious sculptor Auguste Rodin* and the painter John Singer Sargent.

The relationship with Rosamund continued on a highly charged emotional level even after Vita's marriage and she started knocking out babies – which was remarkable in itself as everyone said that there was nothing remotely sexual in the relationship between Vita and her husband. Then, in 1918, Vita seriously started getting down with Violet Keppel. On August 14, after a series of clandestine assignations, Violet wrote to Vita: "Mitya, Mitya, I have loved you all my life, a long time without knowing, five years knowing it irrevocably as I do now, loved you as my ideal, my inspiration, my perfection ... You are the *grande passion* of my life."

When Harold got wind of it he was fiercely jealous.

"Little one – I wish Violet was dead," he wrote to Vita. "She has poisoned one of the most sunny things that ever happened. She is like some fierce orchid – glimmering and stinking in the recesses of life – and throwing cadaverous sweetness on the morning breeze. Darling, she is evil and I am not evil. Oh my darling – what is it that makes you put her above me? ... Oh darling, yesterday I wanted to kiss you as if I loved you, and you turned aside. Such a slight deflection ... and yet it hurt me so, it sent me away so hurt, darling."

Violet made it her business to try and separate Vita and Harold. She did this by constantly ridiculing their love and their home-life. At the same time, she toyed with the idea of marrying Major Denys Trefusis, a career soldier and a hero of Ypres and the Somme. She also fired off passionate letters, missives that would have destroyed Vita's marriage if Harold had read them. In them, she and Vita take on the roles of Eve and Julian from the romantic novel Vita was writing called *Challenge*.

"Mitya, you could do anything with me, or rather Julian could," wrote Violet. "I love Julian overwhelmingly, devastatingly, possessively, incoherently, insatiably, passionately, despairingly – also coquettishly, flirtatiously and frivolously."

She speculated on how nice it would be if Denys and "Julian" met and had to compete for her affections openly. Then she discovered something about Vita's sex life with Harold that repelled her. It was, she said, as if she had "come upon a nest of woolly caterpillars, and my whole nature is polluted".

The shocking information came from Vita's mother.

"Thank goodness I have been spared this horrible knowledge for much longer than most people," wrote Violet. "We will eliminate the words 'lust' and 'passion' from our vocabulary, they are dirty and hideous."

Violet always preferred to live in a world of fairytales. Vita, on the other hand, was a woman of violent, physical passion. She complained to her less-than-discreet mother about Harold being "physically cold".

"I am indeed sorry to hear that Harold is made like that, as he can't help himself," Vita's mother confided to her diary, "but it is so hard on her, poor child, as she misses passionate love not being returned, and he is always so sleepy and has her in a desperate hurry." Presumably to get it over with. "So many men are like that and eventually lose the love of their wife."

Violet tried to profit from this by begging Vita to come away with her. Mama gave Harold a pep talk, however, and the next day at luncheon Vita told her about the "wonderful change that had come over Harold".

"At last he treated her like a lover and she now felt perfectly happy as the one thing that had been missing in him had been altered," recorded mama. "She also admitted that Violet was immoral and she hated that side of her."

However, when Violet threatened suicide, Vita went off to the Côte d'Azur with her, where they were seen dancing together cheek-to-cheek.

"Monte Carlo was perfect. Violet was perfect," she wrote later.

Harold, who was at the Versailles Peace Conference at the time, was distracted by jealousy. He called Violet a swine and compared her to bad odour or a sickness. Vita, he maintained, was merely bowled over by her sycophancy.

"Of course, she flatters you," he wrote to Vita. "That is it – every silly woman is bowled over by flattery. How I hate women."

Now it's coming out. Such frankness, however, was not a good way to get your wife back. I do hope he was a bit more diplomatic at the Peace Conference. Harold hoped that Vita would come to Paris and be by his side as they tried to sort out the mess left by the First World War, but Violet would not let her go. Vita sent a crushing letter to Harold who, in the midst of delicate negotiations, had to cope with the upheaval in his domestic arrangements that her non-appearance caused.

Mama stepped in and persuaded Vita to return to England for the sake of the children. She gave Vita a dressing down "about Violet Keppel, whom she agrees is a sexual pervert and she tries hard to break with that horrible girl". Following this, Violet announced her engagement to Major Trefusis.

After a brief spell of leave in London, Vita returned to Paris with Harold, but warned him that she feared that Violet might come to see her before her marriage.

"I must be away, or I won't be responsible," she said. And she was "absolutely terrified" that she would create a scandal over Violet's wedding.

She also said that she regretted getting married so young. "Women, like men, ought to have their early years so glutted with freedom that they hate the very idea of freedom. Like assistants in a chocolate shop."

Violet was not helping the situation and was deliberately placing temptation in Vita's way.

"Cast aside the drab garments of respectability and convention, my beautiful bird of paradise, they become you not," she wrote. "Lead the life nature intended you to lead. Otherwise Mitya, you'll be a failure – you, who might be among the greatest, most scintillating and romantic figures of all time, you'll be 'Mrs Nicolson, who has written some charming verse'."

As it was the wedding went off without a hitch, but the honeymoon – which began in Paris – was more problematic. The moment the newly-weds arrived in the Paris Ritz, Vita went to see Violet, took her to a small hotel and made love to her.

"I had her, I didn't care, I only wanted to hurt Denys," she said.

The next day Vita saw Denys in what she described as an "awful interview", but it did not dampen her ardour. She began to haunt the Ritz and dined pitifully alone in full view of the Trefusises. In the midst of all this, poor old Harold was trying to secure a lasting peace in Europe – an endeavour that was to come tragically undone 20 years later with the onset of the Second World War. Violet and Denys eventually headed off to the south of France, Vita went home to England, heartbroken, and Harold got stuck into German arms control.

However, when the Trefusises returned to England, they moved into a house just ten miles from Harold and Vita's country house, Long Barn. The liaison continued. This time Harold was cool. He had just shacked up in Paris with the courtier Edward Molyneux, whose skill at cutting out paper patterns must have helped when Harold was redrawing the map of Europe.

"My sweet, are you jealous?" Harold taunted Vita over the Molyneux affair.

Vita was not. She had told her mother that, as chastity and the horrors of male sexuality were Violet's obsessions, she had told Harold that, from now on, their marriage would be platonic. Like the Trefusises, they would have a *mariage blanc* – a union with no sex. Harold, she said, had taken the news "like a lamb". This was not true. Despite his new-found devotion to *haute couture*, Harold wanted a daughter – to dress perhaps?

"I want a little girl who will be like you," he told Vita, "and who will love me as you do – but less selfishly."

He was also angry when he heard that Vita and Violet – now together again in Monte Carlo – had been seen dancing in public.

"I am still cross about it," he wrote. "But I will forgive you anything."

This was so much b.s. – or "backstairs", which was Harold and Vita's code for homosexuality.

Vita told Harold that another child was out of the question, she couldn't handle all that messy business. She also told him that she was going to break with Violet once and for all when she left Monte Carlo. Naturally, she told Violet precisely the opposite. She said she was off to London to make plans so that they could be together forever.

Violet and Denys came to see Vita in her London home for another "unpleasant interview". What Denys wanted to know was, did Vita have the money to keep his wife in the style to which she had become accustomed?

"I felt like a young man wanting to marry Violet and being interviewed by her father," Vita said.

Denys then asked Violet, point-blank, if she wanted to give up everything and live with Vita. Violet replied that she wanted a week to think it over. Four days later though, Vita and Violet decided it was now or never. When Vita told Harold, he collapsed. All this and the inauguration of the League of Nations, too. She agreed to stay with him for his fortnight's leave, but when he returned to Paris to tie up a few more outstanding treaties things were still up in the air.

Vita and Violet then took off to France together, but Vita wrote Harold a little note every day, which must have been a comfort as he tackled the future peace of the world. Denys pursued the lovers and caught up with them at a hotel in Amiens, where he told Vita that Violet was his wife "in all senses of the word". Vita became so hysterical that he had to retract "perjuring himself".

Vita soon realised the truth, though. Violet had been lying to her. The idea that the two women could enjoy their freedom living side by side in two *mariages blancs* was more b.s. Vita left and headed for Harold in Paris to disrupt the worlds of both international diplomacy and high fashion once more. Things were on the mend when Vita's publishers sent the proofs of *Challenge*, which had turned into a thinly disguised version of the Vita-Violet affair so far. A suggestive drawing by Violet, showing herself and "Julian" smoking a cigarette under a lamppost in Paris, was destined for the cover. Fearful of the gossip, Vita paid Collins £150 to halt publication.

Then, following a row with Harold over her "Amazonian theories" and her "truculent virginity", Vita headed off once again with Violet. This time Harold caught up with them and persuaded them to return to England. However, as they were still living only ten miles apart in the country, they often snatched days and nights together.

This was not good enough for Violet. She wanted all or nothing. In contrast, Vita wanted to stay in a chaste marriage with Harold, as she found that she could not write with Violet around. The novelist Clemence Dane tried to persuade the two women to give each other up one "awful morning". Vita agreed, leaving Violet to complain: "You said today that our love had become a debased and corrupt thing."

Violet became ill and Vita rushed to nurse her, but soon she found herself longing for the peace of Long Barn where she could write. When she eventually returned home, she wrote to Harold to say that she and Violet were "separating completely".

"She is going abroad almost at once," Vita said. "I have refused to go."

She then started committing a long confession to paper, which would be published as *Portrait of a Marriage* by her son Nigel Nicolson after her death.

Violet refused to go away. She came over two weeks later with the news that her marriage might be annulled. As the price of their "separation", she insisted that Vita refrain from marital relations with Harold. This caused an enormous strain on their marriage. Vita's mother recorded that, when they were staying in Brighton, "Harold lost his poor little temper in Vita's bedroom, saying all women are cruel." He confided his unhappiness to his mother-in-law, who was very impressed by the brave face he put on the situation when he was in public.

When Vita began to weaken, Violet came flying down to Brighton to strengthen her resolve. From then on Violet reminded Vita of the "promise made at Brighton ... Don't let anything distract you even temporarily from the Great Adventure". She told Vita that there was to be no sex life for this famous lesbian.

Violet was playing a double game, however. She told Vita's mother that "she felt sorry for Denys".

"She said it was different for Vita refusing herself to Harold as they had been married for six years and she had had three children," wrote Vita's mother, "but Denys had nothing and perhaps she would end by giving in to him. She strikes me as playing a wicked game with Vita ... Vita sees nothing and believes blindly in Violet Trefusis."

So the Great Adventure continued. Violet and Vita headed off abroad again in January 1921. Harold, more than a little pissed off, wrote: "You are more selfish than Agrippina* in her worst moments ... more optimistic than the Virgin Mary* at her most light-hearted and more weak than some polypus floating and undulating in a pond."

You old sweet-talker you.

Vita wrote back from the south of France, telling Harold that she loved only him. Now that Violet's mother and Denys had both turned against her she was feeling pangs of guilt.

"I am responsible," she said. She added that she would die if anything separated her from her husband and her babies. Sowing wild oats was all very well, but now they had grown "as high as a jungle".

"I want to be rid of the whole wretched business and live with you again," she told Harold.

Denys was now threatening divorce and the resulting scandal was bound to engulf Harold and Vita. Rumours were spreading and some doors had already been closed to Vita. Mrs Keppel also put her foot down. She paid for Denys and Violet to go and live abroad. Their marriage had become only a front, however, as Denys, denied what he wanted by Violet, went off and found it elsewhere. Violet wrote to Vita, saying: "You have all you want – a lovely place to live in, love, affection. It's not fair."

No comment.

And it wasn't fair. Vita did have all she wanted. To encourage her to break from Violet, Harold had suggested she start a new affair with Dorothy Wellesley.

Thumbing through the *Dictionary of National Biography* – not everyone's bedtime reading, to be sure – it describes Wellesley, Dorothy Violet, Duchess of Wellington this way: "Slight of build, almost fragile, with blazing blue eyes, fair hair and transparently white skin, she was a natural rebel, rejecting all conventions and accepted ideas, loving to proclaim herself an agnostic, a fiery spirit with a passionate love for beauty in all forms" – including the female form? – "whether of flowers, landscape or works of art ... She was a born romantic by temperament, but the bad fairy at her christening had decreed that her intellectual power should never equal her gifts of the imagination ... Dorothy Wellesley loved entertaining her friends ... No biographical sketch of her would be complete without a mention of the charm and gaiety she could display as a hostess."

The author of this paean is one "V. Sackville-West". Her sources, the *DNB* records, were "private information; personal knowledge".

Clandestine letters still flitted through intermediaries between Violet and Vita, but the Great Adventure was over – with Violet at least. The next time Violet came to England, Vita went off on holiday with Dorothy and her husband Gerald. Leaving Gerald in Parma, "Dottie" and Vita sailed for the Dalmatian coast together, but were constantly interrupted by bronzed young men in their swimming trunks. They met up with Gerald and Harold in Rome and, when they returned to England, Vita was invited to dinner at Clive Bell's to meet Virginia Woolf.

Although Vanessa teased Virginia about her "sapphism", it had only been on an emotional and intellectual basis up to this point. She had had a series of close friendships with older women, including Violet Dickinson, who had maintained a maternal interest in Virginia after her mother died, and the composer Ethel Smyth, who was more open about her sexual preferences.

There is no doubt that Virginia was attracted to Vita, who was like a turbocharged Vanessa – even more sexually predatory, worldly and glamorous. Clive and Vanessa's son, Quentin Bell, said: "Vita would seem to have been invented for Virginia's pleasure. In her Virginia found a person of high lineage, but also one in whom there was something better ... a certain literary heritage."

Vita was a beautiful, charming, majestic woman, full of an Andalusian passion – she boasted Spanish blood. Virginia admitted to finding her "lovely, gifted, aristocratic", but after their first meeting she said that Vita was "not much to my severer taste – florid, moustached, parakeet-coloured, with all the supple ease of the aristocracy, but not the wit of the artist. She writes 15 pages a day – has finished another book – publishes with Heinemann – knows everyone. But could I ever know her?"

Four days later, Vita invited Virginia for dinner. Afterwards she wrote to Harold, who was in Lausanne, saying: "I simply adore Virginia Woolf ... At first you think she is plain; then a sort of spiritual beauty imposes itself on you, and you find a fascination in watching her ... She is quite old. I have rarely taken such a fancy to anyone, and I think she likes me. At least, she's asked me to Richmond where she lives. Darling, I have quite lost my heart."

After dining with Virginia in Richmond, where the Woolfs lived briefly before moving back to Bloomsbury, Vita noted that she was "as delicious as ever ... and has had no *grande passion* in her life".

Virginia was aware of what was going on. She told her diary: "She is a pronounced sapphist and may, thinks Ethel Sands, have an eye on me, old though I am. Nature might have sharpened her faculties. Snob as I am, I trace her passions five hundred years back, and they become romantic to me, like old, yellow wine."

Vita took a holiday in the Dolomites in July 1924 and wrote passionately to Virginia. She replied that she was in two minds about the "intimate letter from the Dolomites. It gave me a great deal of pain – which is, I've no doubt, the first stage of intimacy."

Vita wrote back asking her what "pain" she had given. "Or was it just one of your phrases, poked at me? Do you ever mean what you say, or say what you mean? Or do you just enjoy baffling the people who try to creep a little nearer?"

Never mind about "pain", I wonder what "poked" means in this context. Virginia seems to have sensed some erotic overtones.

"These sapphists love women," she wrote. "Friendship is never untinged with amorosity."

The seduction seems to have taken place in Knole, Kent, the Sackvilles' ancestral pile, just before Christmas. It may not have been a terribly successful experience. Several biographers have concluded that Virginia was as unresponsive with Vita as she had been with Leonard. In a letter to Ethel Smyth, Virginia wrote: "Vita also calls me fish."

They think that Vita is saying that Virginia is as cold as a "fish", but that may not be it at all. "Fish" is gay slang for ... well, fish – as in "eating tuna", you know. In fact, since 1850 "fish" has also been English slang for the female genitalia. Clive Bell was the first to call Virginia "a fish", so maybe he got further than most people thought.

At first, in her diaries, Virginia was defensive: "For three days ... I liked her [Vita], I liked being with her and her splendour – she shines in the grocer's shop at Sevenoaks with a candlelit radiance, stalking on legs like beech trees, pink glowing, grape clustered, pearl hung ... What is the effect of all this on me? Very mixed. There is her maturity and full-breastedness; her being so much in full sail on the high tides ... in short, what I have never been – a real woman. Then there is some voluptuousness about her ... the grapes are ripe." Are we talking tits or what?

Virginia was soon bragging to Vanessa: "Vita is now arriving to spend two nights alone with me – Leonard is going back. I say no more as you are bored by Vita, bored by love, bored my me and everything to do with me ... Still, the June nights are long and warm, the roses flowering, and the garden full of lust and bees, mingling in the asparagus beds."

Vita was also open with Harold:

I fetched Virginia and brought her down here [to Long Barn]. She is an exquisite companion, and I love her dearly. Leonard is coming on Saturday. Please don't think that:
a) I shall fall in love with Virginia
b) Virginia will ,, ,, ,, me
c) Leonard ,, ,, ,, ,, me
d) shall ,, ,, ,, Leonard

Vita did fall in love with Virginia, however, though whether Virginia ",, ,," her is not clear.

Virginia recalled that there was a "moment of intimacy" on the Friday evening before Leonard arrived. They were lying on the sofa in front of a blazing fire in the living room together. We do not know if this was a "fish" moment. Vita said she was sensitive to Virginia's "inviolability", but that they were "flapping their gums" – just talking perhaps – until three a.m.

"I was always sexually cowardly," Virginia wrote. "My terror of real life has always kept me in a nunnery." (See *Sex Lives of the Popes* for details.)

Soon after Vita was having lunch with the Bells and the Woolfs when Clive said: "I wonder if I dare ask Vita a very indiscreet question."

Innocently, Vita said that he could.

"Have you ever gone to bed with Virginia?"

"Never," said Vita, vehemently.

Vita told Harold that her vehemence was enough to convince anyone that what she was saying was true. Nevertheless, she was soon having to convince him that Virginia was not going to be another Violet all over again.

Vita had numerous other female lovers at the time, but the affair was passionate nonetheless. On one occasion, Vita threatened to drive over to the Woolfs' country house in Rodmell, Sussex, and "throw gravel at your window, then you'd come down and let me in; I'd stay with you till five, and be home by half-past six".

In reply Virginia telegrammed simply: "Come then."

Vanessa grew jealous.

"Don't expend all your energies in letter writing on her," she wrote. "I consider I have first claim."

She also complained that Vita "treats me as an Arab steed, looking from the corner of its eye on some long-eared mule – but then you do your best to stir up jealousy between us, so what can one expect?"

Vanessa had good reason to be jealous. She had been the model for the central roles in Virginia's novels *The Voyage Out*, *Night and Day* and *To the Lighthouse*, but Vita would be the central character in *Orlando*, a farcical history of England from 1500 to the 1920s based on the history of the Sackville family where Vita changes sex halfway through. It was a bestseller. Vita's son, the writer Nigel Nicolson, said that it was "the longest and most charming love letter in history".

However, as Vanessa was unable to ensnare Duncan Grant* into any heterosexual commitment, she and Virginia stayed close, despite the affair. Leonard declared Virginia's affair with

Vita to be "rather a bore". He did end up liking Vita and published her at The Hogarth Press, the publishing company the Woolfs had established in 1917.

Sometimes the whole of Bloomsbury would go down to Long Barn for summer weekends. Vita wrote to Harold: "I shall make Clive play host. I have put him and Mary [Hutchinson – Clive's latest lover] next to each other, so they can fuck all night if they want to – which they obviously do. I like her awfully – she had the prettiest manners imaginable."

Occasions where Virginia and Vita did what Clive and Mary were doing were marked with an exclamation mark in Vita's diaries. Around that time they were meeting almost every day and there was plenty of !ing going on.

Virginia compared Vita to Sappho* and said that she already reminded her of "a ship breasting a sea" – those tits again. Vita also wrote a cryptic note about Virginia's "inauguration" – to a new variety of sex, perhaps.

While Virginia was writing *Orlando*, Vita began an affair with Mary Garman, who used to drive her husband, the poet Roy Campbell, crazy with the beautiful women she seduced but who he could only dream of. Vita took her to Knole and kissed her in the bedroom, then made love to her on the sofa at Long Barn where she had her first encounter with Virginia. She moved Mary and Roy into a cottage on the estate, so that she would be close. That did not stop her from seducing another friend of Clive Bell's, the young actress Valerie Taylor, or from continuing to see Dottie or Virginia.

For the time being there seems to have been little jealousy between these women. Vita wrote to Virginia: "What a lovely letter you wrote me, Campbell or no Campbell. (How flattered she'd be if she knew. But she doesn't, and shan't.) … But how right I was … to force myself on you at Richmond, and to lay the trail for the explosion which happened on the sofa in my room here when you behaved so disgracefully and acquired me for ever."

The only one who cut up rough was Roy, who threatened murder and suicide after a drinking binge with Augustus John*. The situation was defused when Vita moved on. She was soon spending nights at her Ebury Street residence with Clive Bell's squeeze, Mary Hutchinson, who wrote on June 27, 1927: "I left a pearl earring on the table by your bed. I remember exactly where I put it – at the corner near you. Will you be very nice and post it to me soon? ... Did you sleep among the thorns and petals?" I think it is clear what that might allude to, as well.

Virginia had coped well with Mary Garman, but Mary Hutchinson was a bitch too far. And there were others. Feeling herself no longer young and pretty, Virginia became fiercely jealous. She wrote to Vita begging her not to run off with any of her new lovers.

All Vanessa could do was mock.

"Poor Billy," she wrote, "isn't one thing or the other, not a man nor a woman, so what's he to do?"

Then came an even worse blow. Vita had a male admirer. Philip Morrell had declared his love for her. He was the husband of the wildly promiscuous Lady Ottoline Morrell*, a frequent flier on the Bloomsbury scene. Virginia was going crazy, but Vita stoutly resisted her tantrums.

"I won't be trifled with," Vita told Virginia. "I really mean this."

Vita was going through a distinctly heterosexual phase. She was sleeping with the writer Geoffrey Scott, who bought her a ring after an afternoon session in a borrowed flat in Hanover Terrace and then thought better of it and fled to Italy. And, after a party at Mary Hutchinson's at Chiswick, Vita gave politician, diplomat and author Duff Cooper a lift home.

"To my astonishment he made love to me," wrote Vita, "altogether a queer evening."

You can say that again.

There were still erotic moments between Vita and Virginia, though. For the publication of *Orlando*, Virginia needed some photographs of Vita in her female incarnation.

"I was miserable," Vita wrote to Harold, "draped in an inadequate bit of pink satin with all my clothes slipping off – but Virginia delighted and kept diving under the black cloth of the camera to peep at the effect."

With Harold back in London on leave, he and Vita made a broadcast on the BBC on the subject of marriage.

"We won't be able to mention sex, I presume," he said.

The broadcast had been arranged by Vita's new girlfriend, Hilda Matheson, who was director of talks at the BBC. Vita called her "Stoker" and said she reminded her of a sturdy pony.

"How am I ever to see you, apart from Hilda?" wrote Virginia. "Is an afternoon possible? Not since Rodmell, and then only for two minutes, have we been alone in a room together – let alone the other place." Other place?

Curiously, Vita was jealous of Virginia's relationship with Ethel Smyth, who said that Vita was the only person, apart from Vanessa and Leonard, who Virginia really loved. Just two days after Virginia's appeal, however, Vita recorded that she spent the whole day at Sissinghurst Castle – Harold and Vita's new country home – arranging her bedroom with Hilda.

They had already consummated their affair at the house in South Kensington that Hilda shared with two other single women. Afterwards Hilda wrote: "If anything can save me from becoming the kind of dried-up person I dread to think of, you will, and this will."

Well, Vita certainly knew how to get those juices flowing, eh Virginia?

"Love – all you've given me – all the physical side of it too – seems to me to be life in its very highest expression," Hilda wrote to Vita that Christmas. "It is mixed up for me with any decent thinking or feeling I have got or ever had – with everything, in fact, that is true and beautiful and of good report. And yet I suppose some people would regard it as shameful and vicious."

Hilda's frequent letters were becoming an embarrassment and Vita begged her to be discreet.

"I see you're right," said Hilda in another letter. Doh. "Homosexual love is more difficult in itself and takes a lot more intelligence and sensitivity. Perhaps that is why it usually seems to work badly with men – perhaps they are less sensitive on those things ... It feels very natural and inevitable to love you as I do – in every way – as if it would be wrong if I didn't."

In the meantime, Virginia was whining to Ethel: "Do you think Vita really wants me in her life?" And Ethel was writing to Vita, saying: "The human contact others can achieve is not for her – and would not be even if her life had been full of lovemaking of all sorts."

Vita headed off to Berlin, where Harold had been posted. Virginia and Leonard were to follow.

Vita could not wait for Virginia to arrive. She had been to a "Sodomites' Ball" where a lot of men were dressed as women.

"I fancy I was the only genuine article in the room," she wrote home. "There are certainly very queer things to be seen in Berlin, and I think Potto [Virginia] will enjoy himself."

Among the other delicacies Vita sampled were "photographs of Josephine Baker stripped to the waist – very beautiful – and other photographs of an indecency which I won't describe".

When Virginia arrived, she was ill. Vita had a diagnosis.

"Do you know what I believe it was, apart from flu?" she wrote. "Suppressed randiness."

The two of them had gone to the top of the radio tower, where Virginia was "most indiscreet".

Vita then went off on holiday with Hilda Matheson to Val d'Isère. Virginia got to hear of it and was fiercely jealous. Hilda was hardly a worthy rival.

"Why do I mind? What do I mind? How much do I mind?" wrote a tormented Virginia. An intellectual snob, she looked down on Hilda, saying that there was "a queer trait in Vita – her passion for the earnest, middle-class intellectual, drab and dreary".

When Vita returned to England, she went to see Virginia at Rodmell. She told her that she was not in love with Hilda and swore that nothing had happened between them. She was lying, of course. Soon after, Hilda moved out of the house in South Kensington into a flat nearer to the Nicolsons' townhouse, so that she could be on hand day and night. Virginia, though miffed, had to accept this, and even did a talk on Beau Brummell for Hilda on the BBC.

Hilda then took off for a holiday in Sicily with Dorothy

Wellesley. Vita promptly fell on Evelyn Irons, the Women's Page editor of the *Daily Mail*, who she seduced, again, in front of a roaring fire. Unfortunately, Evelyn was not free. She was living with Olive Rinder, who suffered from tuberculosis and who was inclined to be hysterical. To keep her quiet, Vita seduced her, too.

Vita and Evelyn went off on holiday to Provence, but the situation was becoming too complicated. Evelyn became possessive and tried to take over Vita's life. When Vita resisted, she began to disappear at weekends. It was soon evident that Evelyn was seeing another woman. Eventually she kicked Olive out and moved her new love in. Vita took over the care of the ailing Olive and penned a valedictory poem to Evelyn:

> Do not forget, my dear, that once we loved.
> Remember only, free of stain or smutch,
> That passion once went naked and ungloved,
> And that your flesh was startled by my touch.

In the midst of it all, Harold and Vita lunched with Charlie Chaplin* and dined with Albert Einstein. Then Vita went on a lecture tour of America with the stated intention of seducing Marlene Dietrich*. She was shown around Hollywood by Gary Cooper*. William Randolph Hearst* asked her to stay and everywhere she went she was mobbed by "women, women, women". This should have been a joy, but Vita rued: "If anything could cure me of a weakness for my own sex it would be to sojourn among the Women's Clubs of America."

Writing home to her oldest son Ben, who was now 18, she said: "Sex is probably the most exciting but not the most important thing in life. Its very excitingness easily makes it appear the most important. I remember someone saying to me once, 'I feel I want to live for nothing but this.' And then, years afterwards, I met that person and they said they were sickened … Promiscuity is essentially cheap and sickening. Not on moral grounds – you know that I am without conventional morality – but on, almost, aesthetic grounds. It is cheap, easy, vulgar, lowering, a real prostitution of oneself … I wish I had had someone to give me this advice when I was 18. I had to work it all out for myself. Luckily, I fell in love with Daddy."

Ben promptly announced that he was gay. Surprise, surprise. And Vita fired off another long letter saying that she did not mind in the least. Some of her best friends were gay, she said. Just because he swung the other way, it did not mean that he should give up on the "whole happiness and joy of marriage", however.

"It doesn't follow in the least," she said. "Two of the happiest married people I know, whose names I must conceal for reasons of discretion, are both homosexual – for you know, probably, that homosexuality applies to women as well as to men. And then again, Duncan and Vanessa. (They aren't actually married, but they have lived together for years, and it amounts to the same thing as being married.) They love each other even as Daddy and I do, though Duncan is almost entirely homosexual. So you see, it is not necessarily a bar to happiness of our sort ... I see no reason why you shouldn't achieve it too, eventually, after you have sown your wild oats and got bored by the incessant crop."

Vita herself showed no sign of becoming bored, of course.

Then she came up with the *pièce de résistance*.

"As a matter of fact, you know so few attractive women that you may be wrong about yourself altogether ... I know that a lot of unhappiness comes from a muddle as to what matters and what doesn't matter."

As it turned out, Ben never managed to sustain a lasting relationship with a lover of either sex. Vita's mother blamed Vita and Harold. Virginia rode to their defence.

"The old woman should be shot," she said.

"Virginia, darling, you are an angel," Vita wrote in gratitude, "an angel to understand so unfailingly."

By then Hilda had quit the BBC and moved into Sissinghurst as Vita's secretary. This was something Virginia did not understand at all and, by 1935, her relationship with Vita was over.

It was all down hill for Virginia from there. She met Sigmund Freud* and went into psychoanalysis, but this was no substitute for Vita's more hands-on therapy. As war engulfed Europe once again, her depression deepened. Then, on March 28, 1941, she filled her pockets with stones and drowned herself in the River Ouse, not far from Rodmell.

This was a liberation for Leonard. At last, he could have sex. He immediately got down with South Africa-born "Trekkie Parsons", wife of Ian Parsons, a director at Chatto who Leonard had frequently collaborated with. Not a good business move. Less than a year after Virginia's death, Leonard moved into a house next door to the Parsons. Trekkie and Leonard began to spend the occasional weekend together in the country. These became more frequent when her husband, now in the armed forces, was sent to the United States to teach the interpretation of aerial photography.

Leonard called Trekkie "Tiger" – and also "Owl", "Dove" and "Pussy". She must have been a real animal. In October 1943, he begins a letter to her: "Dearest (I suppose I mustn't say and most beautiful) of creatures ..." It goes on: "... If ever anyone was worth a passion, dearest, it is you. Sometimes when I leave you, a – I daresay unreasonable – terror comes over me ..." In response she sent a poem to him supposedly written by her Persian pussycat, which when it came on heat was to be sent to be mated to a tom named Blue Wave. It read:

> I'm no longer cool, aloof and well bred
> Now I'm calling for Wave and his marriage bed;
> With ears laid back, and head low to the floor,
> I want once again what I've had once before
> I shake with desire
> I burn like a fire
> I'm passion's slave
> As I call for Blue Wave.

We get the picture.

This was a far more passionate affair than he had ever had with Virginia.

"I would rather go with you to Hell than with anyone else to Heaven," he wrote.

Beat that, Ginny.

After D-Day, Trekkie and Leonard moved in together while her husband was doing his bit in France. After the war, the three of them lived together. Eventually Trekkie split her time between living with her husband in London and living with Leonard in Sussex, but she travelled extensively with Leonard and tended him until he died in 1969. She then buried him under an elm tree in the garden where Virginia's ashes had been scattered 28 years earlier.

Vita had died in 1962, after spending her declining years tending the splendid gardens she and Harold had created at Sissinghurst Castle. Harold struggled on alone with his trowel until 1968.

6 The Well, Well, Well of Loneliness

Radclyffe Hall had numerous affairs with society women before blowing the lid off the London lesbian scene with her famous Sapphic novel, *The Well of Loneliness*, published in 1928. It explored, in detail, the love between a young girl and an older woman. The book was banned, but it appears that Hall – or John as she was known – was anything but lonely.

Born Marguerite Radclyffe-Hall in 1880, she came from a distinctly upper-class background. She had one older sister. A few weeks after her birth, her father, a playboy known universally as Rat, lived up to his name and left. Her mother promptly changed her name from Mary to the more fanciful Marie.

Radclyffe Hall's biographer, Lady Una Troubridge*, said that Marie "had, from the hour of birth … disliked her second daughter". Mrs Radclyffe-Hall divorced Rat, and then married Alberto Visetti, the professor of singing at the Royal College of Music and a man who Marguerite despised. He was cruel to her and there is some evidence of sexual abuse.

As Marguerite grew to adolescence, her mother became increasingly concerned about her tomboyish ways. Although she frequently visited Virginia Woolf's* house, her prose style emulated that of the more outré Vita Sackville-West*. Her mother tried to force Marguerite into ruffles, soft draperies and plumed hats so that she would appear, at least, like "a regular society girl".

Like many homosexuals of her age, she returned to classical models for her inspiration. This only confirmed in her mother's eyes that she was not "normal". She became convinced of her daughter's sexual deviance, believing that she "fell in love in turn with several of Visetti's pupils who were lodging in the house". She got so wound up about this that, "in a blind fury", her mother "flew at her and tore her hat (and some of her hair with it) from her head".

Visetti – who Radclyffe Hall referred to as "my disgusting old stepfather" – then took a hand in "normalising" his pretty young stepdaughter. He was well practised at this as he seems to have had affairs with a number of the young students who lodged with the family. We cannot tell the exact nature of these advances, but they seem to have begun when she was 11 years old. She told no one about them until she was in her thirties and living with Una Troubridge, her partner for 29 years. After Radclyffe Hall died, Una wrote her biography. In the first draft she mentioned "the sexual incident with the egregious Visetti" and offered a long description of it, but this was deleted before publication. However, in the day book she kept while she was with Radclyffe Hall, she regularly berates Visetti for his "lechery".

When Radclyffe Hall's mother asked Una to help the biographer she had hired to write a memoir of Visetti, Una refused to help in any project concerning that "dreadful, cretinous, lecherous old man". In her "Letters to John", she indicates that the advances were both violent and frightening. Then there was a contrived photograph of Radclyffe Hall and Visetti that Una described as "pathetic".

"A faded, shiny, *carte de visite* obviously taken to exploit the 'paternal' affection of Alberto Visetti," she wrote. "John a very thin, bony girl of about ten, very unbecomingly dressed and with all the appearance of an unloved child, standing awkwardly beside a seated Visetti, already getting rather portly, the epitome of smug self-satisfaction and conceit."

It's enough to make you hate men.

All was not well between Marguerite's mother and stepfather. His friends, who included Dvorak, Tchaikovsky* and Elgar*, looked down on her. She railed against his frequent infidelities, which he did nothing to conceal; sometimes he even brought his mistresses home with him. This did little to promote the joys of heterosexual love in the household.

In the midst of all this domestic turmoil, Marguerite felt misunderstood. She hung a large wooden crucifix on her bedroom wall and dreamt of being a martyr. She also fancied herself as a "jeaneous" (sic) – not at spelling obviously, she was dyslexic – and a lover, always pining after her piano teacher or some other pretty girl in a silk dress.

"I can scarcely remember the first time I fell in love," she wrote. "I think I was a lover even from my mother's womb."

Well, there's only one person you can love in your mother's womb. That's yourself.

Of course, Visetti's studio was a happy hunting ground for the young sapphist. There she could watch young women, flushed with passion, singing ardent declarations of love in the arias of Mozart*, Wagner* and Verdi*. She saw girls kissing boys and, sometimes, girls kissing girls.

"I came to realise that the desires, which had tormented my childhood and which I was told by my mother were wicked, were merely the usual feelings that animated most of my fellow beings, were indulged in as a matter of course and pandered to as the essentials of an artistic temperament," she said. "This was a great revelation and one which filled me with excitement."

Naturally she wanted to join in. When she was 15, she pushed up the sleeve of the silk dress of one her stepfather's students and kissed the girl's arm. The girl giggled, but did not object, so Marguerite kissed her on the lips. Again there was no problem, so she "repeated the exercise at every opportunity" until the girl left to study in Paris.

Visetti's most promising pupil was Agnes Nicholls, who made her debut at Covent Garden just a year after she left college. Naturally Visetti flirted with her, but Agnes kept him at bay. His stepdaughter was soon a rival for her affections.

Agnes had milk-white skin, auburn hair and blue eyes, but she was a girl with a big appetite and was a little on the plump side. No matter. Marguerite was a bit of a chubby chaser.

"Her voluptuous figure appealed to my youth," she said.

Contriving to be in the studio when Agnes was singing, Marguerite felt a *frisson* from "the look in her eyes".

"These lessons became the focus of my existence," she said. "I lived for them, like the victim of a drug."

Agnes toyed with Marguerite. Sometimes she ignored her. Sometimes she flirted, and if Marguerite showed affection to the girl in the silk dress, she became positively proprietorial. She would send her on errands or tell her to come and sit by her.

"And when I sat by her, she would sometimes slide her hand down where mine lay between us," said Marguerite. "I think it was her desire to see the little shiver that her touch produced, for she would bend forward to watch my face at such moments."

That was not enough, however.

"Her music and her thrilling voice stirred my passion unendurably ... I longed to dominate her, to hurt her, to compel her, to kiss her mouth."

When Agnes began performing, Marguerite would accompany her as her "special property" – although she would have to endure seeing adoring young men in the audience flirting with her. On the way home, however, they sat close together in the carriage and Marguerite would hold Agnes's bare arm under her cloak.

Sometimes Agnes would torment her. Had she seen Lord so-and-so in the audience? She was going to marry him. But usually Marguerite was carried along by the emotion of the moment, regardless of whether the performance had been a triumph or a fiasco.

Seeing that she had rivals for Agnes's affections, Marguerite adopted a more masculine look and started to think of herself as a suitor. But she had a worse rival than other men. Marguerite's mother spotted that Agnes "was in love with her voice ... I would have tramped half the world to hear that perfect organ, so strong, thrilling, chaste and pure".

Marguerite's interest was anything but chaste and pure, but we all like a perfect organ, don't we?

Agnes joined the family on visits to music festivals on the Continent with Arthur Sullivan*. When Marguerite's father Rat died, she inherited everything. She suddenly became wealthy, independent and wanted to travel on her own. Agnes was against this. When Marguerite asked why, Agnes burst into tears. She accused Marguerite of wanting to break off their friendship and, suddenly, kissed her on the mouth. Marguerite was delighted by this, but she also felt "revolted, terrified and … trapped". However, they now shared a secret. It was a bond between them. Marguerite no longer wanted to leave home, or stir far from Agnes's side.

Agnes contrived to have late lessons, the last in the day, so that she would be invited for dinner. Over the meal, Marguerite would watch for a certain look that would come into Agnes's eyes. It was a strange look, half invitation, half warning.

"I never failed to find it there," she said.

Then there would be restless glances toward the clock. At last it would be bedtime. Agnes would stay in a room opposite Marguerite's at the top of the house. They would say their goodnights and part at Marguerite's bedroom door. Inside, alone, Marguerite would torment herself with the "thousand sweet intimacies" she imagined lay behind Agnes's closed door.

She said that they spent weeks "hovering on the brink". She would wait on the landing, or lie in bed hoping to hear the creak of a floorboard. They went out for walks in the park together and identified with the couples they saw there. Then, one day, they had a proper date. They went to a matinee together and after they had tea. That evening the fog was so thick that Agnes had to stay the night once more. This time, once they were outside the bedroom door, there was no hesitation. Agnes went straight into her room. Marguerite went into hers and undressed, "seized with a sense of elation". When she went out on to the landing again, she could see a light under Agnes's door. She paused for a second, but then she heard Agnes whisper: "Come in, kid."

Marguerite did. And when she got into bed with her, Agnes said: "You ridiculous child, why didn't you come before?"

Once Marguerite had possessed Agnes, the thrill was gone. Agnes was now a star and Marguerite, who began calling herself Peter, was not content to be a mere acolyte. The affair petered out. Now at least her sexual orientation was clear. She began wearing well-cut suits, broad-brimmed hats and swept her hair back from her face. She kept dogs and started to ride to hounds.

Unmistakably lesbian, she did not even feign interest toward the opposite sex.

"Men are vile to her," said the novelist Violet Hunt. "I believe that is why she will never marry."

Violet was a neighbour in Campbell Hill, Kensington, a friend of Henry James and a lover of H.G. Wells and Ford Madox Ford. Marguerite/Peter wanted to be added to that list and bombarded her with *billets doux*.

"She loved me so hotly, poor darling," wrote the decidedly cool Violet Hunt, which I suppose is a rather unfortunate name, given the circumstances. "She use to write and say that I erected a brick wall between her and me." Unfortunate wording here. "Why brick, I would say nervously, but I knew. I was always full of someone." Wells? Ford? Some other brick? "And I wear the pearl necklace she gave me." A pearl necklace? Oh, a pearl, pearl necklace.

Having an income of her own, Violet Hunt was not easily impressed by expensive gifts. Marguerite, however, could now buy her way into the beds of many of her impoverished sisters – and did so with a will. There were also some real love affairs, though. At her great-aunt Mary's house in Knightsbridge, she met her mother's cousin, Jane Randolph. Jane lived in Washington, DC, and her husband had brought her and their three children over to London on a business trip.

"I have never seen anything so fascinatingly slender and so adorably ugly as this woman who stood before me," drooled Marguerite. "Her shoes were perfectly cut, I noticed, and her ankles clad in transparent black silk stockings. Her whole body conveyed an impression of suppleness ..."

So far, so good, but dear old Radders knows how to put a damper on things.

"... But it was her face that was the most arresting thing about her, for it was so frankly ugly. Oval in shape with a rather large mouth, projecting teeth, a blunt nose and pale blue eyes set far apart and masses of chestnut hair wound round a small head and you have one of the most perfect examples of the fascination of personality that some plain women possess."

I knew there was a reason I was not a lesbian.

Nevertheless, Marguerite resented Jane's husband because he possessed her. When she said as much, Jane just laughed.

"Oh, Bob," she said. "He's not too bad, he's only rather a bore at times and he's dog poor, that's the worst of him."

Not as far as Radders was concerned, it wasn't. In fact, she said, it was "possibly the only thing in his favour".

The gifts started, the little treats, the trips to the theatre.

"She was quite a new type of woman to me, completely at her ease," Marguerite said.

Sadly, Jane was heading back to America before this leisurely seduction could come to fruition. On their last day together, Marguerite took her on a romantic carriage ride in Richmond Park at sunset.

"I was tongue-tied" – not a good thing if you are a lesbian, I would have thought – "and I could only glare helplessly into her pale eyes," said Marguerite. She gripped her arm and Jane turned her face calmly toward her.

"I know," she said in her slow Southern drawl. "I guess you needn't tell me because I know."

"If you know," said Marguerite, angrily and almost bursting with frustration, "what are you going to do about it?"

Well, nothing. Not for now at least. She returned to Washington. Then, suddenly, poor old boring Bob died. Something in his coffee perhaps? And Marguerite sailed across the Atlantic – under her own steam, I would imagine. Ever lavish with her lovers, she made provision for the grieving widow and her children, then shot off on a tour of the Southern states where they "shared all kinds of youthful escapades".

After a year, she brought the whole family over to England and settled them in Malvern Wells, in Worcestershire, where she could get down to some serious hunting – sorry – and began writing poetry. A lot of it hints of a lesbian liaison – there are trysts, kisses, lagoons, splashing water, flowers, petals and delicate aromas wafting on the winds.

They were back in the United States when Marguerite fell for her teenage cousin, Dolly Diehl, a blonde-haired, blue-eyed beauty. She addresses her in osculating verse as "my sweet little girl" and says:

> I'd waken you out of your valley of dreams
> And open your heart with my passionate beams.

They are words that leave little to the imagination. It certainly made what was going on clear to Jane, who promptly married a wealthy Texan – although Marguerite and Jane's daughter, Winifred, maintained a heartfelt correspondence for years to come. Irritated by Marguerite's infidelity, Jane said: "Radclyffe Hall had probably loved more women than she had read books."

Meanwhile, Dolly came back to England to live with Marguerite and the two of them travelled in France, Italy and Germany. Then Marguerite published a slim volume of her poetry called *Twixt Earth and Stars* and dedicated it to "My Inspiration". It got good reviews and no critic questioned why women were kissing "sweet little girls" or what a "valley of dreams" might be.

Dolly and Marguerite went to watch their friend Troupie Lowther – weight-lifter, fencer and all-round sportswoman – take on the seven-times Wimbledon champion Dorothea Chambers in a tennis match in Homburg. She lost in straight sets. When they returned to England, Marguerite and Troupie checked into the Savoy with Dolly and Miss Douglas, Troupie's ladyfriend *du jour*. Also staying there was Mabel Veronica Batten who, ten years before, had been bonked in the same hotel by the Prince of Wales, now the king, Edward VII*. She was now 50 and, this time, she was staying with her maid Susan Attkins and her 75-year-old husband George – though they had rooms on different floors.

They had married in Simla in 1875, when Mabel was 18. George was a widower of 43 and brother-in-law to the Lieutenant-Governor of Bengal, Sir John Strachey. Marriage, then, was a social necessity. However, it was not unusual for a young wife to take lovers to pass a hot Indian afternoon and, with a big bust and a tiny waist, Mabel had plenty of them. Within months of their marriage, the Prince of Wales* arrived for a state visit and the affair began.

Mabel also had a fling with the Viceroy of India, Lord Lytton, which won George the position of his private secretary. Lytton plied her with poetry, but their affair was fraught with difficulties. After the assassination of the previous viceroy, Lytton was guarded day and night. Mabel could not be smuggled in unobserved and, much to his chagrin, Lytton told the poet and diarist Wilfrid Scawen Blunt that she "consoled herself" with his aide-de-camp.

Lytton asked Blunt not to do the same, but the temptation was overwhelming. In 1880, home in England for the Goodwood races, Mabel was a house guest at Blunt's ancestral home, Crabbet Park in Sussex.

"I found her door ajar at about 12 o'clock," said Blunt, "and stayed with her until daylight."

Such goings-on were commonplace in country houses at the time.

Blunt described Mabel as "gay, fond of pleasure, quite depraved, but tinged with romance". So you had a good time then? She also told Blunt of her numerous affairs and those enjoyed by all the other ladies of Simla.

When George retired in 1882, the couple returned to England and moved into a house in Chelsea where George involved himself in his hobbies – collecting recipes and doing acrostics. Meanwhile, Mabel amused herself with Count de Mirafiore, the son of Victor Emanuel II*, the first king of a united Italy. Mirafiore wooed her with furs and jewellery, including an emerald ring that had once belonged to the King of Serbia and a brooch shaped like two diamond-encrusted tortoises she called Edward* and Sophie*.

She took up singing and Fauré, Delius, Elgar* and Percy Grainger* all wrote songs for her. She also sat for John Singer Sargent, John Koopman and Edward Poynter and wrote songs, including "The Queen's Last Ride", which was performed on the first anniversary of Queen Victoria's* death by Louise

Kirkby-Lunn, a student of Alberto Visetti's, under the baton of Henry Wood, with Edward VII* in attendance.

Mabel and George – nominally – had one daughter, Clara. She painted erotic fantasies – whips, nudes in shoes, mermaids on fishmongers' slabs – under the name Rognons de la Flèche, French for "Kidneys of the Arrow" or "Testicles of the Trick", or "Dog's Bollocks"? She lived with her husband, the Vice-Chairman of Lloyds Bank, who went about turning the lights off, even when people were in a room, to save money, her lover, an orthopaedic surgeon, and a macaw that screeched, "Fuck off, you silly bitch." This bothered Clara only half as much as it bothered everyone else as she was stone deaf in one ear and used an ear-trumpet – something that Mabel abhorred, even though she too was hard of hearing.

By 1906, Mabel was plump and frumpy and short-sighted, slightly deaf with her thinning hair turning grey. Marguerite fell for her immediately and began wooing her with expensive gifts, poems and jewellery – in exactly the same way that men had done in the past.

At the same time, Marguerite was falling out of love with Dolly, who was 19, penniless and alone in a foreign country. Unconcerned, Marguerite took off for a holiday in Scotland with Violet Hunt who, perhaps, had had enough of bricks for the moment.

"Marguerite used to come and sit on my bed in the clearest, coldest Japanese kimono from Liberty's with a streak of blue on the collar and her fine, sandy, auburn hair in a plait," said Violet. "A decent young girl of 25 who knew the world, in spite of her pigtails and her robe of innocence."

The fun was curtailed, however, when Marguerite received a letter from Dolly in Malvern saying that she was having trouble with the servants and the horses. She headed back, but soon mourned in verse the death of her love for Dolly with the following lines:

> A little shiver crept along my heart
> For you and I were strangers, far apart.

Soon after she wrote "Ardour" about "the new-found splendour" of her love for the matronly Mabel.

In June 1908, Marguerite, Mabel, Dolly and George took a jolly little holiday together in a rented house in Sidmouth. Marguerite and Mabel were soon taking off together on long walks down the beach, swimming and sitting on the rocks talking. One can only wonder what Dolly and George got up to while they were away. They must have had so much in common. Then, on Marguerite's birthday, August 12, she and Mabel headed off together to Ostend. There they played roulette in the casino, other games in the bedroom and returned as lovers. Like Violet Hunt, Mabel earned herself a pearl necklace. A pearl necklace? Oh, I've already done that joke.

Dropping round to Marguerite's London home for a bit of hanky-panky, Mabel spotted a painting of Marguerite's great-great-grandfather, the surgeon John Hall. From then on, Mabel called her John. And John called herself John for the rest of her life. Mabel got a nickname, too – Ladye, as a spoof on her sister who was now Lady Clarendon, and she insisted on being addressed as such. They soon fell into these roles and set up home together.

Another book of poems, *A Sheaf of Verse*, hit the streets. There were references to the mists of passion, comforting breasts, submissive lips and the "potent ecstasy" of kissing. Still nobody rumbled them. The *Daily Express* even recommended the *Sheaf* as a Christmas stocking filler – oh, I see what you mean.

There were rumours, of course. This distressed George, who was struggling with prostate trouble. Dolly was unceremoniously dumped. So much for family.

In the summer of 1909, John and Ladye absconded to the Riviera, and then to Italy. Mabel wrote to George advising him not to follow because of the crowds and mosquitoes. When George was persuaded to take a holiday in north Wales instead, Mabel wrote to Clara, saying: "I fancy he was prompted by some little bird or minx." Which may well have been true. He went with Mabel's maid, Susan Attkins, who was soon his dancing partner. George wrote to Clara, saying: "She seems to be enjoying herself."

That autumn Dolly got married to the composer Robert Coningsby Clarke with John as a witness. Ah-h-h!

John continued to lavish expensive gifts on Ladye and, to make the union even more perfect, John took Ladye's religion and converted to Catholicism. They prayed at home together at a little gilt altarpiece with statuettes of the Madonna and Child and pictures of the Pope*. The fact that the Vatican stood out against lesbianism and would have condemned their adulterous relationship never bothered them. They were, after all, bound together by patriotism, royalism, Toryism and class. Foreigners were looked down on. Socialists were sneered at. A few Jewish friends were tolerated but, as a race, were despised. And don't even mention the lower orders.

In February 1910, Marguerite and Mabel set off for a holiday to Tenerife, while George and Susan were despatched to family in Grantham. On the voyage to the Canaries, a young man from Homburg assumed that they were mother and daughter and tried chatting John up.

"Germans never know when they are not wanted," she said. For once she was prescient. The First World War would start just four years later.

Their three months on Tenerife, they both said, was the happiest time of their lives. John rattled out enough love poetry to fill another volume, which included "A Rosary of Love". This contained such memorable verses as:

> By all youth and passion's might.
>   I swear I love thee
> By all thy beauty and delight,
>   I swear I love thee.

And:

> By Love himself, his holy flame,
>   I swear I love thee,
> By those I loved 'ere thy love came,
>   I swear I love thee …

There are 15 verses of this until I want to swear at thee. Nevertheless, when published as part of the *Poems of the Past and Present*, the critics rolled over and kicked their legs in the air. Even when Louise Kirkby-Lunn sang Ladye's setting of John's "Ode to Sappho" at the Albert Hall – the equivalent of Madonna kissing Britney at the Grammies I would have thought – no one said a dickie bird. Were they blind, deaf and dumb?

In 1910, both Edward VII* and George popped their clogs. Marguerite and Mabel both wore black. Then, within a month, it was off with the widow's weeds and off on holiday again. This time Dolly and her new hubby joined them. Mabel wrote to Clara that Dolly "is much improved in every way and seems now to appreciate Johnnie and all her kindnesses in a way she never did when she was living with her". And with George out of the way – despite the strictures of the Catholic church – John and Ladye now considered themselves to be married.

They mixed socially with lesbians of their own class, attending the "suffragette concerts" of Ethel Smyth*, exhibitions of the paintings of Romaine Brooks*, going motoring with Troupie Lowther and having the Princesse de Polignac* and her latest lover, Olga de Meyer, over for tea. They attended lectures on India and theosophy given by Annie Besant and went to an "Arabian Nights" ball, with Mabel dressed as the Lady of Baghdad and John as her Persian slave boy.

There was a beastly miners' strike to put up with. Then there were the antics of some perfectly ghastly suffragettes. The distinctly lower-class Emily Davison threw herself under the King's* horse. Others smashed windows and chained themselves to railings. In outrage, John and Ladye collaborated on a letter to the *Pall Mall Gazette*. It read:

Sir,

Have the suffragettes no spark of patriotism that they can spread revolt and hamper the government in this moment of grave national danger? According to Mrs Pankhurst, they are resorting to the methods of the miners! Since when have

English ladies regulated their conduct by that of the working classes? But indeed, up to the present, the miners have set an example of orderly behaviour, which the suffragettes might do well to follow!

I was formerly a sympathiser with the cause of female suffrage, as also were many women who, like myself, are unrepresented, although taxpayers. Women who are capable of setting a revolutionary example at such a time as this could only bring disgrace and destruction on any Constitution in which they play an active part.

Yours, etc.

A Former Suffragist

Up the ruling classes!

Ladye's health was failing, though. When she was breathless – which must have been often if John had anything to do with it – she had pains in her heart. John took her to see a specialist, who prescribed amyl nitrate. A result there, then. John had her own problems, however. Haemorrhoids. Ooh. Too much horseback riding I guess. When they had to be excised in the Devonshire Street Clinic, Ladye stayed overnight in an adjoining bed.

John, naturally, was incapable of being faithful and began spending afternoons alone with Phoebe Hoare. Their affair carried on, on the understanding that both John and Phoebe had partners they were committed to. All John needed to know was that Phoebe preferred her to the husband she was cheating on. After a heavy afternoon session they sometimes dined with Phoebe's husband, which must have been nice. Ladye was not so sanguine.

John considered the arrangement to be perfectly civilised. While Ladye was her wife, Phoebe was her mistress. John would fix unwanted engagements for Ladye while she spent time with Phoebe and then returned with an expensive gift.

"I never told her an untruth," boasted John, "except once" without saying when that once was. In short, she was behaving as her own father "Rat" – or, for that matter, the hated Visetti – had done.

When Clara fell pregnant, the illusion was complete. John, who had always wanted to sire children, "almost feels like a father," wrote Ladye.

Ladye did not follow the example of John's mother and divorce her errant partner, or rail against her. They said mass together at the Brompton Oratory and dined at the Ritz. In 1913, they went to Covent Garden to see the Ballet Russes and Nijinsky*, and heard the music of Debussy* and Stravinsky*. Then they dined with the Princesse de Polignac*, who read extracts from her manuscript about a trip to Lesbos.

"John was very upset afterwards with *remords de conscience,*" wrote Ladye, not without some self-satisfaction – not that it helped. "I got no sleep at all."

Conscience or not, John spent the next afternoon with Phoebe – and the next ... After a week of hot matinees, John was falling asleep at the dinner table and Mabel was in a sulk. At night, John and Phoebe tangoed openly, caring little for the gossip this caused. However, John could not even be bothered to be faithful to Phoebe. She slipped in a quickie with harpsichord player Violet Gordon Woodhouse, who currently shared her life with a husband and three other male lovers in a scandalous *ménage à cinq*. With so much competition for her time, it must have been a real quick one. John did not bother to hide the fact and dedicated her next volume of poetry, *The Forgotten Island*, to "Morena" – the name she called Violet.

By this time, John and Ladye had been together for five years and they tried to make something of the anniversary. Then John took off with Phoebe and Dolly, leaving Ladye in the hands of family – just as she had done with husband George. They planned to holiday in Spain that summer, but John switched to Italy at the last minute to be near Phoebe. In her diary, Ladye, with a typical grasp of world events, dismissed 1913 as a horrid year and "felt delighted when 1914 set in".

In fact 1914 started out okay for Mabel. Phoebe's husband Oliver put his foot down. He called John and Phoebe in for an "interview" and made it plain that it was his hot crumpets she should be buttering at teatime. Soon after, John and Ladye set off on holiday. They met Alice Keppel* at the casino in Monte Carlo. Ladye swapped notes with her – as the last mistress of Edward VII*, Alice famously remarked that her job was to "curtsy first and then to hop into bed". She was also the great-grandmother of Camilla Parker-Bowles*.

Along the Côte d'Azur, Ladye and John stayed in adjoining rooms. As John was dyslexic, Ladye was employed to transcribe John's latest love poems, which she knew were not for her. Then Dolly joined them, complaining that her husband was not as generous as Marguerite had been, which cannot have improved the atmosphere much. And when they returned to England, John got back with Phoebe again.

John caught the mumps and used it as an excuse to exile Mabel to the Cadogan Hotel. She then took a studio in Tite Street, where she could carry on her affairs in privacy, but this cosy arrangement was disrupted by the start of the First World War. John, naturally, wanted to enlist, to fight, to die a hero – but refrained for the sake of Ladye. Nevertheless, she produced recruitment leaflets urging young men to join up and, when they failed to comply, she wrote to the *Malvern Gazette* demanding to know: "What manner of men have we in these parts?"

"Their women should be ashamed of them," she wrote. The letter was signed: "Mr M. Radclyffe-Hall."

Separated from both Phoebe and Dolly, who was now working for the Red Cross, Johnnie took to knitting to aid the war effort. It bored her, so she gave it up and cranked out another volume of unrhymed verse about forbidden love and the joys of nature, designed to be sung by ladies at tea gatherings – just what the world needed as it sank into the abyss of trench warfare. Like another anonymous victim of the muddy fields of Flanders, the book sank without a trace. Stuck in Malvern with Ladye, who was convalescing after a car accident, John turned her attention to prose. She began an autobiography in which she called herself Michael West.

Taking afternoon tea at Lady Clarendon's, John first set eyes on Ladye's cousin the 28-year-old Una Troubridge*. She, in turn, was very taken with John's 35-year-old face.

Sappho of Lesbos (left and below)

Virgina Woolf

Vita Sackville-West

Radclyffe Hall and friend

Bessie Smith

Mercedes De Acosta

Eleanor Roosevelt

Agnes Moorehead

Barbara Stanwyck

"It was not the countenance of a young woman, but of a very handsome young man," Una said.

Una was feeling lonely and depressed that day. Her husband, a rear-admiral 25 years her senior, had given her syphilis, stepchildren who hated her, an unwanted child of her own and the unwarranted glare of media attention due to a high-profile court martial he had forced on the authorities to clear his name. She accepted John and Ladye's offer of a lift back to her flat in Bryanston Street. They stayed for supper. Soon she was "dropping round" to John's house for morning coffee, afternoon tea, lunch, dinner, then breakfast – after she had stayed the night.

All Ladye could do was look on and record the details of their burgeoning affair in her diary. Una had already separated from her husband – so there would be no Oliver Hoare riding to the rescue – and Una made no secret of the fact that she aimed to oust Mabel and have John all to herself.

The three of them went off on a jolly holiday to Cornwall, but as Ladye was in no fit state to go walking on the cliffs, John and Una had time to themselves. When they returned to London, they all moved in together in a suite in the Vernon Court Hotel. Then John and Una went off to Malvern together and came back "with a bond forged between us". After the misery of syphilis and childbirth brought upon her by her husband, sex with the quasi-masculine John was just dandy.

John was still worried about breaking off with Ladye and taking up with Una; she feared that to do so would be to put all her eggs in one basket.

"How do I know if I shall care for you in six months' time?" she said.

Even so, she bought Una a platinum ring with their names engraved on it.

Una was a sculptor. Having completed a successful study of Nijinsky*, she took a studio in Tite Street and began work on a bust of John. She took over Mabel's transcription work and set about turning herself into John's devotee.

Una's husband turned up at Vernon Court to enquire how the old treatment for syphilis was going and to inform her

THE WELL, WELL, WELL OF LONELINESS

that he had been posted to Belgrade. Later, his son Thomas, Una's stepson, turned up and urged her to return to her husband. He warned her that if any scandal caused by her relationship with John hurt his father, he would make sure that it rebounded on her.

Tired of hotel life, John took a lease on a new flat, but there were wrangles about who would sleep where. It was all too much for Ladye, who had a stroke that left her paralysed and speechless. She died soon after. Even Una's husband, Rear-Admiral Troubridge, turned out for the funeral. John bought a crypt in Highgate cemetery with four shelves in it. One was for Ladye, another for her daughter Clara, a third was for John herself and the fourth was to make the whole thing symmetrical.

Una and John both felt guilty over Ladye's death and began to fray each other's nerves. John went to stay with Dolly after the interment.

Going through her mother's possessions, Clara began reading Ladye's diaries which detailed John's infidelities. She confronted John with the pain that it had caused her mother. John protested that she had given Mabel the best eight years of her life and, "although other people took my surface twice during that time, they never touched my soul or penetrated my mind". Other things, one must suppose, were both touched and penetrated.

As she was somewhat of a drama queen, John talked of killing herself to be with her lost love, but Una pulled her back. She returned like a faithful lapdog. The two of them went to a series of mediums to try and contact Ladye and say sorry. The spiritualist business was booming at the time as a result of the First World War. They were soon fully paid-up members of the Society for Psychical Research and John had her nose stuck in *Spiritual Intercourse* by H. MacKenzie.

The search for the lost Ladye began to irritate Una, especially as some of the mediums, who were female to a man, took an unnecessarily intimate interest in John. For her part, John was irritated by the regular visits of Una's daughter, Andrea – as was Una herself. Nevertheless, in January 1918,

John made the great declaration to Una: "I've married Ladye and I've married you." Una did not have to be asked, as indeed she wasn't.

Now calling herself Radclyffe Hall – which, appropriately enough, sounds like a girls' boarding school – John read a paper to the Society for Psychical Research. For those who had ears to hear, it was a manifesto of lesbian love. Published in the Society's journal, it caused sensational gossip.

The gossip was stoked by Clara, who complained to the Society that Radclyffe Hall had abandoned her mother for Una, and that Una had abandoned her husband for Radclyffe Hall and was mentally unbalanced. Radclyffe Hall responded by saying that it was Clara who was mentally unbalanced. Where's a spirit guide when you need one, eh?

Following the end of the First World War, Radclyffe Hall bought a mock castle called Chip Chase in Middlesex with interconnecting bedrooms. John and Una spent a good deal of time in each other's bedrooms – and each other's beds – but slept alone.

"Nothing has ever led me to believe that comfortable repose can really be achieved with one's head pillowed upon another's breast," said Una, "or with someone else's head riding upon one's bosom." Radclyffe Hall, on the other hand, said that she had not "wanted to sleep the whole of a night with a woman" since she was 20.

She moved her medium in nearby. Both she and Una were beastly to the servants, particularly the serving girls, who deserved it. They were, after all, lower class.

Una's husband, now a full admiral, turned up. He objected to them living together and there was an "unpleasant scene" – but not as unpleasant as the one in Una's solicitors' office, where her specialists sought to lay out the evidence that the admiral had given his wife venereal disease. Wary of further adverse publicity Troubridge signed a deed of separation. It stipulated that their daughter would be looked after by his sisters when he was out of the country – which must have come as a relief to Una – and that "under no circumstances" should she "be left under the guardianship or care of Marguerite Radclyffe-Hall". She would have been relieved as well, though no doubt the intention was to wound and offend.

What really wounded and offended was the legacy of syphilis. The newest of a long line of specialists took a peek up Una's crack and suggested painting her vaginal wall. It was not that he wanted to do a makeover in pastel colours. Although he told her that she "would always be sensitive", he thought that, with a couple of coats of gloss, she would be as right as rain in three years. In the meantime, her diaries were full of discharges, cystitis and the other joys of sex. Her regular doctor had a swab almost permanently up there and another quack tried "electrical treatment" – the thought of which makes your hair stand on end. Every cloud has a silver lining, though. Troubridge got a K to add to his CMG and became a "Sir". It made Una a proper "Lady", rather than a counterfeit Ladye like Mabel. While affecting to be indifferent, Una raced down to the printers to get a new set of visiting cards run off. Perversely, Radclyffe Hall looked down her nose at Una's husband, Sir Ernest. Partnering a Lady, surely, made John a Lord. Meanwhile, Una, Lady Troubridge – as she now styled herself – was undergoing regular hypnosis and psychoanalysis; probably because, like her partner, she was barking mad.

When news came that Radclyffe Hall was to be elevated to the council of the Society for Psychical Research, the gossip circulating in the London clubs said that she had now added witchcraft to her list of vices, along with lesbianism and seducing men's wives. Troubridge himself muttered darkly about how Radclyffe Hall had wrecked his happy home. This came to the ears of St George Lane Fox-Pitt, the pioneer of electric street lamps, the leading light of the Society for Psychical Research and the proud owner of rather too many names. For some reason, Radclyffe Hall's girl-on-girl psychic research paper had not turned old St George on and he now sought to kick her in the all-too-metaphorical goolies. He was, after all, the son-in-law of the ninth Marquis of Queensberry*, who had brought down Oscar Wilde, so he had the family honour to maintain.

He made it plain to the Society for Psychical Research that he objected to Radclyffe Hall's elevation to the council on the grounds that "Miss Radclyffe Hall is a grossly immoral woman" and had destroyed the domestic bliss of Admiral Troubridge. Asked to tone it down a bit, old chap, he wrote to the Society's journal, saying:

> Miss Radclyffe Hall is a thoroughly immoral woman. She lived for many years with a woman mentioned in the paper which she and Lady Troubridge wrote, a woman who was a most objectionable person. Miss Radclyffe Hall has got a great influence over Lady Troubridge and wrecked the Admiral's home. I am quite determined to oppose her election to the council. If I cannot persuade Mrs Sidgwick to withdraw her proposal of Miss Radclyffe Hall for the council, I intend to bring the matter before the council myself and put it strongly so as to carry my point, as she is quite an unfit person to be on the council.

I can't see what he was getting so rattled about. Surely lesbians are the perfect people to get in touch with the other side.

The editor of the journal was a bit worried about that word "immoral", but Fox-Pitt said not to worry. Troubridge would back him up.

When Radclyffe Hall heard of this, she went straight to her solicitors. Never mind the word "immoral", Fox-Pitt had called her "Miss" – twice. That was clearly defamation.

When the case came to court, the press had a field day with the "Spiritualist Slander Suit" and the "Society women versus the Spooks". Old Radders had the money to get the best and she was represented by Sir Ellis Hume-Williams, a Unionist MP. Penniless after losing a previous suit over patents for incandescent street lighting, Fox-Pitt defended himself.

In his sonorous opening statement, Sir Ellis said that St George Lane Fox-Pitt had made "as horrible an accusation as could be made against any woman in this country. The words used by the defendant could only mean that the plaintiff was an unchaste and immoral woman who was addicted to unnatural vice and was consequently unfit to be a member of the council of the Society for Psychical Research."

The case presented all sorts of problems for the law. While the Protection of Women and Suppression of Brothels bill of 1885 strangely (see *Sex Lives of the Famous Gays* for explanation) made "any act of gross indecency" between two males a misdemeanour and buggery had been against the law since the reign of Henry VIII*, there were no equivalent laws concerning sexual acts between two women.

It is said that when the 1885 bill was drawn up, it made all acts of "gross indecency" between members of the same sex a punishable offence. When it was presented to Queen Victoria*, however, she is supposed to have said: "Women don't do such things." So any reference to Sapphic love was removed. There is no record of this.

In another version of the story, lesbianism was excluded from the bill because no one was willing to explain it to her. This too seems implausible. Victoria may have been conservative in social matters, but she had lived too long and was far too inquisitive to have remained entirely innocent. She was, after all, a hot-blooded Hanoverian woman from a family whose depravity knew no bounds.

On the other hand, the 1891 Slander of Women Act made it an offence to "impute unchastity or adultery" against any woman in England, Wales or Ireland. The law did not apply in Scotland, presumably because the men wear skirts up there and it would all have been far too confusing. This law, it is interesting to note, is still on the statute books today.

The Lord Chief Justice, presiding, had to decide whether "immoral" in this case implied "unchastity". And as "unchastity" came next to "adultery" in the 1891 Act, did that imply that it could only take place between people of the opposite sex? Or did tipping the velvet constitute "unchastity", "adultery" or both? I think we need Bill Clinton's* opinion on this one.

And where exactly did the "unnatural vice" fit in? Public interest was at fever pitch. The case was going to be hotly contested in all senses of the word.

Radclyffe Hall's solicitor subpoenaed Troubridge. He was not about to back Fox-Pitt. If he was behind him, he was so far behind him as to be out of sight. Having clawed his way back from a damaging court martial, Troubridge was now a pillar of the establishment – an Admiral and a knight of the realm. He was not about to have his reputation smeared by a full and frank discussion of his wife's lesbianism, her syphilis and her devotion to spiritualism. He claimed in court that he had made no allegations at all concerning Radclyffe Hall.

The bewhiskered Fox-Pitt also dissembled. He had no witnesses to call on and, as his own counsel, he could not submit himself to cross-examination. He claimed that he had in no way tried to impugn Radclyffe Hall's behaviour or character. Perish the thought. What he meant by "immorality" was that the paper she had read to the Society and had published in the Society's journal would produce impure and immoral thoughts in a reader – a reader such as himself?

In an attempt to clarify matters, the Lord Chief Justice said: "You say that you used the word 'immoral' only in relation to her work in the Society … You deny that you used the language complained of as implying unnatural vice, unchastity or sexual immorality. The plaintiff contends that you meant that. Whether you have used language calculated to imply it is a matter for the jury."

Fox-Pitt then got to cross-examine Radclyffe Hall. Unwilling to go into what went on behind closed doors with Una Troubridge – or on the psychic plane with Mabel Batten – he restricted his questions to her paper. The Lord Chief Justice read through it and was intrigued.

"How does a spirit bathe?" he asked. "I see later on that the lady had a private bathing pool in the spirit world. You must bear in mind that hearsay evidence is not admissible."

A titter ran round the courtroom.

Fox-Pitt then began to lose his temper. He questioned her scientific training and put it to Radclyffe Hall that "this paper of yours is scientific rubbish, quite unworthy of the Society, and its publication is extremely harmful. It has produced a condition of mind which I consider immoral."

Again the Lord Chief Justice tried to clarify matters.

"You do not mean by the word 'immoral' anything sexual?" he asked.

"No, my lord, and I will call evidence to prove it," said Fox-Pitt, seeking to flourish a dictionary.

"You are not suggesting that the relationship between the plaintiff and Lady Troubridge led to the separation of the Admiral and his wife?" asked the judge.

"Who suggested it?" asked Fox-Pitt.

"Not a spirit in the other world?" suggested the Lord Chief Justice helpfully.

Fox-Pitt eventually whipped out his *Shorter Oxford* and reeled off definition after definition of "immoral" that did not mention sex in any way. Radclyffe Hall admitted that she had not been aware that the word had so many other meanings. However, Radclyffe Hall would not be caught dead handling a *dict*ionary – being dyslexic, I mean.

Under cross-examination, Una, Lady Troubridge, tried to pull rank. Mabel, she said, "occupied a high social position and lived in perfect amity with her husband".

The Lord Chief Justice asked what this had to do with the case. Sir Ellis Hume-Williams enlightened him.

"There is an allegation made by the defendant that she was a person of low and immoral character," he said.

The judge was not impressed.

"Her position in society would be no answer to the charge that has been made," he said.

Good God, they'll be letting the working classes sit on juries next. Where will it all end?

Under cross-examination, Fox-Pitt babbled on about a plot to oust him from the Society. He was plainly in need of some psychic help, if not some spirits. The jury found against him and Radclyffe Hall was awarded five hundred pounds. That would have bought a few dinners at the Ritz in those days, but Fox-Pitt did not pay up. Radclyffe Hall took some satisfaction that she had cleared her name in court, though – or so she thought. Thanks to the judge's efforts to steer the case towards the question of sexual immorality, jokes about her sexuality were flying thick and fast.

The next day, Radclyffe Hall and Una spent the day in bed together and read the papers. They could not have been very comforting. Later, they sought the reassurance of other sapphists. They had dinner with Gabrielle Enthoven and "Brother" Troupie Lowther, who was just back from France where she had been driving ambulances in an all-woman army unit. Radclyffe Hall and "Brother" danced together to the gramophone. Una said grumpily that she thought Troupie was a hermaphrodite.

Fox-Pitt was not done. He appealed against the verdict and a retrial was ordered. The press and public geared up again in the hope that, this time, they were going to hear all the smutty details. However, Radclyffe Hall was advised that it was stupid to waste a lot of money stirring up a lot of tasteless tattle again and let the case wither on the vine.

It did not wither on the grapevine, though. In the eye of the public, Radclyffe Hall's unwillingness to contest a second hearing proved that she was a lesbian – and that she was guilty of unchastity, gross immorality, indecency and all the rest of it. In parliament, the Conservative MP, Frederick Macquister, proposed an amendment to the 1885 Act, covering "gross indecency by females". MPs blustered about the declining moral standards among women and its effect on the birth-rate. The motion was passed in the House of Commons, but, in the House of Lords, Lord Birkenhead said: "You are going to tell the whole world there is such an offence, to bring it to the notice of women who have never heard of it, never dreamed of it. I think this is a very great mischief."

Once the girls get to hear about it, they will all be doing it in the street, right?

It was considered that it was a greater insult to lesbians that they ignore it. Their Lordships hoped that, if they paid it no mind, it would go away. Besides, the opinion in the Lords was that the current law could be tailored to indict any lesbians who got out of hand, as it were.

Radclyffe Hall became something of a social pariah as a result of the case. Phoebe Hoare wrote to say that her husband said that she could never see her again. This brought Radclyffe Hall to a low ebb. She fell ill and retired to bed with Una. After licking their wounds, they decided that they had to tough it out. So Radclyffe Hall got Una to crop her hair in a distinctly masculine style – Ladye had always liked it longer, but she was no more. Then, at Christmas, Radclyffe Hall finally said that Una could have the last shelf in the Highgate crypt.

"I feel I can never be really unhappy again," wrote a grateful Lady Troubridge.

Radclyffe Hall began banging out barely coded lesbian novels – the first dedicated to Ladye, the second to Una. Ethel Smyth*, a fan, came to tea.

"Why is it so much easier for me, and I believe for a great many English women, to love my own sex passionately rather than yours?" Ethel mused with a male friend.

Jane Randolph and other former lovers came to stay at Chip Chase in a gesture of solidarity, but found the exclusivity of Radclyffe Hall and Una cloying. Many disapproved of the crop-haired, pipe-smoking John they found, rather than the softer more womanly Marguerite that they had known and loved.

Visits by Una's daughter were barely tolerated. Her childhood treats included mass at Brompton Oratory and excursions to Ladye's mausoleum in Highgate. And she was frequently despatched back to convent school, in tears, before the beginning of term if her presence was inconvenient.

Dogs, however, were loved and pampered – but only briefly. A year after moving into Chip Chase they moved out again. Radclyffe Hall missed the London lesbian scene. She wanted to be in the thick of things again. The dogs were kennelled. The servants fired. The furniture stored. And they moved back to Knightsbridge. This was handy for Una. Her clap doctor was just round the corner, a mere waddle away.

Radclyffe Hall now had access to Troupie's literary salon of like-minded lesbians. The cliterati included militant feminist and Mills and Boon author Ida Wylie, May Sinclair, who had been in Troupie's ambulance unit, Vere Hutchinson, who dedicated all of her books to her "undying love" for her partner "Budge", and the animal painter Dorothy Burroughes-Burroughes. There are some posh double-barrelled upper-class names in this circle, but that one takes the biscuit.

They danced together at Soho all-girl clubs the Cave of

Harmony and the Orange Tree. All the girls from Troupie's army unit – Honey, Nelly, Poppy, Lizzie, Susie and Hilly – turned up to a fancy-dress ball at Troupie's and Una feigned shock at the way they all "carried on" together sexually. Troupie also introduced Radclyffe Hall to Romaine Brooks*. Through Romaine, Radclyffe Hall became a fan of fascist poet Gabriele D'Annunzio*, and even named one of her canaries after him.

Troupie fancied Romaine and, after a "fragile commencement", she hounded her with letters and phone calls. Romaine, on the other hand, fancied Radclyffe Hall, but could not prise her away from Una. The three of them were seen out together at the theatre or dining at the Savoy Grill. They sat up late chewing the fat. Romaine even invited the couple to her villa on Capri. Sensing a honey-trap, Una objected. After a late-night tussle, Radclyffe Hall gave way and they did not go. However, Romaine did catch up with them in Paris where she introduced them to Natalie Barney*. There they attended a fancy-dress ball with Radclyffe Hall dressed as an Indian chief. In her novel *The Forge*, there is a scene where an Indian chief appears with a harem of six women. Literary lesbians at the ball knew the scene well and played along.

Back in London, Radclyffe Hall and Una went to first nights with Noël Coward*, Ivor Novello, Arnold Bennett, Somerset Maugham and C.B. Cochran. There were also poetry readings with Edith Sitwell. Radclyffe Hall sent flowers backstage to Tallulah Bankhead* and took her dancing at the Cave of Harmony. All this was a pain to Una, who neither drank nor smoked and got a headache if she stayed up late.

Radclyffe Hall and Una moved once again and now shared a bedroom. This was all the more agonising for Una's daughter Andrea, who was embarrassed that her mother was a lesbian. Nevertheless Una insisted on wearing a monocle, even though she had to scrunch up her face to keep it in. One New Year's Eve, Troupie came to dinner with her new lover Fabienne Lafargue De-Avilla. Gabrielle Enthoven was also on hand and they all danced together to the chimes of Big Ben. It must have been excruciating for poor Andrea. Soon after, the wretched girl got a boyfriend. Una whipped her off to the doctor, who "confirmed her suspicions". A stern lecture followed.

Radclyffe Hall's *romans à* cleft soon had a large following due, partly, to Troupie's literary *Safia* who gave them rave reviews. This emboldened Radclyffe Hall and she decided that it was time to write "the truth about one of the greatest tragedies that exists in the scheme of nature". And I thought you girls were having fun.

"I wished to offer my name and my literary reputation in support of the cause of the inverted," she would say. "I knew that I was running the risk of injuring my career as a writer by rousing up a storm of antagonism, but I was prepared to face this possibility because, being myself a congenital invert, I understood the subject from the inside …"

"If we cannot write books about ourselves, then I ask about whom may we write them?" she asked in a lecture on novel writing.

First, though, after that beastly General Strike was over, they took off to the Riviera, stopping off for a tour of the lesbian clubs of Paris – Regina, Dingo, the Select – with Natalie Barney* and her latest squeeze, Mimi Franchetti. They then went home to Natalie's Temple of Love, where they hooked up with Natalie's ex, the duchesse de Clermont-Tonnerre*, and the Broadway actress, Eva Le Gallienne*, who had just broken up with Mercedes De Acosta*. Radclyffe Hall eventually met up with de Acosta at a dinner at Gabrielle Enthoven's.

Dinner with Troupie and Fabienne was followed by Edouard Bourdet's *La Prisonnière* at the Théâtre Femina, a play based on the affair between Violet Trefusis and the princesse de Polignac*. After putting flowers on the grave of Renée Vivien* and after having had a massage and a rubdown at the thermal baths at Bagnoles, it was on to the casinos of the Côte d'Azur. Only then did she bend herself to the task.

In *The Well of Loneliness*, Radclyffe Hall said, she aimed: "To encourage inverts to face up to a hostile world in their true colours, and this with dignity and courage. To spur all classes of inverts to make good through hard work, faithful and loyal attachments and sober and useful living." So that's what you were doing on the Riviera, was it, Radders? "To bring normal men and women of good will to a fuller and more tolerant understanding of the inverted."

The novel is certainly designed to appeal to "all classes of inverts". It tells the tale of Sir Philip and Lady Gordon, who live in the baronial splendour of Morton Hall in Great Malvern and long for a son and heir to inherit the pile. Their only child is born a girl, however. Undeterred, this down-to-earth couple name her Stephen. As she grows up, it becomes apparent that she is not like other girls. She is more like other Stephens. She cuts her hair short, wears breeches, and learns to fence and hunt. Sounds familiar? The local yokels begin to think she is a bit odd. So she gets down with an older woman, an American who's kinda pissed off with her boring husband.

It has to be said that there is not much sex in *The Well of Loneliness* – not nearly as much as you are getting here so don't rush off and read it. About as hot as it gets is: "She kissed her full on the lips like a lover." Now I know you lot are not going to be satisfied with that.

Okay, they do go to bed together, but they are "in the grip of Creation, of Creation's terrific urge to create; the urge that will sometimes sweep forward blindly alike into fruitful and sterile channels". Hold on, run that by me again. "Creation's urge to create", "fruitful and sterile channels" – is this some sort of code? Then there are "strangely ardent yet sterile bodies", "flaccid embraces" and "sly pornographic expressions". All this is, naturally, done in the best possible taste – not like what you are getting here, I hear you say.

Stephen, of course, becomes a novelist who writes books like *The Furrow*. That should certainly be worth dipping into. Stephen is, naturally, a "true genius in chains, in chains of the flesh". No harm in getting the review in first. In Paris, she lives in rue Jacob where she does up a derelict temple. Then along comes the First World War and she becomes an ambulance driver like Troupie and an all-round, shrapnel-scarred hero, just like Radclyffe Hall wanted to be. Her service in the ambulance corps is a real eye opener, because she sudden realises that there are "many a one who was even as herself" in her unit. In the "whirligig of war", these sisters "found themselves" and "crept out of their holes". I'm not really sure I can go with that last image.

Stephen then starts hitting on a young orphan lass named Mary. Her commanding officer disapproves, but Mary says that she wants to kiss Stephen "more than anything in the world". Stephen is honourable and resolute, however. She says: "If you come to me, Mary, the world will abhor you, will persecute you, will call you unclean. Our love may be faithful even unto death and beyond – yet the world will call it unclean."

You've got to admit that she's got a snappy way with dialogue.

Stephen goes on to say that in the eyes of the world it is okay for "men and women to defile each other, laying the burden of their sins upon their children", and that "unfaithfulness, lies and deceit" are tolerated, as long as you are "normal".

Mary doesn't care, though. She just wants a shag. They piss off to Tenerife together, then shack up in the temple. Stephen takes to wearing men's clothes and writes spectacularly successful novels, while Mary simpers over her seamless prose and does all the housewifely things.

The odd couple find that they are not welcome back at old Morton Hall – or should that be Radclyffe Hall? – so they confine themselves to the Sapphic salons and clitoral clubs of pulsating Paris ...

We could have had a happy ending if it had ended right there, but we couldn't have that now, could we?

Stephen feels that Mary will be "murdered socially" if she does not get wed, so she pretends to spend the night with another woman so that Mary will feel that it is okay to run off with a man and marry him. A martyr to the cause, Stephen spends the rest of her life fighting the good fight on behalf of fellow inverts. The End.

Radclyffe Hall explained to her publisher that the entire novel was about "sexual inversion" and that "having attained literary success I have put my pen at the service of some of the most persecuted and misunderstood people in the world".

Sorry, but it is hard to think of the likes of the mega-rich Radclyffe Hall, Natalie Barney*, the princesse de Polignac*, the duchesse de Clermont-Tonnerre* and movie star Tallulah Bankhead* with their fine houses, long holidays, private incomes, lavish lifestyles and social privileges as being among the "most persecuted and misunderstood people in the world". But then I guess I am a callous bastard. Is there no charity for these people? What can I do to alleviate their suffering? Where do I send money?

These people (see the list in the previous paragraph) were "utterly defenceless" she told Jonathan Cape, who eventually – out of pity presumably – took the book. After signing the contract, Radclyffe Hall and Una went on a shopping spree to celebrate and saw Puccini's *Turandot* at Covent Garden. They were so oppressed. Knopf took the book to the United States and Havelock Ellis agreed to write an introduction.

Radclyffe Hall bumped up the publicity budget with her own money and read *The Ballad of Reading Gaol*, in preparation for suffering the same martyrdom as St Oscar*. However, her bubble was burst by Compton Mackenzie, who wrote *Extraordinary Women*, a spoof on monocle-wearing "Aeolian fauna" and their affairs on Capri set against the background of the First World War – the Aeolians were the people who colonised Lesbos.

Apart from the rave reviews supplied by the *Safia*, the critics found *The Well of Loneliness* "tendentious, lacking form, tedious, humourless, melodramatic and long". Cyril Connolly* pointed out in the *New Statesman* that: "Homosexuality is, after all, as rich in comedy as in tragedy." I hope so, Cyril, I hope so. However, no one had any problem with the subject matter. Two editions sold out immediately and Cape prepared to print a third.

Cape had deliberately not sent review copies of the book to Express Newspapers as they wished to avoid the kind of lurid coverage their titles specialised in. The retribution for this slight was swift. Unable to fill his pages with titillating quotes concerning lesbian love romps, the editor of the *Sunday Express* did the next best thing. He climbed on his high horse, took offence and called for the book to be banned. He would, he said, "rather give a healthy girl or boy a phial of Prussic acid" than Hall's novel. Soon the phones at Cape's offices were ringing off the hook with booksellers desperate to stock more copies. Meanwhile Cape, equally disingenuously, condemned the *Sunday Express* for bringing unwanted publicity to the book. It was no longer reaching the "right class of reader". Instead, Cape complained: "Smut hounds and those with a taste for pornography would now be seeking the book out."

[Note to publisher: Let's not send a review copy of *The Sex Lives of Famous Lesbians* to the *Express* and see what happens.]

In something of a panic, Cape sent a copy to the Home Secretary with a sheaf of the upmarket reviews, saying that he would be perfectly happy to withdraw the book from circulation, if the Director of Public Prosecutions asked him to, but that he would not do so at the behest of the *Sunday Express*. The Home Secretary, Sir William Jonyson-Hick, was a noted prude and the Deputy Director of Public Prosecutions, after examining the 511-page book for less than a day, decided that it could be prosecuted for "obscene libel". He could not be sure that a jury would convict, though, and the publicity a prosecution would bring would only increase sales. So Jonyson-Hick took Cape up on his offer. Cape duly cancelled the third printing. He was way ahead of the game, however. He had the printers make a mould of the plates and sent them to Paris to have it printed there.

Radclyffe Hall was outraged. As she was independently wealthy, she did not care about making a huge heap of money. Instead she railed against the suppression of the book on the grounds of free speech – which was ironic as Cape's tactics were going to ensure that the book reached a far larger audience than it would have done otherwise. Class solidarity came into play. Virginia Woolf*, Vita Sackville-West*, E.M. Forster* and other Bloomsburyites rode to Radclyffe Hall's side, while looking down their noses at the book as indecent and dull and its author as vain, egotistical and mad. After all, Virginia had published *Orlando* that year, a novel that covered some of the same themes, and the Bloomsberries all agreed that it was a much better book. Poor E.M. Forster*, being gay, found "sapphism disgusting". Seeking other support, Radclyffe Hall and Una went to see Noël Coward* in a London nursing home where he was having his piles surgically excised. They found him writing – appropriately enough – *Bitter Sweet*.

By this time, bootleg copies of the book were flooding in from France to fill the unfilled orders at the bookshops and the cover price rose from 15 shillings to 25 – 75p to £1.25. This gave HM Customs and Excise a problem. The Home Office wanted them to intercept the French edition, even though the book had not been banned. The problem was that Customs and Excise comes under the jurisdiction of the Chancellor of the Exchequer and not the Home Secretary. The Chancellor did not find the book obscene and duly released the imported edition. Having been comprehensively outflanked by Cape, the Home Office had no choice but to act and the Chief Magistrate, Sir Chartres Biron, issued warrants under the Obscene Publications Act. Radclyffe Hall characterised this as "a reign of terror", but instead of facing *la guillotine* in the Place de la Concorde, she and Una went on holiday to Rye, where they walked the dogs on Camber Sands and read *Orlando*. Robespierre would have wept.

The trial took place at Bow Street Magistrates Court. Sir Chartres Biron opened the proceedings by saying that the "substantial question before me is, does this book as a whole defend unnatural practices between women?"

The fact that acts of lesbian love were not against the law did not bother him in the slightest, he said, as "the unnatural offences between women which are the subject of this book involve acts which between men would be a criminal offence, and involve acts of the most horrible, unnatural and disgusting obscenity". Well, it's good to start out with an open mind.

Many of those who supported Radclyffe Hall found a reason not to attend. Those who did turn up to testify were not called. Biron – sorry, Sir Chartres as Radclyffe Hall would certainly have called him – said that other people's opinions about what was and what was not obscene were of no interest to him.

In defence of the book, Radclyffe Hall's counsel, Norman

Birkett, claimed that the relationships in the novel, though sentimental and romantic, were "purely intellectual in character" and had nothing do with sex. Radclyffe Hall objected to this. They certainly were sexual, she interjected; she was told not to interrupt.

Following a lengthy study of the text, Biron succeeded in finding one sentence which, he said, clearly indicated that something naughty was going on. It read: "And that night they were not divided."

It may not exactly have been hot stuff, but it was enough to get the book condemned. Biron ordered that it be burned and charged Radclyffe Hall 20 guineas costs. She also had considerable legal fees of her own to meet.

Sales of her other books received a fillip, however. *The Well of Loneliness* flew off the shelves in the United States – where it was not judged to be obscene. The publishers were raking it in as, in light of the scandal, it was priced at five dollars instead of the usual two. And in France, Cape's co-publishers also made a killing, selling copies off a cart outside the Gare du Nord.

Radclyffe Hall appealed against the judgement, but proceedings were hampered by the fact that there were now no copies of the book for the appeal judges to read. She felt particularly let down because *her* party – the Conservative Party – was in power at the time. And instead of becoming a martyr, like Oscar Wilde, Radclyffe Hall found herself mocked by the numerous spoofs of *The Well of Loneliness* that circulated.

Even her mother provided no comfort.

"You can't touch filth without getting filthy," she said.

The controversy died down quickly, however, and *The Well of Loneliness* would have been forgotten if Virginia Woolf* had not satirised Sir Chartres Biron in her feminist essay, *A Room of One's Own*, in 1929.

She refused to be forgotten in lesbian circles, though, and Radclyffe Hall and Una headed off to Paris, where Radclyffe Hall was a celebrity. *The Well of Loneliness* caused a new sensation when it was adapted for the stage in Paris. Natalie Barney* held a reception for her at the Temple of Love and Hall and Una went to tea with Colette*. They took her advice and visited St Tropez, where they swam naked and ate lobster.

Back in England, Radclyffe Hall visited a seaside retreat of her own – Rye. There, she mixed with a lesbian coterie. Noël Coward* and his boyfriend Jeffery Amherst* came to visit, while Una got to work on a stage version of Colette's* *Chéri*, which opened to "unspeakable" reviews. Hall and Una were seen as a couple of English eccentrics on the Sussex coast and were accepted, socially, as a respectable married couple – exactly how they saw themselves. Una, for example, was so appalled by an article advocating sexual freedom in *Twentieth Century* magazine that she burnt it before the servants could read it. The way other lesbian couples in their circle kept changing partners appalled her. She was equally appalled when her daughter, now 23 years old, announced that she was going to get married – to a man.

Middle age was now creeping on. Radclyffe Hall was going through the menopause with the accompanying hot flushes and sleepless nights. Una had a hysterectomy and then suffered a vaginal abscess, infected gums, haemorrhoids and shingles. In Bagnoles she came down with gastroenteritis. The American Hospital in Paris sent a nurse – 30-year-old Evguenia Souline, a White Russian who had escaped with her family after the Bolshevik Revolution. Radclyffe Hall quickly became besotted with her.

"John was obviously ready to fall in love," said Evguenia. "She was waiting for her ideal. I was unprotected, a lonely, pathetic figure; a refugee on whom she could bestow her reserve of deep affection and love, whom she could treat like a child."

At dinner, Radclyffe Hall insisted that Evguenia be served first and given the best portions – even though it was Una that was ill. They took long walks together. Signing a copy of her latest book for Evguenia, Radclyffe Hall said: "I can see how you flushed to the eyes with pleasure that I wrote your name in it."

When Radclyffe Hall was late down to breakfast one day, Evguenia went up to her bedroom to see if she was okay.

"I have come on my own initiative," she said. Radclyffe Hall was flattered, but Evguenia was afraid of her.

"All was not altogether right," she wrote. "She roused my instinct in some perturbing way. I decided that I must go as soon as I could so as not to be engulfed in this contradictory mass of feeling."

Even though Una was now better and the American Hospital was charging 175 francs a day for the nurse, Radclyffe Hall would not let her go. However, after two weeks of idleness, Evguenia managed to escape back to Paris. Then the letters and phone calls started.

"I fought like anything within myself not to fall under her spell and repeated to myself over and over again: no, no, I do not wish to," she said. "I must not let myself be carried away by this undetermined emotion. But John – as she wanted me to call her – was very determined. Her letters became at once very strong and emotional. She would not hear of any reason on my part not to accept her affection, not to write to her or to see her."

Evguenia tried to put her off by replying to her as Miss Hall – the ultimate insult.

"Never again can I be Miss Hall to you," wrote Radders from England.

She and Una were on their way to Italy. Radclyffe Hall planned a two-day stopover in Paris so that they could have an assignation.

"Meet me at Lapeyrouse (you know, on the Quai des Grands Augustins) at 12.30," wrote Radclyffe Hall, "and we will lunch there alone together, just you and I. After lunch we will go back to my hotel where I shall have a sitting room and there (if you are willing) we will spend the afternoon. We shall be quite alone … Take care of yourself and know that I am counting on this meeting in Paris as I have counted on few things in my life."

After Radclyffe Hall and Una had arrived in Paris and checked into the Hôtel Pont Royale, she sent a note saying: "Darling, yes, I am here in Paris and it seems so strange that only a few weeks ago I did not know that Paris meant you. I want to come to you. It is red hell to be here and not to be able to see you until the day after tomorrow and then only for a few hours."

Una knew what was going on. In her diary she notes: "July 26. John gave my ex-nurse luncheon at Lapeyrouse."

Evguenia was nervous and ate nothing at lunch, but Radclyffe Hall still whisked her back to her hotel where they kissed for the first time. Evguenia was shy and awkward. When Radclyffe Hall wrote later from Italy, she said: "I had kissed your mouth many times already, but you suddenly said, 'Do you want to kiss my mouth?'"

Fearing that she was not giving Radclyffe Hall the passionate response that she wanted, Evguenia said: "This is the only way I know how to kiss."

"Your darling lips were so firm and protective, so chaste, so unwilling to respond," wrote Radclyffe Hall. "Why, you kissed me like a sister or a child – or were you really experienced and not intending to do otherwise. But once, just once, your lips gave way a little."

All of the passion came from Radclyffe Hall. Evguenia was unused to such things. In her written recollection of that afternoon, she omitted any mention of the kissing. Instead she merely said: "John invited me to the hotel and we had … a long talk."

Radclyffe Hall had asked her about her attitude to men and her sexual experiences. Evguenia told her that she had a number of gentleman admirers. She had met a promising young artist at a sanatorium in the Alps and they were to have been married, but when she left, he became very ill and had to stay on indefinitely, so "I was free from any romantic ties, and therefore ready to accept any affection given".

And Radclyffe Hall was certainly ready to give her some. Of that afternoon, Evguenia wrote: "Her love, her affection, her nearness, drove me into a kind of ecstasy which only comes once in one's own life … I felt like giving my own life for her."

On leaving, Evguenia said: "I can't believe that this is the last time I shall see you."

On the way home she was elated and "did not know anything

but that I was in love with Radclyffe Hall, the famous writer, the writer of *The Well of Loneliness*".

The following morning, Radclyffe Hall woke before dawn. Tormented by the fact that she was going away and might never see Evguenia – she called her Soulina – again, she began to dash off a letter.

"I am tormented because of you, and this torment is now only partly because of the senses," she wrote, "but it is now an even more enduring thing and more impossible to ease, my sweet, because it is a torment of tenderness, of yearning over you, of longing to help you – of longing to take you into my arms and comfort you innocently and most gently as I would comfort a child, whispering to you all sorts of foolish words of love that have nothing to do with the body. And then I would want you to fall asleep with your heart on my breast for a while, Soulina, and then I would want you to wake up again and feel glad because I was lying beside you, and because you were touching this flesh of mine that is so consumed by reason of your flesh, yet so subjugated and crushed by my pity, that the whole of me would gladly melt into tears, becoming as a cup of cold water for your drinking."

Radclyffe Hall was halfway through writing this when a letter arrived from Evguenia.

"It is a beautiful letter. It is as though I struck the rock with a staff of love and, at last, the spring has gushed out, out of your heart into mine," she continued. "Something tells me that all this was meant to happen, that we shall meet again, that our love will last, that our mutual desire, the one for the other, is only the physical expression of a thing that is infinitely more enduring than our bodies ... Otherwise why did I let you go from me even as you came – I, who needed you so and who could have made you incapable of resisting, who could have made you no longer want to resist? For you are not a woman of ice and this I well know, my little virgin, and I agonised to take your virginity and to bind you to me with the chains of flesh because I had and have so vast a need that my wretched body has become my torment – but through it all my spirit cries out to you, Soulina."

Radclyffe Hall complained that "the flesh may be weak" but "I dare not write any more, and since you have your living to earn and I am a marked woman ... I beg you to lock up this letter".

Although Una knew that something was up, she had no idea that such a grand passion was going on between them and assumed that "this young Russian woman with the curious face was to be ... a bird of passage". They were on Lake Garda, celebrating their 19th anniversary, when Radclyffe Hall told her that she intended to stop off in Paris to see Evguenia on the way back to Rye. Una forbade it and created a scene. She reminded Radclyffe Hall of her hysterectomy and litany of other illnesses and told her that her doctor had told her to avoid emotion. She emphasised the fact that she had stood by Radclyffe Hall during the obscenity trial, that she "stood for fidelity in the case of her inverted unions" and that "the eyes of the inverted all over the world were turned toward her" to set an example. She ended up hurling herself on the floor and behaving as though she was demented.

Radclyffe Hall gradually talked her round. First Una conceded that she and Evguenia could correspond. Then, when Radclyffe Hall said that she could not eat or sleep – let alone write a book – because she was so desolate, Una gave her permission for them to meet in Paris provided that Radclyffe Hall gave her "word of honour not to be unfaithful in the fullest and ultimate meaning of the word".

During the next six weeks, Radclyffe Hall wrote 41 letters to Evguenia, many having a hundred or two hundred franc note enclosed. She also arranged for a bank transfer of one hundred pounds – a huge sum in those days.

Despite her promise to Una, Radclyffe Hall promised Evguenia that she would "make a woman of her" so that she "would know the meaning of passion".

"Sweetheart, were I in very truth your lover in the ultimate sense of the word – I might not always be very gentle," she wrote. "I might try to be so, but I might not succeed, because the sex impulse is a violent impulse – I can't explain this to you very well because you know so little about it, beloved. But this I tell you. Were we lovers in deed, you would not want me to be very gentle – not if you feel for me even half of what I feel for you."

While Radclyffe Hall considered herself a "congenital invert" who could never have sex with a man, she knew that Evguenia was a bisexual who had other needs.

"The other day, I thought 'Would Souline like to have a child?'" wrote Radclyffe Hall, then found it necessary to fill in some of the facts of life. "Dearest, I can't give you that I am afraid ... you mustn't laugh at me, my Souline" – why not? we are – "I suddenly saw you with a child and the child was our child and we were very happy. Would you love me even more if I were a man? In some ways I should probably love you less. I'm not trying to lessen the obvious importance of normal love between men and women – and this love can, of course, be terribly strong – only I think that the other love is stronger."

Radclyffe Hall was going to be back in Paris on September 30 and started to make arrangements. On October 1, she would take Evguenia out to lunch, then whip back to Evguenia's apartment for a matinee.

"You shall tremble in my arms, which even you, *even you* must admit does not constitute either a rape or a 'seduction'," she wrote. And she sent her an allowance so that Evguenia did not have to work every afternoon and evening she was in town.

Evguenia was getting cold feet, however. She said that she was going to the United States with Mrs Baker, a wealthy patient who needed nursing on the trip. This made Radclyffe Hall fume. Mrs Baker "appears to have more claim upon you than I have," she wrote. It was she who paid her bills and her allowance. "If you're anyone's slave, you're going to be mine". After all, she had the privilege of falling in love with the great Radclyffe Hall, not with some lesser mortal.

Radclyffe Hall got Una to change their itinerary and they arrived in Paris sooner. On September 23, Una noted in her diary that John had gone out at 11.30 a.m. and had not returned till midnight. She had spent the afternoon in Evguenia's room.

"I found you a virgin and I made you a lover," said Radclyffe

Hall. "I have made a new discovery through you. I find that to take an innocent woman is quite unlike anything else in life."

For Radclyffe Hall it was "perhaps the most perfect experience". For Evguenia it was quite the opposite. She hated the whole business. Radclyffe Hall dismissed Evguenia's distress as "nerves" and "ignorance of physical passion" – "Remember how you fought me, my darling?" she wrote cheerily. What happened to the trembling in my arms that would not "constitute either a rape or a seduction"?

Afterward Evguenia "sat all crumpled up and in despair". At supper, Radclyffe Hall had to feed her "as though you were a child and consoled and reassured you as though you were a child".

Radclyffe Hall had no regrets – in fact, she was proud of what she had done.

"I was your first lover," she said. "Through me you are now no longer a child. Wonderful, yes, but terrible also – terrible because so achingly sweet."

Despite the fact that Evguenia was in a bit of a state, Radclyffe Hall pissed off back to Una at midnight, pretending that nothing had happened. For the next ten days she came back for another lap at Evguenia's well of loneliness, whether the Russian nurse liked it or not.

"Step by step – very quietly, I led you toward fulfilment," boasted Radders. "And this has made you doubly mine."

That was not how Evguenia saw it at all.

"Very often I would do something which was not what I wanted but which I knew John liked me to do and I usually gave in," she said.

But then again, isn't that what old Visetti did to Radclyffe Hall? What goes around comes around.

Radclyffe Hall also boasted that she had taught Evguenia all the facts of life, though it is clear that she held back some of the secrets of the trade – to make sure that there would be a chance for seconds, perhaps.

Una was not fooled, despite Radclyffe Hall's promise not to be unfaithful.

"Inversion, alas, what things are done in thy name that would be perversion a hundred times over were they heterosexual," she lamented in her diary.

Back in England, poor old Una was forced to make travel arrangements for Evguenia to come over and stay. As Evguenia had been stripped of her Russian citizenship by the Soviet authorities, Una had to intercede with the Home Office to get her a visa – "as I have some standing as the widow of an admiral".

Una was to stay in Rye, while Radclyffe Hall entertained Evguenia in Folkestone and a suite in London.

"The hotel is so nice and we shall have peace," she said. "No servants, no telephone, nothing but ourselves. Darling, that does seem to me to be like heaven."

However, a trip was planned to Rye, just to heap fresh humiliation on Una's head.

Again Evguenia tried to get out of it. She had a nursing assignment with a Russian princess in Zurich.

"Soulina, I need you more than these lesser people," said Radclyffe Hall, feeling particularly lofty. She offered Evguenia even more money to come. And Una, she said, would be no problem.

"I am not and have not been for years the least in love with Una," she told Evguenia. "I feel a deep gratitude toward her, a deep respect and a very deep affection – also an enormously strong sense of gratitude."

For Evguenia, though, she felt "a consuming need that is not the need of our bodies only". For Radclyffe Hall it felt like "first love".

"No face seems beautiful to me but yours," she wrote, "no voice seems beautiful to me but yours. I am only half alive when we are apart."

That's first love all right, and a very bad case of it, but there was also a very strong sexual element to it.

"I feel an overwhelming desire to be with you day and night, both in the moments of passion and in the moments of rest that come after passion," she wrote.

Of those first three rapturous nights together in Folkestone, Radclyffe Hall said: "You have taken me body and soul in your hands."

Looking back later she said: "I feel crazy sometimes remembering our days and nights in Folkestone."

"We were both mad happy," said Evguenia, who was obviously getting into the whole swing of the Sapphic thing. And she must have been really in love because Radclyffe Hall began calling her "Chink Face", "Chinkie Pig" and "Chink Face Little Tartar". I think I would have objected to this on grounds of political correctness alone.

Meanwhile, back in Rye, Una was wrestling with a nice big dollop of Catholic guilt. She realised that she was now suffering in exactly the same way that Radclyffe Hall had made Mabel Batten suffer years earlier.

Radclyffe Hall and Evguenia came to visit. They had lunch, tea and dinner à trois. Then Radclyffe Hall whipped Evguenia back to Folkestone for another night of passion.

After two weeks, Evguenia had to go back to Paris. She went bearing Radclyffe Hall's ring on her finger. Radclyffe Hall spent her time gazing lovingly at her photograph and kissing the bed where she had slept. Life alone with Una was now unbearable. However, after they had spent a miserable Christmas together at Rye, Radclyffe Hall brought Una with her when she went to Paris in January 1935.

"It will be kind of you if you let her come around with us," Radclyffe Hall told Evguenia. "It will give her a lot of fun and pleasure."

Hardly. After dinner à trois the first night, Una retired to bed with chest pains.

"I am perpetually anxious these days and with good cause. I live in a state of fear of what more will have to be met and suffered," she wrote in her daybook. "This girl is being brought into our lives, daily and hourly, so our old treasured companionship à deux hardly seems to exist." Now she was treated to the sight of the "devotion that for 20 years was all mine, overflowing for someone else, and a woman years my junior who has never been to John all that I have been. It hurts and hurts and is never for one waking moment out of my mind and heart."

They went to a party at Natalie Barney's* and the ballet à

155

trois but, though Radclyffe Hall promised never to leave Una alone all day and night, she spent most of her time at Evguenia's.

Even when Radclyffe Hall was with Una, there seemed to be little emotion between them.

"Her mind never seems to leave the girl for a moment," complained Una. "It is Russia, the Russians, the Soviets, the old Russia, Russian music, Russian art, Soulina, her looks, her clothes, her voice, her opinions, her naturalisation, her past, her present, her future, all roads lead back to the same name and face. If we look in shop windows, what would suit her? If we go out anywhere, would she have liked it? And what a pity she was not asked."

It was enough to get on your tits.

When Una complained that Radclyffe Hall did not write any more, or read, or think about anything else but Evguenia, Radclyffe Hall said: "You're quite right. I really don't want to do anything in the world but play around with that girl."

Una consoled herself with the thought that the attraction was entirely physical and would, sooner or later, wear off. There was another thing on her side, too. Radclyffe Hall wanted to keep her affair with Evguenia a secret as, like Una, she liked to play the great example of fidelity in a sea of promiscuity. When Evguenia played ping-pong with Natalie Barney's* lover, Nadine Hoang, she was told to be discreet, or news of their relationship would be all over Paris within 24 hours.

Things had moved on since the days of Mabel Batten. Una was now the wife while Evguenia was John's mistress. What's more, Una was a Lady. All Evguenie had going for her was her nurse's uniform, which Radclyffe Hall adored. How very like a man.

"Beyond excellent teeth and a nice smile, there is nothing at all," wrote Una.

When Evguenia offered to type a manuscript, Una kicked up a fuss that she was trespassing on her territory. She maintained her position as amanuensis and muse, but had to put up with Radclyffe Hall "petting and spoiling and pandering to moods and holding her hand". She longed to return to the time when there was "perfect and complete union between us two and Ladye and no intruder or outsider between us".

Una played a waiting game. She praised Radclyffe Hall and sniped at Evguenia. As she was responsible for making the travel arrangements when they went to the Riviera, she made sure that the "girl with the negroid face and eyes like currants" got a small room with no balcony or bathroom, while she and Radclyffe Hall occupied the suite which had a private bathroom with a balcony overlooking the sea. Nevertheless, every night after Radclyffe Hall had donned her pyjamas, she would make an excuse to visit Evguenia, saying she was going to put some conditioning preparation on her hair.

"I hate this camouflage, these transparent devices which are so unworthy of both of us," said Una suddenly one night. "Why call it that, darling? You are going to sleep with her every night and I suppose it is natural or does you good, or seems to. You know it and I know it."

Radclyffe Hall's response was that Una's disapproval "always spoils it a little". Well, it would, wouldn't it? For Una, Radclyffe Hall's callous behaviour made her cry herself to sleep most nights.

"I am always coming across things that hurt," she said. "The door I must not open, the letter I must not read, the thing I must not say, the caresses that are given elsewhere and not to me."

As the wife, Una was "the tired old routine", while, as the mistress, Evguenia was "the holiday, the excitement and the pleasure". What is more, as secretary and PA, Una was a boring permanent fixture, while Evguenia talked of studying at the Sorbonne, starting a business and making a life of her own.

After a round of parties with Colette*, Maurice Goudeket*, Jean Cocteau*, Natalie Barney* and Romaine Brooks*, the three of them headed for Italy where Radclyffe Hall hoped to meet up again with Gabriele D'Annunzio* who she had been introduced to on her last trip. D'Annunzio had a thing about lesbians. Radclyffe Hall bought black shirts for Una and Evguenia, and openly supported Mussolini's* invasion of

Abyssinia. Her only worry was that a new war in Europe might separate her from Evguenia.

Although Una continued to complain of Radclyffe Hall's "blemished fidelity", she found and decorated a new apartment for Evguenia in Paris and put up with her at Christmas in Rye. Her strategy was beginning to pay off. Radclyffe Hall grew jealous of Evguenia if she was late or if she did not know where she was.

"You belong to me and don't forget it," Radclyffe Hall reminded Evguenia. "You are mine and no one else's in the world. If I left you for 20 years you'd have to starve. No one but me has the right to touch you. I took your virginity, do you hear? I taught you all you know about love. You belong to me body and soul, and I claim you. And this is not passing mood on my part – it's the stark, grim truth I am writing."

Evguenia began to tire of the threesome and avoided meeting Una, especially after she had been making love with Radclyffe Hall. However, when a chest X-ray revealed suspected tuberculosis, she had to put up with being nursed by both Radclyffe Hall and Una. They headed for the south of France on doctor's advice – Evguenia and Radclyffe Hall in first class, with Una in second class with the dogs, canaries and the rest of the livestock.

Despite the TB, Radclyffe Hall wanted to continue making love to Evguenia. Una was terrified of contagion and urged Radclyffe Hall to ask the doctors whether it was safe to continue kissing Evguenia.

When they returned to Paris the cat was out of the bag. The three were referred to in the newspapers as *le trio lesbienne*. The public attention put Evguenia off sex and when Radclyffe Hall turned up at her flat unexpectedly for a bit of nookie and was refused, she trashed the place.

Evguenia managed to get a year-long visa to Italy, but the tensions among the *trio lesbienne* were now uncontrollable. Evguenia said that she could no longer live with Una in tow. Radclyffe Hall said that she could not give Una up – but what did that matter? She was not having sex with Una, as Una herself had asked her to point out when Evguenia's illness "debarred her from physical life".

"Debarred? I wasn't debarred," sneered Evguenia, saying that her illness had brought a welcome respite.

She enjoyed a further respite as Radclyffe Hall was suffering from cystitis at the time. Lack of sex only increased the tensions, however. Una and Radclyffe Hall were at least united in their admiration of Mussolini* and were both delighted that Hitler* had turned against the Jews. And when Edward VIII* abdicated to marry Wallis Simpson*, Una wrote: "The king is captured, like my John, by a worthless woman with whom he is infatuated."

That Christmas, Radclyffe Hall gave Una a pair of gold and onyx cufflinks in the shape of the *fascio* – the bundle of rods with an axe in it that symbolised unity and the power of the state in Ancient Rome and which gave Fascism its name. With them came a touching note. It read: "My darling Squiggie, thank you for being on earth."

After a sojourn in Florence, Evguenia returned to Paris while Radclyffe Hall and Una went to Rye. There they entertained the local lesbian ladies. Una's daughter, Andrea, whose marriage had now failed, came to stay and Una annoyed Radclyffe Hall by constantly referring to her as Evguenia.

"My dear, your child's name is, or used to be, Andrea," said Radclyffe Hall in a state of some irritation.

Evguenia herself visited in September, then they reunited again in Florence. In the meantime there were passionate love letters. When Evguenia wrote asking what Radclyffe Hall wanted for her birthday, she replied: "There is nothing you can give me, except a baby Chink made by me."

Whatever happened to the facts of life that Radclyffe Hall was teaching Evguenia?

Radclyffe Hall decided to shelve her anti-Semitism when Humbert Wolfe, a Jew at the Home Office, granted Evguenia a year-long visa. "Never again will I speak against the Jews," said Radclyffe Hall.

It is good to know that some of her circle thought her the deepest thinker of her generation. However, in this, as in other things, she was not true to her word and she soon started railing against Jews again when it suited her.

Evguenia was to come to "your John's own country England" again that September. Radclyffe Hall spoke of the visit as though it was to be their honeymoon and bought a silk dressing gown for the occasion. She slipped on the doorstep in Rye, though, and broke her ankle. When Evguenia turned up, she and Una fought over who was to nurse her. They also battled it out over who could buy more flowers for her hospital bedroom.

There was another disastrous trip to Italy. Evguenia said that she could no longer endure Una's hatred and wanted a life of her own. Radclyffe Hall said that Evguenia should think of her as a man who was married to Una before they met, and as they were Catholics they could not divorce. There were plenty of people she knew who lived in a *menage à trois*, she claimed, and she couldn't "eat, or sleep, let alone work" without her.

Evguenia was now talking about her desire to marry a man. Radclyffe Hall accused her of having an affair with a Russian soldier. She, herself, was not going to live without sex and would get it wherever she could. The three women continued to squabble, row and slug it out, while Europe mobilised around them. That did not worry them, though, because Radclyffe Hall's medium had given them her solemn assurance that there would be no war.

When war came, Evguenia was trapped in England. Radclyffe Hall's condition continued to deteriorate, but Evguenia and Una still continued to slug it out over the invalid. Evguenia was eventually given resident status and was allowed to do war work. Una took control and prevented her from visiting Radclyffe Hall – she would only allow her to visit her once, at the end, when she was in a coma.

When Radclyffe Hall died in 1943, Una was in complete command. The body was placed next to Ladye's in the mausoleum in Highgate Cemetery. Inscribed on a brass plate on the coffin were a couple of lines from Elizabeth Barrett Browning's sonnet "How Do I Love Thee?": "And, if God choose, I shall but love thee better after death. Una."

She didn't love Evguenia any better, however. She burnt the manuscript of Radclyffe Hall's last novel *The Shoemaker of*

Merano, because it portrayed her love for Evguenia, rather than their own grand passion that had featured in a coded form in earlier works. She gypped Evguenia out of her inheritance, appointed herself guardian of the sacred flame of Radclyffe Hall's genius, then set about telling her version of Radclyffe Hall's life in *The Life and Death of Radclyffe Hall*.

7 The Lust Generation

lthough Gertrude Stein is seen as a lesbian hero, her lesbianism opus, *QED*, was only published posthumously. She hardly hid her proclivities, though. While she was alive, she published *The Autobiography of Alice B. Toklas* after her live-in lover, "The Love Song of Alice B.", and composed an opera based on the life of Susan B. Anthony* and the deliciously named *Tender Buttons*.

A dedicated modernist, much of her work is so inaccessible that it is unreadable. Her defenders said that it was the literary equivalent of cubism, but the Hearst Press asked in exasperation: "Is Gertrude Stein not Gertrude Stein but somebody else living and talking in the same body?" More recent, and more partisan, commentators suggest that her elliptical language is motivated by a "desire to unleash a lesbian tongue" – surely it could be put to some better use.

Gertrude Stein's first love was not a woman at all. It was her older brother Leo, the only one in the family she felt close to. They read widely together, went on long walks and swam in the rivers and pools in Oakland, California, where they grew up. She did not sleep with him, however, but with her older sister Bertha.

"She was not a pleasant person," said Gertrude. "It is natural not to care about a sister, certainly not when she is four years older and grinds her teeth at night."

You'd have thought that would have put her off.

Leo had his problems with women, too. He ran away from any girl who showed any interest in him. At a party where the children were playing kissing games, he jumped out of the window rather than take his turn.

He put his chronic shyness down to a traumatic birth or weaning. He found it difficult to be polite to women, let alone chivalrous or romantic. He explained: "All sex expression toward them was rigorously suppressed and was reserved in later years for prostitutes who are for the most part regarded not as belonging to the real world but to the world of fantasy."

It was not just sex with women that frightened him, however. At school, there was a bright girl called Anne who always got top marks. He fancied her so much that he would go around the block to avoid meeting her. Later in life, when Gertrude's fame outshone his, he felt the same about her.

When Leo went to Harvard in 1892, Gertrude applied to Radcliffe to be near to him – it would be tempting to say that she applied to Radclyffe Hall*. They spent the summer of 1896 in Europe and, when Gertrude was accepted at Johns Hopkins medical school, they moved to Baltimore together. Then Leo dropped out and went to Florence.

After Leo's departure, Gertrude moved into a terrace house with fellow student Emma Lootz. Gertrude quickly asserted herself as the master of the house.

"Once Gertrude got alarmed about her health," recalled Emma. "She thought there was something the matter with her, so she hired a welterweight to box. The chandelier in my room used to swing."

Gertrude would have tea in the apartment of Bryn Mawr college graduates, Mabel Haynes and Grace Lounsbery. They were athletic women with "no dreaminess". Mabel was having an affair with another Bryn Mawr graduate, May Bookstaver.

"A tall American version of the handsome English girl," said Gertrude. "Upright and a trifle brutal."

Soon Gertrude was having an affair with her as well.

This triangular love-match may well have disrupted her studies, but it did provide the material for her first novel, QED. According to the book, it was May that made the first move. Gertrude confessed to being a "hopeless coward" when it came to these things.

"All I want to do is to meditate and think and talk," she said.

While she was talking, May "let her fingers flutter vaguely" near Gertrude's lips. Then, suddenly, Gertrude found herself "intensely kissed on the eyes and lips".

"I was just thinking ..." she continued.

"Haven't you ever stopped thinking long enough to feel?" said May.

It was all feeling from then on.

They had to keep their affair secret from Mabel, who was picking up May's bills. They met clandestinely in restaurants and museums. Later, they managed to organise a more intimate tryst in New York, meeting at a friend's apartment. In *QED*, Gertrude's experience is transposed into the third person.

"Something happened in which she had no definite consciousness of beginnings," she wrote. "She found herself at the end of a passionate embrace."

So here we have no conscious beginning and an end. It's what happened in the middle that I'd like to know.

Gertrude seems to have been puzzled, too. She found herself trapped in "unilluminated" immorality and longed for some moral code that could "stand the wear and tear of real desire". It did not help that her mother kept writing to her, telling her to marry a doctor. Nor did it help that Leo, writing from Paris, seemed to have sorted himself out, albeit expensively. He wrote to her of nights that "cost me 150 francs for champagne, eats, and the lady between midnight and six o'clock".

Back in Baltimore, while May made an effort to hide the truth, Gertrude got so frustrated that she blurted the whole thing out to Mabel.

"If you weren't wholly selfish you'd have exercised self-restraint," May wrote to Gertrude.

Mabel responded by whisking May off to Europe for the summer of 1901, leaving Gertrude desolate.

"I am now convinced my feelings for you are genuine and loyal," Gertrude wrote to her absent lover. "I dread you giving me up ... I dread more being the cause of serious annoyance to you."

"Hush little one," May wrote back. "Oh you stupid child, don't you realise that you are the only thing in the world that makes anything seem real or worthwhile to me. I have had a dreadful time this summer."

The reason that she was having a "dreadful time" was that Mabel had read one of her love letters to Gertrude and it had "upset her completely".

"She said that she found it, but I can hardly believe that," May's sorry tale continued. "She asked me if you care for me and I told her that I didn't know and I really don't, dearest. She did not ask me if I cared for you ... she was jealous of my every thought and I could not find a moment even to feel alone with you. But please don't say any more about giving you up. You are not any trouble to me if you will only not leave me."

When May and Mabel got back to Baltimore, Gertrude tried to avoid her. Inevitably they bumped into one another, however. They were soon spending a lot of time together in May's room "in the habit of silent intimacy", exchanging caresses "that seemed to scale the very walls of chastity".

It was nice but naughty. Gertrude tried to put a stop to it.

"We are more completely unsympathetic and understand each other less than at any time in our whole acquaintance," she wrote. When May received this letter, she fainted.

Despite their resolve to part, a chance meeting in the street was enough to set the whole thing off again. While they were apart, Gertrude said that she felt "sad with longing and sick with desire".

Mabel caught them kissing under a lamppost and made a scene, but May was not prepared to give either of her lovers up. This fraught situation dragged on for the next three years and it had a devastating effect on Gertrude's academic work. Her grades faltered and she flunked out. The other women medical students on her course thought that, with her failure, she "had done harm to their sex".

In 1902, she met up with Leo in Italy. Then they went to London where they rented rooms at 20 Bloomsbury Square (two minutes' walk from my front door). Leo bought his first painting from artist William Steer and they rubbed shoulders with intellectuals who included the art historian Bernard Berenson and the philosopher Bertrand Russell. Leo moved to Paris where he began drawing, using a rather astonishing technique.

"When I got back to the hotel, I made a rousing fire, took off my clothes and began to draw from the nude," Leo told his friend, the conductor Pablo Casals.

Surely it's more fun to have a nude model, Leo. (See *Sex Lives of the Great Artists*.) I trust that he did not employ the same technique when he spent a week drawing statues in the Louvre.

Gertrude stayed on in London, spending many hours in the reading room of the British Museum – where the *Sex Lives* books used to be written – determined to read English literature from the 16th century to the present. She claimed to have done this in a matter of months. I must try it when I've got a little free time.

Leo moved into a studio at 27 rue de Fleuris and wrote to Gertrude asking her to come and live with him. It was there that she wrote *QED*, which she finished in 1903. She then locked the manuscript in a cupboard. It was rediscovered in 1932. There was talk of publication, but her agent advised against it because of its explicit portrayal of lesbian love. Alice B. Toklas read the manuscript and then, in a fit of jealousy, destroyed all of May Bookstaver's letters to Gertrude.

In September 1907, Alice B. Toklas and her friend Harriet Levy arrived in Paris. On their first day, Harriet, a friend of the family, said: "Let's go and see the Steins."

They found Gertrude surrounded by paintings and Persian rugs.

> She was a golden presence burned by the Tuscan sun and with a golden glint in her warm brown hair. She was dressed in a warm brown corduroy suit. She wore a large, round, coral brooch and when she talked, very little, or laughed, a good deal, I thought her voice came from this brooch. It was unlike anyone else's voice – deep, full, velvety like a great contralto's ... She was large and heavy and with delicate small hands and a beautifully modelled and unique head.

That was how Alice remembered her. In contrast, Ernest Hemingway* said that she looked like a Roman emperor: "That was fine if you liked your women to look like Roman emperors."

Alice, on the other hand, had a cyst between her eyebrows which Pablo Picasso* said made her look like a unicorn. She combed her hair forward to hide it and was slight, compared to the enormous girth of Gertrude. If she walked behind her, you could scarcely see her.

Visiting Gertrude's cousin Julian Stein in Baltimore for Christmas in 1934, one of Julian's children, aged three, said that Gertrude looked like a man, before asking: "Why did the lady have a moustache?"

Although Alice was only two years younger than Gertrude, she felt that she was "so much younger in experience".

That's true. Alice had had little sexual experience. Brought up in San Francisco, she had danced with young men at Mardi Gras and kissed the boys goodbye as they went off as soldiers to the Spanish-American War of 1898. She had had a number of romantic friendships with the girls at school, particularly Nellie Joseph and Lilyanna Hansen. These affairs left her emotionally confused. Her mother was terminally ill, however, and there was no one to talk to about her feelings.

The day after their first meeting, Alice and Gertrude took a walk together in the Luxembourg Gardens. They ate cakes in a patisserie off the boulevard St Michael. From then on, until Gertrude's death 39 years later, they were never apart. Only the arrival of Lilyanna Hansen competed for Alice's attention.

Gertrude whisked Alice and Harriet off to Tuscany. Under the warm Italian sun, Gertrude asked: "Did Nellie and Lily love you?"

There was no need for an answer.

Gertrude told Alice that she intended to "win my bride".

"Care for me," she implored. "I care for you in every possible way."

She proposed nothing short of marriage. Alice was to be the wife, she the husband and it was to be a sexual match.

"When all is said, one is wedded to bed," she said.

"Pet me tenderly and save me from alarm," begged Alice. Then she began to cry.

"I understand the language," said Gertrude. "I love my love and she loves me."

Alice said later: "She came and saw, and seeing cried I am your bride."

The crying went on for some time. "Day after day she wept because of the new love that had come into her life," said Harriet. Alice was getting through 30 hankies a day.

They began to call each other Lovey and Pussy – Alice was Pussy – and did not care who heard them. Gertrude also called Alice kitten, gay, wifie, queen, baby, cheribum, cake, lobster, Daisy and her little Jew. Alice, on the other hand, called Gertrude, he, husband, hubby, king, Mount, fattuski or Baby Woojums. I think I feel sick.

They wrote notes to each other inscribed "DD" – Darling Darling – and "YD" – Your Darling. Letters to others were signed: "Gertrude and Alice Stein." And on the wall hung the proclamation: *"Mon epoux est a moy et je sui a luy"* – "My husband is mine and I am his."

Gertrude even put some of her passion into her poetry, saying: "Little Alice B. is the wife for me … She is very necessary to me. My sweetie. She is all to me …"

Then there's:

> Tiny dish of delicious which
> Is my wife and all
> And a perfect ball.

And:

> You are my honey suckle
> I am your bee.

And:

> Kiss me kiss … I'll let you kiss me sticky

I think we get the picture, ladies.

Leo gave up his study so that Alice could have a room of her own and discreetly went out when they wanted to get it together.

"It was very considerate of him," said Gertrude.

Gertrude was soon glowing with health and Leo became "more and more impressed by the supreme importance of nutrition and sexuality".

He soon solved his own problems with an artist's model called Nina Auzias; she was also known as Nina of Montparnasse, in recognition of the area around which she distributed her favours. He first saw her posing naked in a friend's studio, kneeling in a pose of supplication. Later, she poked her tongue out at him in a billiards hall. He asked her to pose naked for him, too.

Now you've got it, Leo.

She refused, but suddenly kissed him. However, no matter how he implored, she refused to pose nude for him. Instead, he paid her four times the going rate for her to be his "psychological model". She had to sit on the sofa and tell him of her adventures around Montparnasse. Despite periods of separation and numerous other sexual encounters on both sides, they stayed in contact and finally married in 1921, when he was 50.

Together Leo, Gertrude and Alice began collecting the work of Picasso*, Henri Matisse* and Georges Braques*, and began to define what we now think of as modern art. In 1913 came the inevitable falling out between Gertrude, Alice and Leo. The bone of contention was, naturally, who owned which painting. Leo moved to Italy and Gertrude and Alice vowed never to see him again.

After the First World War, expatriate American writers, including Sherwood Anderson, John Dos Passos, F. Scott Fitzgerald and Ernest Hemingway*, found their way to Gertrude's salon. She called them the "Lost Generation". She then began to write and publish on her own account.

The *Encyclopaedia Britannica* notes that Stein's style is too convoluted and obscure for the general reader, for whom she remains essentially the author of such lines as "A rose is a rose is a rose is a rose." Some of her unpublished work reaches new levels of uxorious awfulness. Try this:

> I marvel at my baby. I marvel at her beauty I marvel at her perfection I marvel at her purity I marvel at her tenderness. I marvel at her charm I marvel at her vanity … I marvel at her industry I marvel at her humour I marvel at her intelligence I

marvel at her rapidity I marvel at her brilliance I marvel at her sweetness I marvel at her delicacy, I marvel at her generosity, I marvel at her cow.

A "cow", Steinian scholars tell us, is an orgasm. Gertrude herself said: "Cows are very nice. They are between the legs." And she gets very worried when Alice does not have a cow.

> A cow has come he is pleased and she is content as a cow came and went … And now a little scene with a queen contented by the cow which has come and been sent and been seen. A dear dearest queen.

Are you following this stuff so far?

Then there are "caesars", which have something to do with cows, but no one is quite sure what. She said: "Having caesars is a duty. Yes, their duty is to a cow. Will they do their duty by the cow. Yes, now and with pleasure."

Gertrude wrote a lovely story called "A Book Concluding As A Wife Has A Cow. A Love Story". She compared it to Tristan and Isolde. Here's an extract:

> Having it as having having it as happening, happening to have it as happening, having to have it as happening. Happening and have it as happening and having to have it happen as happening, and my wife has a cow as now, my wife having a cow as now, my wife having a cow as now, my wife having a cow as now and having a cow as now and having a cow now, my wife has a cow and now. My wife has a cow.

Is there any wonder people gave up on literature? Gertrude Stein was single-handedly responsible for a lost generation of readers. Alice B. Toklas said that Gertrude Stein was a genius. I say she was a cow.

8 The Blues Get Bluer

esbians were not confined to white literary circles where
Sappho was discussed in the drawing room before her
philosophy was put into practice in the bedroom. The birth
of the blues threw up a number of black African-American
lesbian, or at least bisexual, stars. And in the early years of the
last century, they were ready to get down and dirty.

The mother of them all was "Ma" Rainey. Born Gertrude
Malissa Nix Pridgett on April 26, 1886 in Columbus, Georgia,
she began her singing career at the age of 12 when the locals
put on a small show called the "Bunch of Blackberries Revue".
She was spotted by William "Pa" Rainey, who was wooed as
much by her talent as by her personality and looks. They
married in 1904 and she toured with him in F.S. Wolcott's
Rabbit Foot Minstrels and other shows. In 1905, she claimed
she discovered, if not invented, the Blues – this was seven years
before W.C. Handy wrote "The Memphis Blues", the first
published Blues song.

The way "Ma" Rainey told it was that in 1902 she was
appearing in the tent show in a small town in Missouri. One
morning, a girl from the town came to the tent singing a song
about a man who had left her. The song was so strange and
poignant that "Ma" Rainey used it as an encore in her act.
Three years later, when someone asked her what kind of song
it was – on account of it being moody and sad – she said: "It's
the Blues."

She was a short, heavy, dark-skinned woman – though, in the
manner of the time, she lightened her skin for the stage with
heavy greasepaint, powder and rouge so that she looked gold
coloured under the amber stage lights. She draped herself in
jewellery – necklaces and earrings made of gold pieces,
diamond-studded tiaras, rings and bracelets – and her mouth
was a mass of gold teeth.

"Yes, she was ugly," said her trombone player Clyde Bernhardt. "But I'll tell you one thing about it, she had such a lovely disposition, you know, and personality, you forgot all about it. She commenced to lookin' good to you."

She was, of course, famous for her "Black Bottom".

Officially billed as Madame Rainey, she was known as "Ma" because of her warm and nurturing personality and also because she was ten years older than most of the other girls in the troupe. She was particularly nurturing towards young Artiebelle McGinty of the Smarter Set Company which she and "Pa" Rainey set up in 1916.

The name "Ma" had some other spin-offs. After she began recording in 1923, it allowed Paramount to push her as the "Mother of the Blues". It also had the connotation of "mama" – African-American speak for a lover or a voluptuous and desirable woman. On stage, she became "Big Mama" – a sex symbol that she played with slightly comical overtones.

She was supported by a chorus of dark-skinned girls – which was unusual for the time as lighter-skinned "sepia lovelies" were generally preferred, but "Ma" did not want anyone looking lighter than her. One of these dark girls was 18-year-old Bessie Smith.

On stage "Ma" told jokes and of her craving for the flesh of young men – "pig meat" or "bird liver" as she called it. Both "Ma" Rainey and Bessie Smith were bisexual. They may have had an affair.

Sam Chatmon, who played guitar for "Ma" Rainey's tent show in Jackson, Mississippi, certainly thought that they were lovers.

"I believe she was courting Bessie," he said. "The way they'd talk, I believe there was something going on. Bessie said, 'Me and "Ma" Rainey had plenty of big times together.' I'd talk to Ma and she'd say her and Bessie had big times … she was acting so funny, I believe that one of them was the man, the other one was the girl."

And Rainey would get jealous.

"If Bessie'd be round, if she'd get talking to another man, Ma's run up. She didn't want no man to talk with her," Chatmon said.

There is no doubt that "Ma" Rainey was interested in women. Later, she appeared in an ad dressed as a man, flirting with women, and wrote and recorded the openly lesbian song "Prove It On Me Blues". Its lyrics are explicit:

> Went out last night with a crowd of my friends,
> They must have been women, 'cos I don't like no men.
> Wear my clothes just like a fan,
> Talk to gals just like any old man
> 'Cos they say I do it, ain't nobody caught me,
> Sure got to prove it on me.

"Ma" Rainey always had a number of like-minded chorus girls on hand and, by the 1920s, she and "Pa" Rainey had separated. In 1925, she threw a lesbian orgy for her chorines at a hotel in Chicago. They were drinking and making so much noise that a neighbour called the police. When the cops arrived to investigate, the party had just got into its swing. There was pandemonium as the naked girls scrambled for their clothes and fled out of the back door in a state of undress. Clutching someone else's dress, "Ma" was the last to the exit and she was apprehended after she fell down the stairs. Accused of running an indecent party, she was thrown in jail. Bessie Smith bailed her out the next morning.

Later, "Ma" Rainey married a much younger man who had no connection to show business. She continued performing and recording until 1935, when she retired back to Columbus, Georgia, where she was active in the Baptist Church. She died on December 22, 1939 and was interred in the family plot at Porterdale Cemetery in Columbus. Her death certificate listed her occupation as "housekeeper".

"Ma's" protégée, Bessie Smith, was born on April 15, 1894 in Chattanooga, Tennessee. It is said that she was kidnapped by "Ma" Rainey at the age of 18 and initiated into the rites of Sapphic love. The kidnapping story seems unlikely – what talented black singer would *not* have wanted to get out of Chattanooga in 1902. The bit about Sapphic love has more of a ring of truth about it, though. Neither Bessie nor "Ma" Rainey made any secret of their desire for other women and both performed both on and off stage with their chorus girls.

Bessie was promiscuous and also had affairs with men, with a strong preference for partners of a darker complexion. She made an exception, however, in the case of the light-skinned Sidney Becht, who got her her first recording session. Bessie's first release, "Downhearted Blues", established her as the most successful black vocalist of the time. More than any other performer, she was responsible for introducing the Blues into the mainstream of American popular music.

In 1922, she met Jack Gee, who had seen her perform in Atlantic City. An illiterate night watchman, he often pretended that he was a policeman with the Philadelphia Police Department. As they were preparing to go out on their first date, Jack got shot. She visited him every day in hospital and, when he came out, she moved in with him. On June 7, 1923, they married. Bessie already had a hit on her hands and also had enough money to afford a honeymoon.

The marriage was fine when they were at home in Philadelphia, but once she went out on tour, things started to turn sour. Soon Jack began beating Bessie up.

"She was afraid of Jack because he beat her so," recalled Jack's niece, Ruby Walker, who toured with Bessie. "If he was around she didn't allow you to talk to her about nothing except maybe the show – she didn't want to be bothered, she'd go into her room, afraid you might whisper something and Jack would think she was planning something terrible."

Of course, when he was not about she was partying. Her appetite for drink and uninhibited sex was legendary. Rumours reached the ears of Jack, fuelling his jealousy. He wasn't the only one who was jealous and violent, though. Bessie behaved just as badly over an attractive young dancer in her show called Agie Pitts from Detroit.

"Some way or another Bessie fell for that boy," said Ruby. "And he was a boy compared to her."

One night Ruby was in Agie's dressing room and they were fooling around. Suddenly the door flew open and there stood Bessie.

"Everything I like, you like," she told Ruby. "And I am going to break you out of the habit of trying to be Bessie Smith – I'm gonna let you know you ain't Bessie Smith."

Bessie then launched herself on Ruby while Agie fled the room. Ruby managed to fight Bessie off until someone heard her screams and called the police.

"I kept on hollerin' even when I saw the cops coming," said Ruby, "I was that mad. They asked me what happened and I said: 'That woman beat me.' I acted like I didn't know Bessie. They took Bessie, me and Agie in, and put us all in jail. Bessie was drunk. I was half-drunk and they locked Agie up because we were fighting over him. But I wasn't fighting. It was Bessie. She was so jealous."

Next day someone paid their fine and they got out, but Bessie was not contrite.

"I beat you up this time in this town," Bessie told Ruby, "and you'd better get ready to be beat up in the next town if you don't stop messin' around with my men."

Frightened that news of this altercation might have reached Jack's ears, when she went to Philadelphia for a couple of days to see him, she took him a diamond ring that cost over two thousand dollars. She did not bother to hide her sexual indiscretions when she was out on tour without him, however. Occasionally, he would turn up unannounced. It became a cat-and-mouse game.

"Jack was the fightingest man you've ever seen," said Ruby. "He'd walk into a room hittin'. Every time they had their fights he'd hit her so hard I'd think he was going to kill her, and I'd butt in and he'd slap me down like I wasn't even there – and I got tired of getting beat up on account of Bessie."

After all, Bessie was the one who got all of the benefits. There would be a period of loving reconciliation after a fight when Bessie would be on her best behaviour. In addition to that, she was the one who had all the fun with other lovers. And Jack benefited, too. She lavished him with expensive gifts. He was supposed to have some hand in her management, but neglected his duties, often without any legitimate excuse for his prolonged absences.

It was fortunate that Jack could not read, as news of Bessie's broad sexual tastes filled the pages of the black gossip sheets. Hot on her case was the *Interstate Tatler*. One small item appeared in the "Town Tattle" column of February 27, 1925, under the byline "I. Telonyou". It read: "Gladys, if you don't keep away from B., G. is going to do a little convincing that he is her husband. Aren't you capable of finding some unexplored land 'all alone'."

The Gladys was the male-impersonator Gladys Ferguson, who Bessie was close to at the time.

Meanwhile, Ruby had a 16-year-old school-friend called Lillian Simpson, who was desperate to get into show business. She taught her a few steps and, in 1926, organised an audition for her with the troupe. Bessie said that she did not need any more chorus girls, but Lillian's mother had once been her wardrobe mistress so she gave her a job. After an intensive training course, Lillian joined the chorus line of the new show *Harlem Frolics* on tour, and waited on line to become Bessie's new lover.

Bessie was fiercely jealous about her dancing girls. The train was just getting ready to pull out of Ozark, Alabama, with the troupe on board, when one of the dancers told Bessie that Jack had been "messing around" with another girl in the chorus line while she had been away recording in New York. Without bothering to check out the story, Bessie got hold of the girl concerned and threw her out on to the track, injuring her. Then she flung her belongings out after her.

She then went looking for Jack.

"Come out, you motherless bastard," she yelled, storming down the train while the rest of the troupe braced itself for the inevitable confrontation.

Jack was not on the train. He had gone into town on a last-minute errand. Bessie found his gun. He had just returned when Bessie came storming out of their state room to find him, out on the track, stooping over the sobbing girl.

A shot rang out. Bessie stood on the rear platform of the train waving the pistol.

"You good for nothing two-timing bastard," yelled Bessie. "I couldn't even go to New York and record without you fuckin' around with these damn chorus bitches. Well, I am going to make you remember me today."

"Put that gun down," said Jack, starting down the track toward her.

Another shot changed his mind. He made a strategic run for it and Bessie chased him down the track firing off the rest of the bullets.

"I've never seen Jack run so fast," said Ruby. "Everyone was scared to death that Bessie would kill him this time, but I think she missed on purpose."

Discretion being the better part of valour, Jack left the tour at this point.

Bessie made no secret of the fact that she fancied Lillian. At a Christmas party she put on for the girls, where eggnogs had quickly been abandoned in favour of straight corn liquor, a drunken Bessie looked over at Lillian and said: "I like that gal."

"I'm glad you like her," said Ruby, thinking that Bessie was referring to Lillian's dance routine. "She's doing good, ain't she?"

"No, I don't mean that," said Bessie. "I'll tell her myself, 'cos you don't know nothin', child."

Whereupon Bessie whispered something in Lillian's ear and the two of them left the room together. They were gone all night. The following day, Lillian told Ruby that she did not know what she was missing.

Ruby shared a room with Lillian and, while Jack was away, she found herself sleeping alone.

Nobody was surprised that Lillian now shacked up with Bessie. They were just terrified that Jack would come back and catch them at it.

Filled with the thrill of lesbian love, Lillian urged Ruby to "try it" with another girl named Boula Lee, who was also the wife of the show's musical director, Bill Woods. Boula regularly made passes at Ruby, but Bessie warned Ruby that if she caught her messing with any of her chorus girls, she would be sent home.

Ruby developed a painful boil under her armpit and was

waiting backstage for her cue at the Frolic Theatre in Bessemer, Alabama, when chorus girl Dinah Scott came up behind her and grabbed her under the arms, bursting the boil. Another chorus girl called Helen ran forward with some tissues and began dabbing the wound. Boula Lee saw this from the other side of the stage and misunderstood what was going on. After the show she dragged Ruby into the alley outside and, in a fit of jealousy, warned her: "You ain't gonna mess around with them other bitches."

She then lunged at Ruby, scratching her face. This sparked a full-scale catfight until Bessie appeared and separated them.

"I know Jack's gonna blame me for this," she said, looking at Ruby's scratched face. Jack was due to return that evening and, with one blow, Bessie knocked Boula clean across the alley.

When Jack showed up, he found Bessie and the troupe in her room.

"What y'all doin' up here drinkin'?" he said.

"Nobody been drinkin' any liquor, nigger," said Bessie. "You're not in the police force, you're in show business, so don't come in here pushin' on people all the damn time."

At that point, Jack noticed the scratch on Ruby's face and asked her how it had happened. Ruby said, as Bessie had instructed her, that it had got scratched when some of the girls were fighting over costumes.

Then Bill Woods piped up: "It was one of them bulldykers who's after Ruby."

"What do you mean, one of them?" yelled Bessie. "It was your wife."

Jack turned to Boula, grabbed her, dragged her out of the room and threw her down the stairs. He then ordered Bill to send her home. Lillian was now in a panic, fearing that she was in for the same treatment. However, while Jack was out of the room, Bessie turned to Ruby and said: "Whatever you do, you'd better not tell on me and Lillian."

They kept their secret as far as St Louis, where Jack left the tour again. Bessie was eager to resume the affair the moment he was gone. She went into the room Lillian was sharing with Ruby and kissed her. Embarrassed, Lillian pulled away.

"Don't play around with me like that," she said.

"Is that how you feel?" asked Bessie, grabbing her around the waist.

"Yes," said Lillian. "That's exactly how I feel."

"Well, to hell with you, bitch," said Bessie. "I got 12 women on this show and I can have one every night if I want it. Don't feel so important, and don't you say another word to me while you're on this show, or I'll send you home, bag and baggage."

They ignored one another for three days. Then, on the fourth night, Lillian did not show up at the theatre.

"She's just tryin' to pout," said Bessie and the show went on without her.

When the curtain fell, Bessie's sister-in-law, Maud, burst into the dressing room. She had gone back to the hotel and, passing Lillian's room, saw an envelope sticking out of the door. The door was locked. The envelope contained a suicide note and she came racing back to the theatre to get Bessie.

Bessie, Ruby and Maud then hightailed it back to the hotel. They could smell gas outside Lillian's door. They called the proprietor, who smashed the windows that Lillian had nailed shut. Lillian was rushed to hospital. Bessie had a sleepless night. The next day she went to the hospital and discharged Lillian. Lillian lost all her inhibitions from that moment on.

"She did not care where or when Bessie kissed her," said Ruby. "She got real bold."

Lillian may well have lost her inhibitions, but she did not lose her fear. She knew that Jack would find out about them sooner or later. When they reached Chicago she tried to quit, but Bessie persuaded her to stay on. However, by the time they got to Detroit, Bessie gave up and let her go.

While Lillian was around Bessie was relatively sober, but, once she left, Bessie began to indulge once more in her excessive appetite for home-cooked Southern food and moonshine. Bessie was intimately acquainted with the tenderloin districts of the cities she performed in. On a previous trip to Detroit, she had become friendly with a woman who ran one of the notorious "buffet flats". Sometimes known as "good-time flats", these were private establishments that provided gambling, bootleg liquor, sex shows and any conceivable type of erotic entertainment. Originally set up for Pullman attendants – who were highly respected in the black community – they had a reputation for being safe. They were usually run by women, who would also act as bankers, taking a gentleman's money for safekeeping and then doling it out as and when he needed it during the course of the evening.

Bessie knew that the proprietress would send two cars to the theatre when she was in town to bring her and a party of the more discreet girls over. Bessie would admonish them at the door of the theatre: "If any of you tell Jack about this, you'll never work in my shows again."

The night after Lillian left, there was a party of six, including Ruby. When they reached the flats, Ruby took a good look around.

"It was nothing but faggots and bulldykes, a real open house," she said. "Everything went on in that house – tongue baths, you name it. They called them buffet flats because buffet means everything, everything that's in the life. Bessie was well known in that place."

Even though the girls had been sworn to secrecy, Bessie was still afraid that word might get back to Jack. Perhaps she was just missing Lillian. So – that night at least – she limited her activities to drinking and voyeurism.

The flats' most popular attraction was a live show in which one young man expertly made love to another. Bessie, however, was more taken with a fat woman who could perform amazing vaginal tricks that involved a cigarette and a Coca-Cola bottle.

"She was great," said Bessie. "She could do all those things with her pussy – a real educated pussy."

The show closed the following night and the girls had a pyjama party back at the hotel. They were all drunk and a young girl called Marie was doing a ballet-tap number for them.

"C'mon, Marie, show your stuff," shouted Bessie.

It was at this point that Ruby passed out. When she came to, she was back in her room and all hell had broken loose. There was pandemonium outside. Ruby rushed to the door and opened it. She saw Marie come running down the corridor followed by Bessie. They pushed past Ruby into her room and locked the door behind them.

"If Jack knocks, you don't know where I'm at," said Bessie.

It transpired that Jack had turned up to find Bessie and Marie together in an extremely compromising position. Marie had apparently been showing her stuff.

As the three women quaked in her room, Ruby could hear Jack outside on the landing. He was yelling: "Come here, you bitch. I'm going to kill you tonight."

She heard him approach her door. Then she heard one of the other girls step out into the corridor and appeal for calm. It seemed to do the trick. Ruby heard Jack say, in a more peaceful tone: "I think I know where she is, but when she comes back, you tell her I am looking for her."

After that they heard his footsteps going down the stairs and out into the street.

There was no time to dress. The girls grabbed what they could and made a dash for the railroad depot. Bessie told them not to switch the lights on as they clambered on to her railroad car. Then, with the girls still in their pyjamas, the train pulled out of the station.

Like most Blues singers, Bessie made a big play of a voracious heterosexual attitude and distanced herself from homosexuality. In "Foolish Man Blues", she sang:

There's two things got me puzzled,
There's two things I can't understand
That's a mannish actin' woman
And a skippin', twistin' woman acting man.

She was okay when her lovers, both male and female, were black, but she was not so cool when it came to white women. When she sang at a party given by Carl Van Vechten, music editor of *The New York Times*, she was just leaving when the hostess, Fania Marinoff Van Vechten, threw her arms around her.

"Oh, Miss Smith," she cried. "You're not leaving without kissing me."

Bessie, who had just downed a pint of gin, said: "Get the fuck away from me. I ain't never heard such shit," and pushed Mrs Van Vechten to the floor.

It looked as if things were going to turn nasty, but Ruby and Bessie's piano player, Porter Grainger, took her by the arms and gently led her away. This was particularly courageous of Grainger, who was a fey gay, but then he was so afraid of Bessie that he even obliged her when, occasionally, she ordered him to visit her bed.

Jack Gee finally split from Bessie in 1929 when he took some of her money and financed a show for "brown-skinned beauty" Gertrude Saunders. Gertrude was slim and a good deal younger than Bessie. When Bessie found out about Gertrude's show she was furious. She took a car to the Columbus Hotel where Jack was staying. Gertrude was registered there, too. Fortunately she was out. While Ruby waited outside, Bessie went in to confront Jack. She trashed his room and emerged bleeding. Jack said they later made it up. Others said she never forgave him. Either way the marriage was over.

Not everyone was surprised. It seems that the affair had been going on for some time.

"A lot of nights when we'd be on the train," said Maud, "I'd get off to go in the station and get sandwiches, or something like that, and I'd catch Jack and that woman in there, but I never told Bessie because then we'd never have reached our destination – Bessie would have killed both of them, so I just kept my mouth shut."

That same year, 1929, Bessie appeared in the movie *St Louis Blues*. She was now so confident that her career was on a solid footing that, like "Ma" Rainey, she began to sing songs with explicit lesbian content, such as "It's Dirty But Good" from 1930.

However, as the Depression hit the recording and entertainment industry, Bessie's career went into decline. She was helped out by an old friend, Richard Morgan, who was the biggest bootlegger on the south side of Chicago and who was also a patron of the arts.

"She was like a new woman," said Maud. "Richard was everything that Jack should have been. They got along very well, they both loved a good time and they respected each other. Richard was very jovial when he'd had a few drinks, but he never got nasty, and when he was sober you had a hard time getting a word out of him. He was a good businessman, he didn't throw money around, but he wasn't tight either. Also, he was tall and handsome, a real sharp dresser. He was perfect for Bessie, he understood her."

He could not stop her from binge drinking and smoking weed, though. She was arrested under the Volstead Act, which had introduced Prohibition, and missed a show, incurring a heavy penalty as a result. Clubs were closing and she made her last recording in 1933. Soon she could not support herself and was totally dependent on Richard.

After a three-year hiatus, she started to appear in clubs and shows again, but died before another recording session could be arranged. In all she made over two hundred recordings, including some famous duets with Louis Armstrong.

Bessie Smith died following an automobile accident on September 26, 1937 in Clarksdale, Mississippi, after being refused treatment in a "whites-only" hospital. Although Richard Morgan was on hand at her funeral, it was Jack Gee who stole the limelight.

Numerous other bisexual black entertainers of the time were present, including Ethel Waters, her lover of many years Ethel Williams and Alberta Turner, who married as a cover for her bisexuality but did not live with her husband. Her lover was Lottie Tyler.

Then there was Gladys "Fatso" Bentley, a bisexual three-hundred-pound male impersonator who sometimes performed under the name Bobby Minton. Born on August 12, 1907 in Pennsylvania, she ran away to New York as a teenager and found her way to the clubs of Harlem. She gained a reputation there for improvising obscene parodies of popular songs, honing her shows at the Clam House, a hangout for gays in Harlem.

During Prohibition, there was a vogue for "Pansy Acts" and "Hot Mama" lesbian or bisexual singers. Gladys Bentley was the hottest of these. Dressed in her signature white top hat and tuxedo, she openly flirted with women in the audience.

She recorded solo for OKeh Records, and with the Washboard Serenaders for RCA Victors, recording "Thrill Me Till I Get My Fill".

In the 1930s, she opened the Exclusive Club, where she arranged and directed her own shows, including the famous Ubangi Club Revue, where she was supported by a chorus of men in drag.

Bentley retained her drag off stage as well as on. She boasted to a gossip columnist that she married white woman in Atlantic City, New Jersey while dressed as a man.

In 1937, she and her mother moved to California, where she drew a lesbian crowd to the Monas club in San Francisco and Joquins' El Rancho in Los Angeles. In the early 1940s, she quit to begin a new career as a Blues shouter, recording for various independent labels.

When the mood in the United States became more conservative in the 1950s, she took to wearing dresses and *Ebony* magazine carried an article called "I Am A Woman Again", where she claimed to have cured lesbianism by a course of female hormones. She was finally at peace, she said, after a "hell as terrible as dope addiction".

She then claimed to have married a newspaper columnist called J.T. Gibson. He promptly denied it. In 1952, she married Charles Roberts, a cook 16 years her junior. The two eventually divorced. She continued to perform and appeared twice on the Groucho Marx television show. By then she had become a devout member of "The Temple of Love in Christ, Inc" and had become an ordained minister in the church by the time she died on January 18, 1960 in Los Angeles at the age of 52.

9 Mercedes Bends

At the back of this book you will find instructions on how to play the "International Daisy Chain" game developed by the novelist Truman Capote*. The idea is to pick any two famous people and to link them via a chain of interconnecting sexual partners. The player using the fewest beds wins. Capote said that Hollywood scriptwriter and socialite Mercedes de Acosta was the best card you could hold.

"You could get to anyone – from Pope John XXIII* to John Kennedy* – in one move," he claimed. In other versions of the story, it was from the Duchess of Windsor* to Cardinal Spellman*, which I would have thought was a good deal easier as Spellman was a well-known fag and the Duchess of Windsor was a noted fag hag.

Although Mercedes de Acosta is largely forgotten now, it is interesting to note what a key figure she once was. In a letter to Anita Loos in 1960, the lesbian literata Alice B. Toklas* said: "You can't dispose of Mercedes lightly. She has had the two most important women in America – Greta Garbo* and Marlene Dietrich*."

(According to some sources, Toklas actually said in private that Mercedes had had "the *three* most important women in America", prompting speculation about who the third might have been – Eleanor Roosevelt*, Gertrude Stein*, Shirley Temple*...?)

What made Mercedes such an important card, though, was that while she liked to hang out in drag clubs – and her lesbian lovers were legion – she was also married, occasionally seduced men and often went with bisexuals. In International Daisy Chain, bisexuals count double.

De Acosta had been confused about her sexual identity from an early age. She said she thought that she was a boy until she was seven. Her family encouraged this delusion. Her mother had wanted a boy, so she called Mercedes "Rafael" and dressed her in an Eton suit. As Rafael, de Acosta played as a boy with the other boys until one day, she said, "the tragedy occurred". One boy said that she could not throw a ball as far as they could because she was a girl. She challenged him to a fight. Instead of fighting, he took her behind the bathhouse and showed her his penis. She thought it was horrible and said that he was deformed.

"If you are a boy and you haven't got one, you're the one that's deformed," he said.

The other boys came around the back of the bathhouse and showed her their penises, too.

"Prove that you're not a girl," they screamed.

Mercedes ran back home to her mother and forced her to admit that she was, in fact, a girl. She was then sent to a convent where she vexed the nuns by claiming that she was neither a girl nor a boy – "or maybe I'm both".

Later in life de Acosta would say: "Who of us are only one sex? I, myself, am sometimes androgynous."

As well as failing to sort out her gender identity, the convent also opened her eyes to new possibilities. Her teacher, Sister Isabel, had fallen in love with another nun, Sister Clara. Mercedes acted as their go-between, carrying notes and standing as lookout during their brief trysts. Inevitably, the affair was discovered by the Mother Superior, who arranged for Sister Isabel's transfer to China. Mercedes witnessed their heart-rending farewell:

Sister Clara came in rapidly and for a second they stood there mutely before each other. Then, suddenly, Sister Clara folded Sister Isabel in her arms, and they clung to each other. Not a word was exchanged between them, and Sister Clara pulled herself violently away and rushed from the room. A cry, like the cry of death, came from Isabel and she crumpled and fell to the floor. I rushed to her. The Mother Superior and two other nuns came in, and I was taken away weeping hysterically myself. I remember sobbing wildly in the Mother Superior's office, and beating my head against the wall while two nuns tried to calm me and make me drink a cup of tea. Later on, I went back to class and when I saw another sister presiding and calmly sitting in Sister Isabel's place, I ran out of the room and pulled the fire-alarm bell.

Mercedes also got a sentimental education outside school. At nine o'clock Mass at St Patrick's Cathedral, not far from where the de Costas lived New York, the young Mercedes caught the eye of the theatrical producer Augustin Daly, the owner of the Daly Theatre on Broadway.

"After some weeks of flirting and making faces at each other, Mr Daly went to the Mother Superior and enquired if he could adopt me," Mercedes said.

When Daly pointed out which child he meant at Mass the following day, the Mother Superior said: "That child does not belong to the orphanage. I know her mother quite well."

The childless Daly persisted, however. He was used to negotiating with actors and actresses – and was also used to getting what he wanted. Mercedes' mother was obdurate. Her daughter was not for sale. However, she would allow him to take her out on Sundays.

Daly would pick her up in the afternoon, but instead of taking her home with him, he took her to the home of the actress Ada Rehan, who was under contract to Daly at the time. The three of them would make scenery and costumes, and perform plays on a puppet theatre. Mercedes was hooked. She had such a good time on Sunday afternoons that her mother felt obliged to go around and thank Mrs Daly. Mrs Daly protested that she had never set eyes on young Mercedes, then burst into tears. Her husband, she said, always spent his Sunday afternoons with his mistress.

After that, there were no more Sunday afternoons with the puppet theatre. However, as a special concession, Mercedes was allowed to go backstage on matinees at the Daly Theatre, or sit on Mr Daly's lap in the front of house during rehearsal.

Mercedes' oldest sister, Rita, was an internationally acclaimed beauty who had been painted by both John Singer Sargent and Giovanni Boldini. Through Rita, Mercedes met the writer Anatole France*, the sculptor Auguste Rodin*, the composer Igor Stravinsky*, Queen Marie of Romania and the actresses Constance Collier, Sarah Bernhardt* and Ethel Barrymore*, who swung both ways. She also met the theatrical agent Bessie Marbury, who Mercedes called "Granny Pa", and the reclusive actress Maude Adams – Broadway's first Peter Pan, who later became one of Mercedes' lovers. After a backstage romp, Maude gave her a copy of the novel *Kim*, inscribed and annotated by Rudyard Kipling.

In 1915, Mercedes met the freeform, Sapphic-style dancer Isadora Duncan*, who was visiting a friend on Long Island. They kicked off their shoes and went running down the beach together. She told Mercedes of her great tragedy. She had seen the car carrying her two children and their nanny roll into the Seine. All three of the car's occupants had drowned. In an empty barn, she danced a dance of resurrection and Mercedes, now a dedicated lesbian, comforted her in the only way she knew how.

The following year, Bessie gave Mercedes tickets to see the movie *War Brides* (1916), starring the Russian actress Alla Nazimova*, who was famous for her all-girl orgies in Hollywood. She even had an affair with famous anarchist Emma Goldman. She made no secret of her sexual preferences either.

"Most of my friends are young girls," she told *Photoplay*.

When Nazimova came to New York to perform in a wartime benefit for Russia in Madison Square Garden, the benefit's organiser employed Mercedes to cater for the star's every need. She took the job very seriously indeed. When they met backstage, Alla was dressed as a Cossack:

"Her eyes were the only true purple-coloured eyes I have ever seen. Her lashes were black and thick, providing a setting for the intensity they surrounded. I was always fascinated and conscious of Nazimova's eyes," Mercedes said. "We took to each other instantly. I felt completely at ease and as if we had always known each other."

Nazimova asked Mercedes to walk her home.

"Aren't you tired after running and leaping around all Madison Square Garden?" asked Mercedes.

"Heavens, no," purred Nazimova. "I'm as strong as a lion and I need as much exercise as a tiger."

Big cats. Umm.

After that night, Mercedes began devouring Russian literature.

The affair with Alla Nazimova led Mercedes to believe that she could have sex with any of the gorgeous creatures she saw on the silver screen. However, Nazimova was soon summoned back to Hollywood. At a party given by Mrs John Jacob Astor at her home on Fifth Avenue, Mercedes noticed the "charmingly shaped head and ... delicate and slightly turned-up nose" of the "lovely looking" debutante Hope Williams.

"We were introduced and 'clicked' at once," said Mercedes. "It was a meeting which resulted in a friendship which has grown and ripened through the years."

Both of the girls had a passion for the theatre, but it was not the done thing for society girls to tread the boards – that was reserved for a different type of girl altogether. They soon found their way around that, though. It was socially acceptable, they discovered, if they were to put on productions for charity. Mercedes wrote and directed *What's Next?* in 1918.

Mercedes appeared with her hair daringly bobbed, playing opposite Hope as the Swedish maid, Brunhilde. This launched the two girls into the theatre's Sapphic sisterhood. And, as this was before the birth of the actors' union, Equity, they could combine their work with pleasure.

"We 'sprinkled' the chorus with as many beautiful society girls as possible," she said.

Wearing black, with cropped hair, reddened lips and rouged ears, Mercedes cruised the upper echelons of society both in the United States and in Europe, both of which were well known for their enthusiastic love of women. In those days, though, every society woman needed the ultimate accessory – a wealthy husband. Her mother picked one out for her. He was Chicago-born artist and socialite Abram Poole, rich, talented and ten years Mercedes' senior.

Mercedes did not pretend to be a virgin for the wedding on May 11, 1920. She was dressed in daring sheer-grey chiffon.

Marriage for Mercedes changed nothing. Hope Williams joined them on their honeymoon in Venice, and when they returned to New York, the pretty young debutante, Billie McKeever, came to live with them.

"She was wild, untamed and had a delicious fey quality," said Mercedes. "She could completely twist Abram around her little finger."

What is more, this "Gypsy child" was completely besotted by Mercedes. Abram thought nothing of it. Despite his artistic background, he knew nothing of the tide of lesbian chic that was sweeping certain sections of society. He had four sisters and was used to their "romantic friendships" with other girls.

There was cloud on the horizon, however. Three days before her marriage, Mercedes had met the actress Eva Le Gallienne, another lover of Alla Nazimova*. The two women also shared an obsession with the Italian actress Eleonora Duse, whose love affair with Gabriele D'Annunzio* was celebrated in his novel *Il Fuoco – The Flame*. He wrote numerous plays for her. Sarah Bernhardt* and George Bernard Shaw* were also admirers.

Although there was an instant attraction between them, Mercedes was about to get married and Eva was involved in a long-term relationship with actress Mimsey Duggett. Soon after, Eva went out to the West Coast to try her hand in the movies and Mimsey seized the opportunity to make herself respectable and get married.

Once in Hollywood, Eva moved into the legendary Garden of Alla, Nazimova's housing complex set around a swimming pool which was the home to numerous scantily clad – and often completely unclad – young women trying to make their way in the movie business via Alla's harem. Eva, having already established herself as a Broadway star, felt out of place there. In addition, her position in Alla's affections had been replaced by the dancer Natacha Rambova* – real name Winifred Hudnut – who went on to become the second wife of Rudolph Valentino*. Eva soon escaped back to New York – and into the arms of Mercedes de Acosta.

By this time the 18th Amendment to the Constitution had

been ratified, introducing Prohibition and banning the sale of alcohol, so Mercedes was spending her time in the speakeasies of Harlem, getting ratified herself. It was also a happy hunting ground for her.

"I can get any woman from any man," she used to boast.

Together, Mercedes and Eva cruised society soirées and down-at-heel bootleg parties. They slummed in the gay and lesbian bars in Harlem and visited the "buffet flats" to complete the night's entertainment.

"I suppose it was the newly found excitement of homosexuality which, after the war, was expressed openly in nightclubs and cabarets by boys dressed as women," said Mercedes. "Youth was in revolt and outwitting the government, and getting the better of the police lent zest to our lives."

The best-known torch singer of the time, Libby Holman, and her lover, the Du Pont heiress Louisa Carpenter, would be seen in Harlem dressed in men's business suits and bowler hats. The stripper and stag-movie star, Lucille LeSueur, later known as Joan Crawford*, was another regular. The pianist Oscar Levant* would squire the lesbian chorus girls Marjorie Main and Barbara Stanwyck*. And comedienne Bea Lillie would turn up with what she called the "Four Horsewomen of the Algonquin" – Eva Le Gallienne, her ex, Tallulah Bankhead*, Blythe Daly and Estelle Winwood.

Following this baptism of fire, Eva and Mercedes swore fidelity to each other as Eva set out on tour with a production of Ferenc Molnar's *Liliom*, the play the Rodgers and Hammerstein musical and 1956 movie *Carousel* is based on. On the way, Eva wrote over one thousand pages of frenzied passion to Mercedes. Mercedes herself spent her time writing *Jehanne d'Arc – Joan of Arc* – which she considered to be her *magnum opus*.

Despite her passionate missives, Eva could not live up to her vow of fidelity. Out on tour she began sleeping with her co-star, Joseph "Pepi" Schildkraut, who would "pinch my tits" as she prayed over his lifeless body in the play's climactic scene. At one point her period failed to appear, and so started a series of scalding baths and downing gin and quinine, all of which seemed to do the trick. All of this was duly conveyed to Mercedes. It appears that doing it with a man did not constitute infidelity.

Eva's self-medication may have rid her of an unwanted child, but her health collapsed and the tour was cancelled in Chicago. The two women then decided to spend the summer together in Europe. Mercedes went first, stopping off in London where she met celebrity photographer and all-round self-publicist Cecil Beaton*, before moving on to Paris.

"I think you will simply have to marry me – in order to keep me alive," wrote Eva before rhapsodising on "such wonderful days and nights of work and love and dreams and silences".

As we have already seen, Paris was certainly the place to be if you were two horny chicks who wanted to get it on together. Staying together in the Hotel Foyot on the rue Tournou, Mercedes gave Eva a gold wedding ring. They danced together in nightclubs and visited restaurants, bars and theatres where two women holding hands did not even merit a raised eyebrow. They then headed for Rouen, the resting place of Joan of Arc – or her ashes, at least.

Their bliss was only marred by the fact that Abram was in Europe that summer, too. However, his presence merely added some piquancy to their relationship. Eva would wait at night for a low whistle under her window. This was Mercedes' signal to come down for a goodnight kiss.

Mercedes dutifully set off to Munich with Abram, though the presence of Hope Williams there might well have been an added incentive. Eva, meanwhile, trawled the dives of Montmartre with wealthy male friend Al Lehman. In the Moulin Rouge, they picked up *cocottes*.

"I danced with one of them," Eva told Mercedes. Adding that it was "most interesting to talk to those women".

She insisted that it went no further. Fidelity – at least as far as other women were concerned – was now a "badge of honour" between them, she said.

The two of them managed to get off alone together to Genoa, Venice, Vienna and Budapest – where Eva received an official reception as the city was the home the playwright Ferenc Molnar.

Mercedes then headed back to Abram in Paris while Eva went to see her former lover Constance Collier in England. By this time, Abram had twigged that there was a little more going on between his wife and her girlfriends than just a little girlish giggling. His jealousy made Mercedes' life a misery – to the point that she was contemplating suicide – before they all returned to New York that autumn to find Alla Nazimova* back in town.

Eva went back on tour and the passionate correspondence resumed. Mercedes, now with a little time on her hands, had a fling with Tallulah Bankhead*. Her relationship with Billie McKeever was also revived. Mercedes also confessed to having had an affair with a woman named Sheila.

While she could handle Tallulah and Billie, Eva said that the mysterious Sheila set "every nerve quivering" and made her "sick with worry". When Eva's play reached Baltimore in November, however, Mercedes went down by train for a rapturous reunion in the Belvedere Hotel, then Eva came to New York for Christmas. They were apart again for New Year's Eve, but Eva wrote tearfully, thanking Mercedes for "the most wonderful year I have ever had".

The following year, 1923, saw Alla Nazimova's* all-homosexual movie version of Oscar Wilde's* Salomé. It bombed at the box office, leaving Nazimova broke.

With Abram away, Eva moved in with Mercedes, who wrote The Birth of Venus, a play based on Sandro Botticelli's* painting, for her. That bombed, too, so the two of them went to Europe together. The talk of Paris was André Gide's* new book Corydon, a Socratic dialogue on homosexuality. They had tea in Natalie Barney's* Temple of Love in rue Jacob and saw their idol Eleonora Duse wrapped in a blanket on the balcony of her room in the Hotel Regina.

"We should kneel," said Mercedes, ever the drama queen.

They took a walking holiday in Brittany, which they thought of as their honeymoon, swimming in the sea and making love on the linen wedding sheets of the fisherman's widow whose cottage they stayed in.

In London, they saw Eleonora Duse on stage and sent

flowers. In New York, Eva was summoned to the great actress's dressing room. Later, Mercedes wangled an introduction. It is clear that she paid tribute to the great Italian's acting skills with her own well-honed erotic skills. In gratitude, the 66-year-old Duse promised to star in *The Mother of Christ*, a play that Mercedes had written for her.

"I will tour the whole world with this play," said Duse, at least that's Mercedes' story. "After it I will never act again."

Sadly, after being caught in a downpour in Pittsburgh – following a dust storm in Arizona and a snowstorm in Detroit – the ageing, asthmatic actress died. Benito Mussolini* sent a battleship to carry her home and she was buried with a copy of *The Mother of Christ* on her coffin, again according to Mercedes.

Meanwhile, in New York, Abram was back on the scene, so Eva had to move out. She set up a love-nest nearby and wrote that this new apartment would "bring us each day closer and closer together". It didn't work. By the autumn of 1924, Abram was cutting up rough again. When Eva asked: "Why now?" Mercedes confessed that she had been playing around. That was okay, because Eva had been doing the same. They decided that their love was intact, but fidelity was now plainly out of the question. As neither was willing to play the "cold policeman" and limit the other's fun, they agreed that they would have an "open marriage" from now on.

Their affair was given a new lease of life when Firmin Gémier of the Odéon Theatre in Paris agreed to put on a French translation of *Jehanne d'Arc* with Eva starring. It would be funded by Alice de Lamar, an American mining heiress who had a crush on Eva. The girls set off for Paris, where they met up with Alla Nazimova*. To keep her lesbian activities under wraps in Hollywood, she had pretended to have married actor Charles Bryant, whose claim to fame was a fling with the star of the London stage, Mrs Patrick Campbell*. Now that Nazimova's career was on the skids, he wanted out and was very publicly wooing the 23-year-old daughter of a New Jersey judge, while also having the pick of Alla's poolside pussycats.

The opening night of *Jehanne d'Arc* was a social triumph. The French cultural minister was there along with the

American ambassador. Also on hand were celebrated wit Dorothy Parker, songwriter Cole Porter*, playwright Zoë Akins, pianist Artur Rubinstein, actress Constance Collier and socialites Mrs Vincent Astor and Elsie de Wolfe. The production was a fiasco, though. Huge sets by Norman Bel Geddes completely overwhelmed the action. The electrical system went haywire. Some 150 extras filled the stage. Half of them were Russian and could speak neither English nor French. The Russian hunk who was supposed to hand Joan over to the English fought so hard to protect her that Eva had to beg him, in a whispered aside, to die.

The production stumbled on for four weeks. Then Eva went off to Alice de Lamar's villa in Italy to make it up to her, while Mercedes hung out with Natalie Barney* and Alla Nazimova* got off with Oscar Wilde's* niece Dolly*.

When Eva returned to Paris, she and Mercedes hit the lesbian nightspots with a vengeance. They adopted the latest ladies-who-love-ladies' fashion of wearing men's dinner suits in the evening.

Noël Coward* bumped into them on their way back to New York on the *Majestic*. He noted that they dressed in black for the entire trip and that their mood "alternated between intellectual gloom and feverish gaiety" – the latter he thought had been induced by the drug *du jour*, cocaine.

Eva spent most of her time in the company of Coward's set designer, Gladys Calthrop. By the time they sailed into New York harbour, they were an item and Eva had developed a lifelong loathing of Mercedes that matched the intensity of their four-year passion. There were better things awaiting Mercedes, however.

In 1924, Mercedes had seen Greta Garbo* filming in Constantinople. As a descendant of the Duke of Alba – famous for his conquest of Portugal and subjugation of the Netherlands for Philip II of Spain* – de Acosta was inordinately proud of her own aristocratic background and when she first clapped eyes on Garbo she thought that the actress was so distinguished and noble-looking that she must be a Russian princess. She only discovered that she was an actress later.

"Several times after this I saw her in the street," she recalled. "I was terribly troubled by her eyes and I longed to speak to her, but did not have the courage."

She did not even know what language to use and, as a result, no meeting took place.

"As the train pulled out of the station which carried me away from Constantinople, I had a strong premonition that I might again see that beautiful and haunting face on some other shore," she said.

Greta Garbo* arrived in the United States in 1925. Mercedes, who shared a publicity photographer with her, saw her pictures and swooned. She was invited to meet Garbo in New York, but missed the opportunity because of a prior engagement. Soon after, Garbo was whisked off to Hollywood.

When Garbo's first American movie, *Torrent*, came out in 1926, Mercedes took Alla Nazimova* to see it. After sitting through it twice, Mercedes declared herself to be "greatly moved". She was determined to have the film's shimmering star.

At the time, drugs had overtaken the gay and lesbian scene and most of Mercedes' lovers were junkies. She spent her evenings with singer Yvonne George, trying to get her into a fit state to perform, and she would spend her weekends with actress Jeanne Eagels, who was a hopeless addict.

Actress Marie Doro – another lover – encouraged her to finish writing her play, *The Dark Light*. Mercedes hoped that Alla would star in it, but she told Eva that it was no good. Even so, Mercedes and Alla headed off to summer in Europe together. In London, Mercedes discussed the rival merits of their respective plays about Joan of Arc with George Bernard Shaw*. Then, after a round of Paris nightlife with Nazimova, she went to visit John Barrymore* in Normandy.

During their stay, Mercedes claimed to have prevented Barrymore from murdering his wife Blanche Thomas – a "New Woman" who wrote poetry under the name "Michael Strange" – with a knife. The altercation, it seems, was provoked by Blanche's affair with Mercedes – which was handy because Mercedes also admitted to knowing Barrymore "intimately".

Back in Paris, Mercedes met up once more with Isadora Duncan*, who was penniless. She paid her hotel bills and got her started on her autobiography. It was then that she discovered that she had not been the only one comforting Isadora after her children had died. At that time Eleonora Duse was living in complete seclusion in Asolo. Hearing of Duncan's loss, she wired Isadora and invited her to come and stay. One day while she was staying at Asolo, Duncan went out for a walk. She lay down on the grass under a tree and, thinking of her dead children, began to sob. Then she felt a hand being placed gently on her shoulder. When she looked up, she said, she beheld "a Greek god". In fact, it was a young Italian painter who lived nearby and who was going down to the mountain stream naked for a plunge in the cool water. He asked why she was crying and she told him about her lost children.

"Let me give you another one," he said.

No further words were necessary. Isadora gave herself.

"I floated back to Eleonora on wings, because I knew that God would surely not be so unkind as not to give me another child," she said, rather tortuously.

When she burst into Eleonora's room and told her about her encounter with her Greek god, Duse was disgusted. She heartily disapproved of such promiscuity, even though she had been pretty wild herself in her day. Isadora protested that her quick shag on the mountainside was not a "sexual adventure" but merely a means toward producing another child. It did not help matters and Isadora was asked to leave. As it happened, God was no kinder than Duse. Isadora's hillside encounter did indeed result in her pregnancy, but the child was born the day war was declared in 1914.

This heterosexual escapade did not inhibit the affair that developed between Mercedes and Isadora in any way. The following year, Isadora wrote a poem to her saviour, which read:

> ... A slender body, soft and white
> Is for the service of my delight.
> Two sprouting breasts
> Round and sweet

Invite my hungry mouth to eat
From whence two nipples firm and pink
Persuade my thirsty soul to drink
And lower still a secret place
Where I'd fain hide my loving face

My kisses like a swarm of bees
Would find their way
Between thy knees
And suck the honey of thy lips
Embracing thy two slender hips.

Back in New York, lesbianism had made it on to Broadway with *The Captive* starring Helen Menken, then wife of Humphrey Bogart*. Following a run of four months and a vehement press campaign by Hearst Newspapers, it was closed down by the police along with Mae West's transvestite comedy *The Drag*.

Mercedes must have been going through something of a rapprochement with her husband at this time. She used her influence on Broadway to get famous actresses into Abram's studio where he could paint them and she could, possibly, seduce them. Their first pick was Katherine Cornell, who provided a successful endeavour on both fronts. He painted Helen Menken, Charlotte Monterey, Ruth Gordon and Greta Kemble Cooper – though Valentina Sanina Schlee must have presented more of a challenge, or at least she must have been more demanding, as she was painted twice.

Then it was back to Paris and Isadora, where Mercedes spoilt her with caviar, champagne, asparagus and strawberries. She then produced what was to be Isadora's last public performance. She died two months later when her trailing scarf wound around the axle of her Bugati, breaking her neck and killing her instantly.

After the show, Mercedes toured Italy with Gladys Calthrop, sojourned with artist Marie Laurencin in Toulon and then headed to London for an orgy with Alla. She was back in New York with Abram when she heard about Isadora's death and consoled herself with Natacha Rambova, who had just opened a dress shop on West 55th Street.

Broadway was buzzing that year and all the stars were in town. Mercedes organised an all-girl "cat party", with many of her past lovers, in her townhouse, expecting it to degenerate into an orgy. There was an all-star cast on offer – Constance Collier, Alla Nazimova*, Katherine Cornell, Laurette Taylor, Jeanne Eagels, Elsie Ferguson, Helen Hayes and Mrs Patrick Campbell*. Eva wisely declined. The party was a disaster. Every one of the stars wanted to be the centre of attention. Only Mrs Campbell deigned to speak and she was so catty that she turned everybody else off.

In 1929, Jeanne Eagels was starring in the movie version of Somerset Maugham's* *The Letter*. Mercedes would accompany the drug-dazed actress to the Paramount lot in New York's Astoria. The talkies had just started and Mercedes dreamed of becoming a scriptwriter. By this time, she was completely obsessed with Greta Garbo* and she passed on every nugget of gossip about her that she heard via the lesbian grapevine to Cecil Beaton* who was similarly enamoured. These included that fact that Garbo strode around like a boy, that she never looked in a mirror, that she was moody and silent and the only time she got noisy and excited was when a tailor sent her some riding breeches with a fly, which she went about ostentatiously buttoning and unbuttoning.

News came from actress Marie Dressler, via Bessie Marbury, that Garbo "wasn't a lesbian but could be". Dressler was 59, as round as a beer-barrel and well past her best, so Mercedes simply assumed that she had made a pass at Garbo and that she had been turned down. Already an accomplished star-fucker, she was determined to possess Garbo's slender, Sapphic body.

She tried to sell some of her plays – including *Jehanne d'Arc* – to the movies, but failed. Then, in 1931, she was summoned to Hollywood to write a script for the silent-movie star Pola Negri*. She did not have to be asked twice.

"The whole world thought of it as a place of mad nightlife, riotous living, orgies, careers that shot up like meteors and crashed down like lead, uncontrolled extravagances, unbridled love affairs and – in a word – sin," Mercedes wrote in her memoirs *Here Lies the Heart*. Hollywood, in short, was her spiritual home.

Mercedes was not interested in writing scripts. It was simply a means to an end – Garbo. Before leaving for the coast, she celebrated her 11th wedding anniversary. Abram wrote in a card with his gift to Mercedes: "Thanks for 11 wonderful years and I hope for many more, with a little love added."

He was ruthlessly abandoned.

Mercedes prepared for her conquest of Garbo in the same way that a general would plan for a campaign. Remembering the riding breeches incident, Mercedes ordered a series of new outfits for all occasions, all of which featured trousers that had been hand-tailored to fit her slender form.

Through Marie Dressler and Bessie Marbury, she knew that the home of sexually avant-garde German actress Salka Viertel was the centre of émigré life in Hollywood. Salka was the key to Garbo's door. Mercedes worked on her connections. One of her former lovers was an actress from the Max Reinhardt* Berlin theatre called Eleanora von Mendelssohn – the great-niece of composer Felix Mendelssohn*. For good measure, she was also the goddaughter of Eleonora Duse and living in the Garden of Allah – as Alla Nazimova's* home had been renamed after it was sold off as a hotel complex – and she was in Salka's magic circle. Hope Williams was another friend of Salka's, while Marie and Helen Menken put in a good word for her with Garbo herself.

The weekend before she took the train to California, Mercedes partied out on Long Island with former lovers Hope Williams and Tallulah Bankhead* – who were now getting it on together – and the dancer Marjorie Moss, who was going to the West Coast with her. There was a much-publicised story – which no doubt Garbo read – that Tallulah produced a pack of cards. Mercedes was to draw a card and make a silent wish – to have a good old girlie time grazing with Garbo. This, of course, was exactly what Tallulah wished for herself. It was reported that Tallulah, after consulting the cards, prophesied: "You will get your wish three days after you arrive in Hollywood."

The more cynical commentators said that the two women made a bet.

Soon after Mercedes arrived in Hollywood, she learned that, professionally at least, the trip had been a waste of time. The bisexual Pola Negri* was considered all washed up. She lunched with Douglas Fairbanks* and Mary Pickford* – two other stars from the silent era – and British musical star Elsie Janis, who, on observing Mercedes' pants, said: "You'll get a bad reputation if you dress this way out here."

That, however, was exactly what Mercedes wanted – a bad reputation, or, at least, a reputation for being bad.

Then, just as Tallulah had predicted, three days after arriving on the West Coast, Mercedes was invited to tea by Salka Viertel where, like a good German, she served coffee. Mercedes wore a German steel slave bracelet for the occasion, having read in a German magazine that Garbo liked heavy jewellery. A few minutes after she arrived, she heard the doorbell ring. In the hall she heard a very low voice speaking in German. It was unmistakable, even though Garbo had only released one talking picture, *Anna Christie* (1930), by that time.

"As we shook hands and she smiled at me, I felt I had known her all my life; in fact, in many previous incarnations," she said. Jeez, I didn't know you were meeting Shirley MacLaine.

As Mercedes already knew, Garbo was even more beautiful in the flesh than she was in the movies. She was particularly impressed by Garbo's eyes "which held in them a look of eternity" and by the fact she, too, wore trousers. Fortunately, Garbo had a penchant for slim, dark, amusing women.

After a brief chat about Eleonora Duse, their host made an excuse and left the two of them together. There was an awkward silence, then Greta's eyes fell on Mercedes' wrist.

"What a nice bracelet," she said.

Mercedes pulled it off and handed it to Garbo.

"I bought it for you in Berlin," she said.

Garbo rued the fact that she was shooting *Susan Lenox (Her Rise and Fall)* (1931) at the time.

"I never go out when I am shooting," she said. "Or perhaps I never go out. Now I will go home to dinner which I will have in bed." I bet Mercedes wished she was eating there, too. "I am indeed an example of the gay Hollywood nightlife." It was about to get gayer.

Mercedes wanted to ask whether she could see her again but, unusually, her courage deserted her. Salka walked Garbo out to her car. When she came back, she told Mercedes: "She likes you … and she likes few people."

Two days later – a Sunday – they met for breakfast at Salka's. Garbo was wearing shorts and Mercedes was impressed by the exquisite tan she had on her legs. As Garbo always sunbathed nude, she was in for a real treat later.

"At this second meeting, she was more beautiful than I had ever dreamed she could be," said Mercedes. "Her face was fresh and glowing. She was in high spirits and full of mischief."

They spent the morning dancing alone at the unoccupied beach house of a Paramount screenwriter. They waltzed and tangoed, then talked at length of *tosha* – the Russian word for a sentimental yearning that Mercedes had learned from Alla and which Greta was feeling in her heart. Greta then invited Mercedes back to her house for lunch. Mercedes said that she had already accepted a luncheon engagement with Pola Negri*. Greta told her to phone and tell Pola that she was not coming. Mercedes said that she could not do that at the last moment as it was "an intimate lunch for six".

Garbo laughed.

"More like six hundred," she said. "You don't know Hollywood, but go to Pola's today and learn your lesson. You will see for yourself."

As the driver pulled away, Greta plucked a flower from the garden and gave it to her.

"Don't say I never gave you a flower," she said.

At lunch, Mercedes was fawned over by Basil Rathbone – another of Eva Le Gallienne's lovers – and Ramon Navarro*, who was said to have owned a lead cast of Rudolph Valentino's* erect penis, signed by the owner of the original in silver.

In the middle of the lunch, Mercedes got a telephone call from a "Mr Toshka". It was Garbo.

"Are there six or six hundred?" she enquired.

"More like six thousand," replied Mercedes.

She sneaked out of the party and sped over to Garbo's house. Garbo was waiting for her outside dressed in a black silk dressing gown and wearing men's slippers. They walked in the garden together, then stretched out on the lawn as the sun turned a fiery red in the sky. When it slipped over the horizon, Garbo said: "You must go home now."

Mercedes had little to do in Hollywood. Her job was largely to keep the now-redundant Pola mollified until her contract ran out. Then, one hot July afternoon, Garbo called to invite her over, saying that her "current prison term" – the shooting of *Susan Lenox* – was over.

"I never invite anyone to my house," she said, "but today, as a great exception, I am inviting you. Will you come?"

When Mercedes arrived, she noticed that there were flowers strewn across the threshold. They bypassed the living room.

"I never use this room," said Garbo. "I live in the bedroom."

It was a simple, starkly empty room. In it there was a desk, a dressing table, some straight-backed chairs – and a bed. There was not a single personal thing in it, except for a thin, leafless, dead tree.

"This tree is my one joy in Hollywood," said Garbo. "I call it 'my winter tree'." For most people holly would be a winter tree. "When my loneliness for Sweden gets unbearable, I look at it and it comforts me. I imagine that the cold has made it leafless and that soon there will be snow on its branches."

She turned sadly from the window and said: "I have never told anyone before about this tree."

It was then that she noticed tears in Mercedes' eyes.

"Oh, I have made you cry," she said.

"That is such a sad story," said Mercedes, reaching for a Kleenex. "Tell me about your childhood – about your life."

Way to go, Mercedes. What a seductress.

Then Greta opened her heart. She talked about her childhood in Stockholm, her dreams, her aspirations, the many things that she had done, the many things she still had to do. In the course of her ramblings she touched on her dead sister whose name was Alva. Mercedes quickly pointed out that she was descended from the Duke of Alba – which was close, fairly. She also pointed out that her screen name "Garbo" meant grace or elegance in Spanish. You certainly know how to get around a girl.

"I have never spoken like this before," said Garbo.

The two of them had a midnight feast in Garbo's bedroom. Then they drove out to the beach in Garbo's black Packard, which Garbo called the "bus". It was, Mercedes said: "Every inch a car Queen Mary* would drive in." And she told Garbo, who sat beside her, that she was "a perfect footman".

On top of a hill, overlooking the moon-silvered sea and listening to nightingales singing, Garbo got all profound.

"Do you believe in God?" she asked.

Now we've all been there – early morning after the party with someone we intend to shag, then whack, the big question. How to sound deep without risking offence? However, Mercedes was, yet again, the master of the situation.

"I wish there was no such word," she said. "How can anyone express God by using a word like God? I just think of God as all creation. Everything is God on its own level. Those nightingales singing are God. If God is God, then there can be no separation between any of his creatures. And by 'creatures' I mean trees, rocks, animals, insects, as well as people."

Wow. Perfect late-night student-speak. You could be talking to a dyed-in-the-wool atheist or a born-again Christian and get away with that. And she ended, perfectly, with: "Perhaps I am right or wrong. I don't know."

Pass the spliff, I feel something deep and meaningful coming on.

The conversation continued in this banal – I mean, deep and meaningful – fashion. As I say, we've all been there. Then, when the moon set and tiny flecks of light streaked the sky to the east, they fell silent. As dawn broke, they walked back down the hill, picking rambler roses as they went. At the bottom the "bus" was waiting.

"It seemed like something alive – faithful and patient," said Mercedes. "We got in and drove away."

The next day, Garbo told Mercedes that she had planned a

long vacation in a shack on a little island owned by Wallace Beery* in Silver Lake in the Sierra Nevada mountains – because she wanted to be alone. After she had gone, the Pola Negri movie was shelved and Mercedes was sacked. To cheer her up, Ivor Novello* took her to dinner with Douglas Fairbanks Jr* and his new wife, Joan Crawford*.

After two days Garbo phoned. She was returning to Los Angeles to get Mercedes. She arrived at midnight and they stayed the night together. The next day, Garbo's chauffeur, James, drove them back out to Silver Lake. He was told to tell no one where she was – not even Garbo's producer Louis B. Mayer* or her own maid, Whistler. Then Garbo rowed Mercedes out to the island.

When they arrived, Garbo said: "We must be baptised at once."

She threw off all her clothes and plunged into the water. Mercedes was impressed. She stripped off too, even though the water was cold for her hot Spanish blood, and swam beside her.

"How to describe the next six enchanted weeks?" Mercedes wrote in her memoirs. "Even recapturing them in memory makes me realise how lucky I am to have had them. Six perfect weeks out of a lifetime... In all this time there was not a second of disharmony between Greta and me or in nature around us."

As a memento of the holiday, Mercedes took some topless photos of Garbo flashing her tits by the washing line, but it was her legs, rather than her breasts, that she was particularly taken with. In an extract she omitted from the final draft of her autobiography, she wrote: "They are not tan or sunburned in colour, which is commonly seen, but the skin had taken on a golden hue and a flock of tiny hairs growing on her legs were golden, too. Her legs were classical. She has not the typical Follies girl legs or the American man's dream of what a woman's leg should be. They have the shape that can be seen in many Greek statues."

Greta and Mercedes moved into adjoining houses on Rockingham Road in Brentwood. Greta would come and whistle outside Mercedes' house if she wanted to go for a walk and they spent time together every day. Silent movie star Louis Brooks* said that Garbo, all too well aware of her own humble background, took on Mercedes for "snob reasons". George Cukor* said that Mercedes certainly helped correct Garbo's "undistinguished" pronunciation, while even the peeved Eva Le Gallienne said that the "divine ecstasy" of Mercedes' "wonderful passion" radiated through on to the screen in Garbo's next movie, *Mata Hari** (1932). Garbo repaid Mercedes by getting her back on the payroll at MGM. Mercedes, meanwhile, involved herself with what was left of Alla Nazimova's* lesbian "Sewing Circle". Most of the girls were now bisexuals, known at the time as "Gillette Blades", because they cut both ways.

On a typical afternoon, Maria Huxley would drop her husband Aldous off at a bookshop or a museum and then meet up with Salka Viertal, Mercedes and, sometimes, Garbo. Mercedes would often wear a tuxedo, like Marlene Dietrich* – who was soon to be another lover – had worn in the movie *Morocco* (1930).

Mercedes was one of the most visible lesbians in Hollywood and frequently wore men's clothes. She encouraged Garbo to do the same. The two of them were famously pictured striding down Hollywood Boulevard in drag, under the headline: "Garbo in Pants!"

"Innocent bystanders gasped in amazement to see Mercedes de Acosta and Greta Garbo striding swiftly along Hollywood Boulevard dressed in men's clothing," read the story.

Tallaluh Bankhead* fumed with jealousy. It should have been her striding down Hollywood Boulevard with Garbo in pants.

Garbo immersed herself in lesbian literature and had a short-lived affair with Eva von Berne, the so-called "second Garbo" that Irving Thalberg* discovered in Vienna. She always dressed in men's clothes at fancy-dress balls and often expressed a desire to play men's parts in films.

When, at Mercedes' behest, she asked Aldous Huxley to write a screenplay about St Francis of Assisi for her, he replied: "What, complete with beard?"

Mercedes attracted the wrath of Thalberg when she wrote a screenplay in which Garbo would be disguised as a boy for most of the film. Thalberg said: "You must be out of your mind. We have been building Garbo up for years as a great glamorous actress. Now you want to come along and try to put her in pants and make money out of her."

When that project was canned, Garbo insisted that Mercedes write a screenplay based on Oscar Wilde's* novel *A Picture of Dorian Gray* for her. Mercedes said: "You go and tell Irving the idea and have him throw you out of the window – not me."

Director George Cukor* saw another side of Garbo. He told Cecil Beaton*: "Of course she's a sensuous woman, will do anything, pick up any man, go to bed with him, then throw him out, but she reserves her real sensuousness for the camera."

And the audience responded. At the height of her fame, she received fifteen thousand fan letters a week, many of them pornographic. She read none of them. Her real interest lay in other women and Tallaluh Bankhead* was now in town.

One night, Garbo's great rival, Marlene Dietrich, spotted Mercedes with her English chum Cecil Beaton* and was immediately lovestruck. The next morning she turned up at Mercedes' house with a huge bunch of white roses, explaining that she knew few people in Hollywood and that no one would introduce them. She had brought the flowers "because you looked like a prince last night". Mercedes de Acosta, the woman who chased stars, was being chased – by a star.

Dietrich also mentioned that Mercedes looked sad. Mercedes explained that Garbo was out of town.

"I am sad, too," said Marlene, "sad and lonely. You are the first person here to whom I have felt drawn. Unconventional as it may seem, I came to see you because I just could not help myself."

"I appreciate your coming," said Mercedes, speaking in barely disguised innuendo. "It must have been difficult to ring a stranger's bell."

"No, it's funny, it was not," said Marlene, responding. "Somehow, I feel at my ease. I feel, even, that I would like to tell you something that will make you laugh. I am a wonderful cook … I want to ask if you will let me cook for you."

Marlene invited Mercedes to dinner, but Mercedes declined, saying that she was too busy writing scripts. Instead Marlene must come to dinner at hers. The table was set with white roses and champagne. Marlene then went into the scene from *Morocco* (1930), where she plays with the petals of a rose to signal her Sapphic intentions. These were soon fulfilled. Each found in the other a lover whose passion, skill and romantic inclinations matched their own. That night, when Mercedes dropped Marlene home, she jumped hurriedly from the car and ran indoors, frightened that her seven-year-old daughter Maria might see her. She then found she could not sleep without the warmth of Mercedes' body near her.

Marlene wrote numerous love letters to her "adored woman" in schoolgirl French because, she said, it was difficult to express love in English. They were written in green ink on blue paper in a matching envelope, closed with sealing wax and stamped with a monogrammed "M".

In response, Mercedes addressed Marlene as "wonderful one", writing: "It is one week today since your beautiful naughty hand opened a white rose. Last night was even more exciting and each time I see you it grows more wonderful and exciting. You with your exquisite white pansy face – and before you go to bed will you ring me so that I can just hear your voice." And she signed off: "Your 'Rafael'" – after the boy she thought she once was.

Of course, Mercedes may well have made up the story of being called "Rafael" in later life – after Marlene told her that her mother had been expecting a boy and had called Marlene "Paulus" as a child for fun.

Dietrich said that she had thought of leaving the US before meeting Mercedes. In one letter, she said she longed to kiss Mercedes' hands to thank them for all the happiness they had brought her. She craved only to see her from time to time, but if Mercedes no longer fancied her, she would descend slowly into her grave and be no more trouble. Her heart, though, would be Mercedes' for ever.

"Don't say for ever," replied Mercedes. "That's blasphemy in love. You never know if you truly have a lasting love, or if you are making oaths that you will forget. In love, nothing binds you."

I think you may have forgotten some of your oaths somewhere along the line, Mercedes.

They also swapped poetry. Mercedes wrote verses of the "Your face is lit by moonlight/ Breaking through your skin" variety, while Marlene translated Rainer Maria Rilke.

Marlene bombarded Mercedes with flowers – first tulips, which Mercedes rejected because they were too phallic, then dozens of roses and carnations, sometimes twice a day. On one occasion she had ten dozen rare orchids flown in from San Francisco. When Mercedes' maid complained that Dietrich was sending so many flowers that they were running out of vases, Marlene sent Lalique vases – and more flowers.

"The house became a sort of madhouse of flowers," complained Mercedes. "I was walking on flowers, falling on flowers and sleeping on flowers. I finally wept and flew into a rage."

She sent the maid off to the hospital "with every damn flower in the house" and threatened to throw Dietrich in the pool if she sent any more. So Marlene began sending other gifts. Box upon box arrived from Bullock's on Wiltshire Boulevard containing dressing gowns, pyjamas, slacks, sweaters, lamps and lampshades.

"Bullock's Wiltshire moved into my home," said Mercedes and she sent the gifts back to the store.

Marlene and Mercedes spent a lot of time together at the Santa Monica beach house that Marlene rented from Marion Davies* and romped on the beach with the gay actors Martin Kosleck and Hans von Twardowski – Martin, who was also a painter, went on to become the fourth husband of Eleonora von Mendelssohn, Mercedes' old flame. Marlene would cook for Mercedes, while Mercedes encouraged Marlene to go without make-up and wear slacks. Garbo in pants may well have caused a worldwide sensation; Dietrich in pants, however, sparked a worldwide fashion.

There was an unspoken rule between Marlene and Mercedes. Garbo must not be mentioned by name. Dietrich referred to her as "that other woman", while Mercedes called her "the Scandinavian child". The truth was that Garbo had a place in Mercedes' heart that no other could attain – "Dietrich was a pro, but Garbo was an artist," she wrote in her memoirs.

Garbo, meanwhile, was back in Sweden, researching her part for *Queen Christina* (1933), Sweden's 17th-century lesbian queen. On her arm in Stockholm was Miss Mercedes de Acosta, the Swedish papers confidently reported. In fact, it seems to have been Mimi Pollak, an early actress friend of Garbo's.

When the studio began to get worried about rumours of Marlene's lesbian affair, Dietrich set Paramount producer Ben Schulberg* straight.

"In Europe," she said, "it doesn't matter if you're a man or a woman. We make love to anyone we find attractive."

She continued to buy gifts for Mercedes from Bullock's, but began to concentrate on items from the men's department. Mercedes responded with love poetry and letters, calling Dietrich her "Golden One".

The affair between Marlene and Mercedes seems to have been encouraged, if not engineered, by Salka Viertel, as she sought to replace Mercedes in Garbo's affections. It was announced that Greta would be moving in with Salka when she returned. Meanwhile Salka's husband, Berthold Viertel, headed for London, where he developed a close relationship with the writer Christopher Isherwood*. Salka was soon galled to find that she was mistaken for Mercedes when she was out with Garbo.

Salka also put the skids under Mercedes at MGM for having a fling with Marlene, one of Paramount's stars. As a result, Thalberg fired her. Marlene stuck around for a while to comfort Mercedes, but in May 1933, Marlene, her daughter Maria, Marlene's husband Rudi Sieber* and his mistress Tamara "Tami" Matul* took off on a family holiday in Europe.

Marlene was planning to visit Brian Aherne*, her English co-star in *Song of Songs* (1933). Marlene had baked him a cake that she presented to him on set. Mercedes, having been a recipient of Marlene's catering in the past, knew what this meant. It was

Mercedes who took to sending flowers as she tried to cling on to their relationship.

"I will bring anyone you want to your bed," Mercedes wrote in desperation. "And this is not because I love you so little, but because I love you so much, my beautiful one."

Marlene apologised for her shabby behaviour, but just as had been the case with Mercedes in her youth she needed a constant and changing diet of affairs. She, too, was happy to pass on the lovers that she had finished with. From then on, there was a constant exchange of pretty young starlets on the make. Marlene tried to pass on the delightful Anna May West, who she had met on *Shanghai Express* (1932), to Mae West*, who was in the next dressing room at Paramount.

Anna offered to wash her hair for her.

"I had to turn her down," said Mae. "I was afraid she didn't mean the hair on my head."

Marlene was on board the *Europa* when Mercedes sent a telegram bearing news of Garbo's reaction to the still-to-be-released *Song of Songs*. It read: "Golden one the Scandinavian child saw your picture and thought you and your acting beautiful ... Will make you smile to know she had decided on the same director and so life goes on Stop I am missing you and worried about the European situation you must return home soon my love ..."

After recording some songs in Paris, Marlene missed out going to London to meet Brian Aherne as planned. Instead she headed to Vienna where her old lover Willi Forst* was directing his first feature film which, it was rumoured, Dietrich was financing. She immediately fell in love with the star of the movie, 28-year-old matinee idol, Hans Jaray*. They were inseparable and were often seen around Vienna in the company of Forst or the ever-tolerant Rudi.

With Marlene away, Mercedes fell into a black depression. Even the return of Garbo had not cheered her up, as she had been replaced by Salka, who made sure that Mercedes was barred from the MGM lot. The best Mercedes could do was write some poetry to Greta, lamenting that her hot land of Spain was now "swept by wind and snow".

While she was out driving with her maid, Mercedes said that she wished a car would hit them and kill her. She almost got her wish. She was thrown from the car and landed on her head.

Recovering in Santa Monica Hospital, she got a cable from Marlene offering to pay her medical bills. She sent recordings made in Paris and kisses for Mercedes' face "and the scars particularly".

The accident also brought Garbo to her bedside and Mercedes did not hide the fact from Marlene.

"Golden Beautiful One," she wrote. "Today your letter arrived and I was so happy to get it because it seemed to me months since I had word directly from you. I know you had a great success in Vienna and I read about you in the French papers. I also read that you are buying many feminine clothes. I hope not too feminine! And I hope that you will not give up your trousers when you return because then people can say (as they already do) that it was a publicity stunt.

"I see the 'Other Person' all the time, who is completely changed toward me – beautiful and sweet – and completely unlike last year ... I will be happy to see your beautiful little face again. Your White Prince."

That summer, Garbo moved out of Salka's house and Mercedes helped her find a new home in Brentwood, just a couple of blocks from her own house on San Vincente Boulevard. The night she moved in, Mercedes filled the place with flowers and lit fires in all the fireplaces. She evidently lit a fire elsewhere. Garbo planned a winter vacation with Mercedes in Yosemite after she had finished shooting *Queen Christina*. In Mercedes' mind it was going to be a snow-clad re-run of the episode at Silver Lake – presumably without the topless photography. However, the day they were supposed to leave, Mercedes waited and waited outside her house for Garbo to turn up.

Eventually, she drove over to Garbo's house only to find that she had taken off with Rouben Mamoulian – Marlene's director on *Song of Songs* who Garbo had pinched for *Queen Christina*.

The trip was a disaster. They got pinched for speeding, with all the resultant press hoo-ha, and Garbo came back with the clap. Meanwhile Marlene had returned to the fold.

In the days before penicillin, the treatment for gonorrhoea was long, painful and debilitating, but when Garbo recovered, she lived up to her promise and took Mercedes on a winter break to Yosemite. However, one evening, while they were out skating, they got lost as night fell. They were lucky to find a hut belonging to a woodcutter, who let them sleep on the floor. Garbo blamed Mercedes, but evidently forgave her.

One day, in 1934, Greta and Mercedes were doing a little nude sunbathing on the balcony of Mercedes house when the actress Katharine Cornell called. She was a former squeeze of Mercedes. Garbo also knew her, but had neglected to tell Mercedes about it because their meetings had been conducted behind Mercedes' back.

"Send her away," Garbo said.

"Don't be foolish," said Mercedes. "I wouldn't dream of being rude to Kit. You would like her yourself if you knew her. If you don't want to meet her, stay here in the sun."

Mercedes pulled on a sweater and some slacks and went down to greet Katharine. The situation was tense and, in an effort to lighten the situation, Kit asked Mercedes if she could introduce her to Garbo, who she knew lived nearby. Mercedes said that she could not take her to see her as she was not at home. At that moment, Garbo appeared at the top of the stairs and said: "Hello, may I join you?"

"This is the moment I have been waiting for all my life," said Kit, showing off her acting skills. The situation remained tense; until they all got stuck into the brandy, that is.

Mercedes was seen on the set of *The Scarlet Empress* (1934) with Marlene and she appeared at "intimate dinners" with her. Dietrich did not conceal the fact that Mercedes was her lover. Despite this, Mercedes managed to swing a job back at MGM. Salka still held sway over Greta professionally, but Mercedes reoccupied her position as best friend, lover and all-round guru. Naturally, Salka reported back to Marlene that Mercedes was two-timing her.

Called to account, Mercedes told Marlene: "To try to explain my real feelings for Greta would be impossible since I really do not understand them myself. I do know that I have built up in my emotions a person that does not exist. My mind sees the real person – a Swedish servant with a face touched by God – only interested in money, her health, sex, food and sleep." Both Marlene and Mercedes thought that they belonged to a higher social class. "And yet her face tricks my mind and my spirit builds her up into something that fights with my brain. I do love the person I have created and not the person who is real ..."

She also explained that she had to keep on the right side of Garbo if she wanted to keep her job with MGM. Marlene was not to worry on the sexual front at least.

"Darling One," she concluded, "I kiss you all over – everywhere. And I kiss your spirit as well as your lovely body."

Throughout all of these toings and froings, Mercedes had managed to maintain her status as a respectable married woman.

"After all, we loved each other," Mercedes said of Abram. "We were friends and had been married for 15 years. That we could no longer make a success of our sexual life seemed to me to be no reason to separate. I was too European to feel, as Americans do, that the moment the sexual relationship is over one must fly to the divorce courts."

Abram was getting restive, however. Mercedes wrote to him in New York suggesting that he take a model called Janice Fair – a woman he had always fancied – as his mistress. He wrote back protesting at this "immoral suggestion". In fact, he had already done so and, the following year, he asked Mercedes for a divorce. She was devastated.

She travelled to New York and quickly became convinced that this was a ruse on Poole's part. Janice wanted to marry Abram and had pushed him into asking for a divorce. He was hoping that Mercedes would refuse him so that he would not have to go through with it and marry Janice. Mercedes became sympathetic to the other woman, however.

"Although it was against my own interests and what I wanted, I insisted that he go through with the divorce and marry her," Mercedes said.

Abram went to Reno, while Greta travelled to New York to

visit Kit Cornell, Ona Munson and Alla Nazimova*, before going on to Europe. In Stockholm, she hooked up with Noël Coward*. They rumbaed in fashionable nightclubs and went to all the right parties. Soon there was unlikely press speculation that they were going to marry. Coward and Garbo jokingly called each other "my little bride" and "my little groom".

As Marlene was involving herself with a number of heterosexual affairs, Mercedes set off to Europe after Greta. She bombarded her with letters, begging to have dinner alone with her. Garbo wrote only to Salka. After finishing *Camille* (1936), she wanted to make *Conquest* (1937), which told the story of Napoleon's* Polish mistress, Marie Walewska*.

During that summer, chasing back and forth across the Atlantic, Mercedes and Salka ended up on the same ship together and spent some time closeted tête-à-tête. Garbo feared that they were forming the third side of a love triangle.

"I hope, poor Salka, that you do not have the 'black and white'" – the only colours in Mercedes' wardrobe – "running after you and making your life a misery or the opposite," she wrote to Salka in London.

Soon Greta was desperate to know what had gone on between the two girls. She wrote to Mercedes in New York – addressing her only as "Black and White" – saying that it would be a "waste of time" to come and see her in Stockholm as she could only give her one day – and she could not even promise that. If Mercedes was in the Grand Hotel, Stockholm on October 10, though, she would call for her. Greta did not even bother to sign her name at the bottom of the letter.

Mercedes quickly figured that if she sailed immediately for Bremen, then flew to Malmö, she could make it and wired back to say that she would meet Garbo for dinner at eight o'clock in the Grand Hotel, Stockholm, as suggested. It was a terrible journey. The seas were rough; the weather was cold. When she arrived, she found there was only one room available – the hugely expensive Royal Suite. She was just climbing into bed when Greta called. It was six in the morning. Minutes later Greta was at the door. Although it was dark and freezing outside, she dragged Mercedes to the Stockholm Zoo for breakfast. There a monkey reached out of its cage and scratched Garbo's face. They raced to find a doctor, who tended the wound and assured them that it would not leave a scar.

That evening they had dinner at eight o'clock in the Grand Hotel as planned.

"The evening was a sentimental one," Mercedes recalled. "We sat at a table in the corner which Greta had reserved and the same one she had described to me so many times in Hollywood. And we did the traditional things, ordering caviar, champagne, and our favourite tunes from the orchestra ... I felt that I was moving in a dream within a dream."

Afterwards they went to see a movie. Garbo was mobbed on leaving the theatre. Mercedes later found her hiding under the counter in a shop.

Instead of being dismissed after one day, Mercedes was taken to stay with Garbo's old friend, the Countess Ingrid Wachtmeister. They frolicked together in the fields and Mercedes wrote new love poetry. Her happiness was only marred when Garbo and the Countess disappeared for hours on end. Greta also took Mercedes to see the cold-water flat where she had been born.

"I was very much moved," said the expensively reared Mercedes.

When they parted, Greta told Mercedes not to write.

Back in Hollywood, Marlene was going through male lovers at a rate of knots. She also set up her own "Sewing Circle" of what lesbian character actress Majorie Main called "glamour gal Sapphics". Marlene was also generous with the club's facilities, handing on girls she had finished with to her first husband, the shadowy Soviet spy, Otto Katz.

The Sewing Circle would often meet for cat parties at the home of Mexican actress Dolores del Rio*. Her husband, MGM set designer Cedric Gibbons, found her fondling Garbo's breasts by the side of their pool one day. Also on hand were Lili Damita*, the former lover of King Alfonso XIII of Spain and wife of Errol Flynn*, Virginia Bruce*, former wife of silent star John Gilbert*, Elizabeth Allan, who played the hero's mother in *David Copperfield* (1934), Anita Louise, who had played Garbo as a child in *A Woman of Affairs* (1928), and Countess Dorothy di Frasso*, the lover of Gary Cooper* and Clark Gable*, of whom it was said: "It is hard to tell whether Dorothy throws one party that lasts all summer or a series of weekend parties that last all week." Mercedes was also a member but, like so many other things, she omits any reference to it in her memoir.

Then Alla Nazimova* turned up again in town, touring in a production of Ibsen's *Ghosts*.

Marlene, always interested in her lovers' lovers, paid a visit to her dressing room after the show and helped her unwind.

Garbo, meanwhile, was on her way back from Europe. She bumped into her old lover Fifi D'Orsay* on the ship.

"Hello G.G. Do you remember Fifi?" she said. Garbo was icy.

Back in Hollywood, Mercedes had taken a spacious new home near to Barbara Stanwyck*, Joan Crawford* and Jeanette MacDonald*, anticipating that Garbo would move in with her. However, the property had neither a swimming pool nor a tennis court. So, employing a certain amount of bribery, Mercedes managed to secure Jeanette MacDonald's place, which had both. Salka was much put out, but managed to install her own housekeeper as a spy.

Garbo was now working on *Camille* with George Cukor*, whose lover Billy Haines* had fallen foul of the law for picking up sailors. Haines and a bunch of gay friends, including Cukor, had been chased off El Porto beach by an angry mob after one of their number had approached a young boy. The incident had made the front page of the *Los Angeles Times*. Soon after, Cukor, Haines and Robert Benchley* were having a dismissal dinner, with Tallaluh Bankhead* rattling on about a rotten review she had just got for her latest play, *Reflected Glory*, which compared her performance to that of a circus acrobat.

"For God's sake, Tallaluh," cried Haines. "It's not the same thing as being called a cocksucker on the front page of the *Los Angeles Times*."

Then Benchley piped up: "Oh, I'd much rather be called a cocksucker than an acrobat."

Garbo was paying a visit to Cukor's when she got a rare

treat. Katharine Hepburn* had just arrived in town and, taking lunch chez Cukor, had spotted the pool, stripped off and jumped in, just as Garbo arrived.

Garbo was always on the lookout for new talent. She had spent hours watching Eleanor Powell*, a new dancer in town, rehearsing. Then she pursued Deanna Durbin and although they did not click, she met the charismatic conductor Leopold Stokowski* on the set of *One Hundred Men and a Girl* (1937). He was married at the time, but quickly decided that Garbo should play Cosima Liszt* to his Richard Wagner*. She got Anita Loos* to invite the two of them to dinner at her Santa Monica home. Then the two of them travelled together in Europe for several months. While this was going on, Mercedes was fired from MGM once more.

"There will be no marriage for at least two years, owing to contracts and engagements in Hollywood," Garbo told reporters. Soon after, Stolowski married heiress Gloria Vanderbilt*.

Meanwhile Marlene was off in Europe again. Her daughter Maria was on vacation from her Swiss boarding school and the two of them took a trip to Paris, where they visited Colette*. According to Maria, Marlene promptly disappeared with their hostess for some private *hommage*. Then they went to visit Gertrude Stein* and Alice B. Toklas*; the same thing happened with Gertrude.

At the opening night of a Maurice Chevalier* musical, Marlene pulled Frederique Baule, girlfriend of Erich Maria Remarque*, the author of *All Quiet on the Western Front* and also a lover of Marlene's.

"Marlene was a marvellous woman," said Frede. "I was just a kid and she could make me do anything she wanted, but she was always kind and generous."

Marlene had an assignation with Frede every time she was in Paris until the start of the war. They hung out in lesbian clubs, sometimes accompanied by Lili Damita* and Errol Flynn*, who described "young ladies necking in dark corners, in the cubicles, at distant tables, beneath the dimmed lights ... There was an air over the whole place of an illicit wonder going on."

Frede would wear a tuxedo with a winged collar and long, flowing bow tie.

"The overall effect was of an English schoolboy," said Flynn. "Her man's haircut looked better on her than any man … She had such a distinguished air that you felt like putting a cloak on the ground before her."

There was nothing Flynn liked better, however, than watching Frede and Lili dancing together in "a strange, rhythmic, silent accord".

When Mercedes turned up, Remarque recalled that all of them were going to a sex show. He remembered "some house … which had flagellation, a fat Madame, a very well-built Negress from Martinique and gin".

When movie mogul Jack Warner* and his wife Ann turned up in Paris, the party moved on to Monaco, where Marlene could be seen in the nightspots dancing alternately with Jack and Ann. She also took Ann to a lesbian club called the Sphinx, where they watched two women making love. Remarque noted in his diary that Ann was "very interested in this". That night Remarque found himself sleeping alone and, back in Hollywood, Ann Warner joined the Sewing Circle.

Other nights, Remarque often found himself paired off with Marlene's husband Rudi, while she went about other business. Although he was not jealous of Mercedes – he even sent flowers to her – he got heated when Marlene started to get close to an old friend of his from Berlin, Margo Lion. Things got worse when Marlene began spending the night on board the yacht of her old flame, the crop-haired oil and whiskey millionairess and speed-boat racer, Joe Carstairs. The island she owned in the Bahamas, Whale Cay, was a lesbian paradise. When Marlene went back to the United States – meeting Ernest Hemingway* on the ship on the way – Mercedes stayed on in Paris, enjoying love games with Frede.

Back in Hollywood, Marlene was seen wearing tails at one of Basil Rathbone's parties and "dancing with all the girls".

"Evidently spring is having a decided effect on your glands," said actor Clifton Webb, an old friend of Mercedes.

Marlene began using Douglas Fairbanks Jr* as a beard to hide her lesbian affairs, but he grew so jealous that he took the house next door to hers to keep an eye on her.

Meanwhile, Mercedes returned to Garbo in time to drive her to the studio for the first day's shooting of *Conquest*.

"This is prostitution," complained the precious Garbo, who was suffering from period pains at the time.

It did not help matters when an admirer loaned her some jewellery that Napoleon* had actually given to his second empress, the Archduchess Marie-Louise* of Austria, for the movie, because Marlene had been seen wearing jewellery of a similar provenance while reading a script in the Paramount commissary – she did not have to borrow hers.

With Marlene busy elsewhere, the Sewing Circle moved to the home of Aldous Huxley and his wife, Maria, who had studied ballet under Nijinsky and who had tried to commit suicide by taking poison after splitting up with Lady Ottoline Morrell*. At these dos, the German painter and caricaturist Eva Herman would sprawl naked on the Huxleys' mirrored coffee table to be photographed, sketched and petted by the other guests. Eva was one of a number of lovers that Maria and Mercedes shared, as well as having a torrid affair themselves. Aldous did not mind.

Lesbianism turned him on. In 1939, he published *After Many a Summer*, based on the story of William Randolph Hearst*. In it, the tycoon's fictional mistress, Virginia – plainly Marion Davies* – only strayed with other women because that did not really count as being unfaithful.

In 1939, Garbo starred opposite Ina Claire*, John Gilbert's* ex-wife, in *Ninotchka* and made a pass at her. It was declined. Then Garbo said: "I must go to the little boys' room." Claire reported that the next time she went to the bathroom, the lavatory seat was up. *Ninotchka* was Garbo's last film. She was 36 and retired to seclusion in New York, saying famously: "I want to be alone."

By this time, the relationship between Garbo and Mercedes had cooled. Mercedes was involved in a torrid affair with the actress Ona Munson – a one-time teenage protégée of Alla Nazimova* – who had also had an affair with the Countess di

Frasso*. She had married comedy actor Eddie Buzzell* and had been involved in a famous fracas at a party at the Embassy Club held by Douglas Fairbanks* and Mary Pickford*. Ona had been dancing with the director Ernst Lubitsch*, while Lubitsch's wife was dancing with screenwriter Hans Kraly*, who Lubitsch had brought with him from Germany. Kraly and Mrs Lubitsch followed Ona and Lubitsch about, taunting them in German until Lubitsch finally hit Kraly. Mrs Lubitsch then slugged her husband. It was the sensation of the season. Later Lubitsch found Kraly in bed with his wife and hounded him out of Hollywood. Kraly and his son committed suicide, and Ona became Lubitsch's mistress – until the all-consuming Mercedes came along. She found Ona "extremely pretty, but the thing that struck me most were her eyes. They were very sad, and there was something about them that touched me deeply."

Once their respective partners were out of the picture, they became an item.

"She came many weekends to stay with me," said Mercedes. "When she started shooting, she often came from the studio directly to my house and spent the night."

Looking back, Ona said that they "shared the deepest spiritual moment that life brings human beings" and claimed that they "created an entity as surely as though we had conceived and borne a child". Did no one teach these women the facts of life?

Mercedes was soon deeply in love with Ona and her main priority was to keep her away from Marlene and Greta, who always expected her to share her lovers. She hid her away in a new love nest, hung with pictures of nude women and dominatrices in boots. The Ona-Mercedes affair was soon the talk of the town. Salka checked Ona out with Dorothy di Frasso* and reported what she discovered to Marlene, whose interest was piqued.

One night, when Mercedes was away in New York for some important dental work, Ona was all done up and dancing at Ciro's when Marlene, Remarque* and Ona's former lover, Dorothy di Frasso, came in.

Remarque remarked: "But it just can't be the same girl."

"Marlene was doing her stuff too and kept looking over and smiling at me," Ona wrote to Mercedes. "I long to hold you in my arms and pour my love into you. With all my heart and soul, Ona."

Mercedes, who knew Marlene all too well, was worried. Ona misinterpreted this, believing that Mercedes thought that her former lover Dorothy di Frasso was the danger.

"I couldn't possibly know Dorothy as well as I do and still be in love with her," wrote Ona. "So – darling for heaven's sake put that out of your head once and for all. Feel me in your arms as much as I want to be there and know that you have my complete love. I'll say goodnight now as I kiss you. Your own, O." O!

It was Marlene who was the danger.

"I went to Ciro's again on Thursday night and Marlene came in with a party and once again she turned the eyes of everyone on me until I blushed up to the roots of my hair," Ona said.

Eventually, Dietrich's stares made her so uncomfortable that she had to leave.

"Darling mine, hurry home because I love you terribly and miss you very much," Ona begged.

When she reported the incident to Mercedes, it provoked her to jealousy. Was Ona flirting with Marlene while she was away? Ona ended up pleading that she was "not interested in any chi-chi with Marlene or anyone else". Mercedes sped back to Hollywood.

Marlene was quite busy at the time. She was supervising an affair between Orson Welles* and Dolores del Rio*, while having an affair with Dolores herself. Welles never cottoned on, even when Dolores ran off to Mexico City for a lesbian fling with jazz singer Billie Holiday. Marlene was also shooting *Seven Sinners* (1936) at the time. On that movie was six-foot-four bit-part actor John Wayne*, who was invited back to Marlene's dressing room for a private conference.

Marlene promptly lifted her skirt to reveal a garter belt with a watch on it.

"It's early, darling," she purred. "We have plenty of time."

Marlene turned up to the premiere with an entourage of

seven – her own seven sinners – husband Rudi*, Erich Maria Remarque*, her latest acquisition, French actor Jean Gabin*, Douglas Fairbanks Jr*, photo-journalist Stefan Lorant, John Wayne* and Mercedes herself. She left screenwriter Hans Rameau, who she had just begun an affair with, off the guest list so as not to spoil the head count.

Garbo was having a brief affair with the health expert Gaylord Hauser*, who she had met through Mercedes. They met Marlene and Remarque at a party in New York in 1941. Back in Hollywood, Garbo began going for long walks with Remarque. One night after a candlelit dinner, they went upstairs.

"She entered the bedroom, the light of the dressing room behind her, softly flowing over her shoulders, enchanting her outline, the face, the hands, the trembling," he wrote in his diary. "Something imperceptible shook her, then the voice, the dark ... the absence of any form of sentimentality or melodrama – yet full of warmth."

Her "beautiful tanned back and the most beautiful straight shoulders," he said, were "more beautiful that Puma's [Marlene's], whose shoulders are a bit too high".

For several months he was in love with her. A veteran of the German trenches in the First World War, Remarque wrote admiringly: "Garbo, all the nights with her, sitting in the dark. Never liked to switch on the lights. A strong solitude. Take her as an example, soldier."

However, Paulette Goddard*, who married Remarque in 1958, said that he had told her that Garbo was "lousy in bed".

Despite sharing Remarque, Marlene and Greta were seen together at Hollywood's foremost gay and lesbian nightspot, the Gala.

"The other night Marlene Dietrich, at the Club Gala, sang her entire repertoire of songs," wrote Hedda Hopper* on October 24, 1941, "and who should be there lapping it up but Greta Garbo and Gaylord Hauser?"

Marlene and Greta did not speak, but a few days later, when Marlene was taking publicity shots for *The Lady Is Willing* (1942), a satisfied smile played around her lips. She had seduced Ona.

She had used the oldest device in Hollywood. While playing a whore in *The Shanghai Gesture* (1941), she got the director and former lover Josef von Sternberg* to hire Ona to play another of the girls. Faux-Prussian martinet von Sternberg's brutal bullying wrung a star performance out of her, earning him, in the end, her "love, friendship and admiration". In the meantime, Marlene was on hand to dry her tears and to accept her gratitude.

Ona was so embarrassed about her infidelity that she avoided Mercedes altogether. When they did bump into each other at an exhibition, she could not bring herself to speak. Eventually Ona pretended that she had taken up with a man. Mercedes wrote to say that she fully understood that Ona needed the protection a man could afford, but that did not need to be a problem. They could go on seeing each other. Surely her new man would understand.

On November 10, 1941, Mercedes wrote: "As I've told you many times, I think of you always with great love and could never change in that respect. There is no reason for asking Dick" – Dick! – "to bring us together, as we have no need for any subterfuge. My only reason for not seeing you is due to circumstances in my life and until that changes we had best leave matters as they are. The demands on my strength of both pictures and radio are pretty strenuous … I think about you often and our paths will join again when the time is right."

Meanwhile, Marlene was having a more straightforward correspondence with Jean Gabin*, who had heard about her Hollywood bed hopping with Ona and many, many others. When he fired off a barrage of jealous accusations, she sent back a telegram saying innocently: "Shit and more shit my angel."

Mercedes consoled herself by taking a vacation on Whale Cay, where she mooned over Joe Carstair's latest, Charlotte Landau. When the United States was belatedly dragged into the Second World War, Mercedes went back to New York to work on *Tomorrow* magazine. A number of new gay establishments had opened up in the Big Apple. There was the 181 Club on Second Avenue, where the waiters were lesbians in drag and the chorus girls were drag queens, Lucky's in Harlem, which catered for interracial gay couples, and the Beggar's Bar, the most sophisticated lesbian nightspot in New York, run by Valeska Gert*, who had played madam to Greta and Marlene's whores in *The Joyless Street* (1925). Garbo was soon a regular.

Hauser often took Garbo to New York to escape from this sexual hothouse of Hollywood. He took her to the Russian dress designer Valentina*, an old amour of Mercedes. George Schlee*, Valentina's husband, turned up at his wife's salon to find Garbo posing stark naked for a simple fitting. Soon Schlee was the only man to whom she would reveal both body and mind. Truman Capote* said he was "unattractive, grotesque, ugly" and the legendary editor of *Harpers Bazaar* and *Vogue*, Diana Vreeland, said that he had bad breath. He was a Russian aristocrat, though, and Garbo was a snob.

Schlee, Valentina and Garbo were seen out and about everywhere together. It was not unusual for Schlee to turn up to a party with both his wife and Garbo wearing identical blue sailor suits.

Returning to California in 1942, Mercedes was eventually reunited with Ona, while Marlene was touring the US selling war bonds. She hosted a birthday party for her on June 16. But no one would hire Mercedes, so she had to go back to New York to edit the Office of War Information's magazine *Victory*, leaving Ona to run an all-girl musical revue called *Victory Belles*.

"I have seven girls on my hands in this show," complained Ona.

The rest of the Sewing Circle benefited from the wartime shortage of men, though some of her old friends sought to comfort the young men who were going away to fight. Actor Gilbert Roland recalled a night of consolation with Marlene.

"On parting I gave her a gold ring, and took her silk panties with the initial 'G'," he said. "We kissed goodbye. I boarded the Army Transport plane back to the field, her panties still inside my coat pocket."

Mercedes had no intention of doing her bit, though. She invited Beatrice Kaufman, wife of playwright George S. Kaufman, to luncheon at her apartment. Bea was surprised to find that lunch was to be *à deux*. After they had finished eating, Mercedes disappeared and returned in a diaphanous yellow negligée. Beatrice fled. Later she told her daughter Anne, who was less than sympathetic. Anne became the last lover and long-term companion of Eva Le Gallienne. In 1977, Anne found a gold ring in Eva's attic.

"It was from Mercedes," said Eva.

She threw it down the well outside her house.

Garbo moved into the Ritz tower near Mercedes' modest quarters at 471 Park Place. Defying the blackout regulations, they signalled to each other by candlelight at night if they needed company. They went separately to the Beggar's Bar, where Garbo picked up any number of Marlene's exes, while Marlene was away single-handedly winning the war.

When peace came, Mercedes took the opportunity to go back to Paris, which was fast becoming, once again, a haven for women who love women. She took a job writing about Europe for an American syndicated newspaper. She was paid in dollars – which went further in Europe – and returned to New York each Christmas. The first year she brought heroine of the French Resistance, Claire, the Marquise de Forbin, with her to fatten up the half-starved aristocrat. They remained intimate companions for the rest of her life. Then, in 1948, Mercedes began an affair with Poppy Kirk. Born Maria Annunziata Sartori and a former model, she was the wife of British diplomat Geoffrey Kirk, but was also the veteran of numerous glamorous lesbian affairs. After an attempted reconciliation with her husband in Panama, she lived with Mercedes in Paris, where she worked for the Schiaparelli* fashion house.

One Christmas trip to New York, Mercedes hooked up with an old lover, 76-year-old theatrical costumier Marion Stevenson. When she met Garbo, Garbo asked: "May I ask you a personal question?"

"Of course," said Marion. "I have no secrets from Mercedes."

"Are you a virgin?"

Laughing, Marion conceded that, technically, she was.

"How extraordinary," said Garbo.

By this time, Garbo had locked horns with Mercedes' old friend Cecil Beaton*. At a party that Christmas Eve, Garbo called Cecil "Mr Beaton", while Beaton, in his affected way, called everyone "darling". Garbo whispered menacingly under her breath: "Don't you dare call anyone darling but me."

Later, at dinner alone with Beaton, Mercedes begged him to marry Garbo. Neither Gaylord Hauser*, Stokowski* or "the little man" – Schlee* – was suitable for her. They didn't marry, but they did visit Mercedes and Poppy in Paris together. They also paid a call on Alice B. Toklas*, who was trying to sell some of the Picassos* collected by her late partner, Gertrude Stein*.

After Garbo left Paris, Eva Le Gallienne arrived with her lover, the director Margaret Webster. They dined with Mercedes and Poppy and laughed about old times. Ona also turned up in Paris with her Russian-born husband Eugene Berman, who she had married in 1949 in the house of Igor Stravinsky*. They lived near to Mercedes and Poppy for a time, but returned to New York when Ona was ill. She wrote to Mercedes about the "strenuous and active" life she had lived with Eugene in a letter that was full of the joys of marriage.

"I have not changed my feelings toward you," she said, "but life has changed and I do not have the vitality and strength of extend it further."

Soon after, she took an overdose of sleeping tablets and died.

In 1955, *Hollywood Confidential* began publishing "The Untold Story of Marlene Dietrich" – including her affairs with Joe Carstairs, Frede Braule and Mercedes. Marlene ignored it. She was a war hero, decorated by both the US and French governments, and, as far as the world was concerned, a respectable married woman. Besides, the *Confidential* did not know the half of it.

Garbo was afraid that the truth about her would come out in a forthcoming biography. She snubbed Mercedes, though Beaton tried to bring them together.

"I am sure she needs you," he wrote to Mercedes, who was now ailing, "and have always thought that the two of you would end your days together."

Garbo changed her phone numbers frequently to stop

Mercedes calling. In Europe she was seen with Cecile de Rothschild, while in New York she hung out with Libby Holman, the former lover of Mercedes and Tallulah.

Mercedes was now down on her luck and both Hope Williams and ex-husband Abram Poole sent money regularly. Eventually, she moved back to New York to be near her doctors. Then, one day in 1957, after two years of silence, there was a knock on the door. It was Garbo. And she was in tears.

"I have no one to look after me," she sobbed.

"But you don't want anyone to look after you," said Mercedes.

"I'm frightened," cried Garbo. "I'm so lost."

Mercedes clutched her to her bosom and introduced her to her doctors. The reconciliation was short-lived, however. After Garbo pulled back, Mercedes threatened suicide. Garbo responded with a telegram addressing her as "dear boy" and promised to take her to a clinic in Switzerland. She did not deliver on this. After taking Mercedes and Beaton out to dinner, she hightailed it back to Schlee, who took her to visit Aristotle Onassis* and Winston Churchill* in the south of France.

Mercedes began to work on her memoir but, given the McCarthy*-ite atmosphere in the US at the time, she found it impossible to hint at any form of lesbian activity. Published in 1960, it was called *Here Lies the Heart*.

"And lies, and lies, and lies," said Salka.

Mercedes phoned Greta, who said simply, "I don't want to talk to you," and put the phone down. Though they bumped into each other once more in a health-food shop, Garbo never spoke to her again.

Although she was now terminally ill, Mercedes hung out with Andy Warhol*, spending the Thanksgiving of 1962 with him. She continued to support her old friends, including sculptress Malvina Hoffman, and picked up new young ones. She took up with a young British actress who waited tables at Chock Full o'Nuts and went walking with Kieran Tunney, author of *Tallulah – Darling of the Gods*.

When Mercedes de Acosta died on May 9, 1968, Cecil Beaton wrote in his diary: "Now, without a kind word from the woman she loved more than any of the women in her life, Mercedes had gone to a lonely grave."

However, if you now play International Daisy Chain, she will live again – and she'll be in excellent company.

10 The First Lady

As the wife of wartime US President Franklin D. Roosevelt, Eleanor Roosevelt* had a walk-on part in *Sex Lives of the US Presidents* (*Sex Lives of the Presidents* in the US). Now she comes into her own. In fact, she came into her own at the time. As First Lady, she instituted the first regular White House press conferences for women correspondents – which is probably why one of them became her co-respondent. After her husband's death, she became the US's first delegate to the United Nations and, as chairman of the UN Commission on Human Rights, played a key role in the writing of the Universal Declaration of Human Rights. More recently Hillary Clinton*, while First Lady herself, said she "communed" with Eleanor on the White House roof. There was some speculation at the time that Hillary swung both ways, but when I'm asked how many First Ladies were gay, I have always hedged my bets and said: "One-and-a-half."

The niece of President Theodore Roosevelt*, Eleanor was considered the ugly duckling of the family – though, as it turned out, she did not turn into a swan. As it was she was delighted that her handsome and debonair cousin Franklin made a pass at her. Most considered that – as an accomplished womaniser and drinker – he was no good for her. Besides, he had a reputation as a causal flirt and may just have been leading her on. On a trip to England, he wrote to his mother, explaining his technique: "As I knew the uncivilised English custom of never introducing people … I walked up to the best-looking dame in the bunch and said 'howdy?' Things went like oil and I was soon having flirtations with three of the nobility at the same time."

What Franklin said to Eleanor about this incident, we will never know. Eleanor burnt all the letters from their courtship, perhaps because they contained pledges of everlasting fidelity that he singularly failed to live up to.

He kept her letters, though. In one of them, she quoted Elizabeth Barrett Browning: "Unless you can swear, 'For life, for death!'/ Oh, fear to call it loving." Franklin may have sworn because, in 1903, they got engaged. On the other hand, frumpy old Eleanor was not getting a lot of offers.

Her mother-in-law-to-be was against the match and took Franklin off on a five-week cruise around the Caribbean. He promptly began a shipboard romance with an older French woman, who his mother disapproved of even more. The woman in question must have had quite an effect on him though. In 1936, over thirty years later, when he heard that she had moved to Trinidad, he tried to get in touch with her again.

Ignoring these warning signs, Eleanor bagged her man at a lavish ceremony where she was given away by the sitting president, Uncle Teddy*. They toured Europe on their honeymoon, sailing on the *Oceanic*, a precursor of the *Titanic*. Because of their kinship to the president, they were given the Royal Suite at Brown's Hotel in London. It cost one thousand dollars a day even then. He began calling her "Babs" – short for "Baby" – not because of any resemblance to busty *Carry On* star Babs Windsor, who had not even been born then. Hard to believe, I know. Anyway, Franklin called Eleanor "Babs" for the rest of his life.

In spite of this intimacy, two things disturbed Eleanor on their honeymoon. One was his sleepwalking, which she considered to be a sign of an uneasy conscience. The other was the thing she thought might lead to that uneasy conscience – his compulsive flirting. Nevertheless, they had some success on the sexual front. When they returned to New York, she was pregnant with the first of their six children, one of which died in infancy.

During the First World War, Franklin was the assistant secretary of the Navy and while he remained in Washington, DC, Eleanor spent her time at their holiday home on Campobello Island in New Brunswick, Canada. This left him free to party with his old buddies from Harvard. Women flocked to him and there was the occasional flirtation and more.

Eleanor had always taken an active part in her husband's political life and hired herself a social secretary called Lucy Page Mercer*. She was a beautiful young woman in her early twenties. Coming from a prominent Maryland family, she mixed easily in the Roosevelts' social circle and, when Eleanor was away, Franklin courted her openly.

The affair was in full swing when Franklin came down with pneumonia. He went to Campobello to convalesce. When he arrived, Eleanor was unpacking his bags when she came across a bundle of letters bound up with a ribbon. They were from Lucy.

"The bottom dropped out my own particular world," Eleanor said.

Devastated, his affair with a beautiful young woman confirmed everything that she thought about herself – that she was ugly, unattractive and unloved. After 13 years of marriage, she offered Franklin a divorce.

"Don't be a goose," he replied.

At a family conclave, it was decided that they must stay together. In those days, divorce would have meant an end to his political career. Even worse, Franklin's mother threatened to cut him off without a penny if he divorced Eleanor. Besides, Lucy was a Catholic and, even if he divorced Eleanor, she would not marry him.

Eleanor agreed to stay with Franklin, but laid down conditions. First, he was no longer to share her bed. This was no hardship. She had never enjoyed sex – with men, at least. She told her daughter that sexual intercourse was an unpleasant burden that a married woman simply had to endure.

"Father and mother had an armed truce that endured until the day he died," wrote their son James.

Eleanor also insisted that he give up Lucy. He had no choice but to agree. He was a politician, however, and was quite happy to say one thing and do another. Lucy had already left Eleanor's staff and had joined the Navy as a yeomanette, working directly under him at the Department of the Navy. She also had an apartment conveniently close by. Eleanor hung on in Washington that summer to keep an eye on them, but as soon as her back was turned the affair resumed. They continued seeing each other for the next 26 years. He died in her arms on April 12, 1945.

While Eleanor was away at Campobello, Lucy and Franklin went on boat trips up the Potomac and took drives in the countryside. Socially, she was accompanied by British diplomat Nigel Law, who acted as a beard in public, but they were seen out alone together, while out on a drive, by Eleanor's cousin Alice Longworth, who even had Franklin and Lucy to dinner. She took pity on him because he was married to the unattractive Eleanor. That did not stop her from spilling the beans to Eleanor, though.

"She enquired if you had told me," Eleanor told Franklin later. "I said I did not believe in knowing things that your husband did not wish you to know, so I think I will be spared any further secrets."

She was not spared. Her son James said that she had evidence that Franklin and Lucy had checked into a hotel in Virginia Beach together as man and wife. After the war, Franklin took on a new secretary, Marguerite "Missy" LeHand*, who also became his mistress. Eleanor knew about this and tolerated it, perhaps because Missy was from a lower social class and it was generally permitted for nobs to knob the hired hands.

Besides, Eleanor now had fish of her own to fry – though I trust she did not actually fry them. She mixed in lesbian circles and began to share an interest with her husband, praising on one occasion the "lovely ladies who served luncheon for my husband and worshipped at his shrine". She did not even mind the fact that the pretty young Miss LeHand was always on hand when he was out campaigning. Franklin himself was not quite so sanguine and was devastated when he heard that Lucy had married Winthrop Rutherford, a wealthy sportsman and dog-breeder 30 years her senior.

In 1921, while vacationing in Campobello, he went swimming in the Bay of Fundy and caught polio. His mother wanted him to retire to the family estates at Hyde Park, in upstate New York, but he was unwilling to give up politics, so Eleanor travelled the country as his political eyes and ears, while Missy LeHand stayed at home to administer a vigorous programme of hydrotherapy and massage to his paralysed nether regions.

Franklin and Missy lived together openly on a houseboat during winter vacations in Florida, where he strengthened his muscles swimming. Although Missy ostensibly had a room of her own, she would have had to go through Franklin's bedroom to get to the bathroom. They were seen lolling about in their swimming costumes and night attire and lived what one guest called a "negligée existence".

As she did not look good in a swimsuit – or in a negligée for that matter – Eleanor stayed away. When she did visit, she usually turned up with one of her lesbian chums.

The Roosevelts also established a foundation for polio victims at Warm Springs, Georgia, where there was more therapy on LeHand. They kept a cottage there, but Eleanor seldom visited. When she did, she was the guest and Missy the hostess. Despite Missy's dedicated attention to Franklin's lower half, he never recovered the use of his legs. However, it is plain that some things were working below his waist.

Things were working below the waist for Eleanor, too. She set up homes in Greenwich Village, known for its homosexual denizens, and at Val-Kill, near Springwood, Virginia. There she entertained lesbian couples Esther Lape and Elizabeth Read, and Nancy Cook and Marion Dickerman – which Franklin referred to as her "squaws" or "she-men". Although they lived separately, Eleanor and Franklin kept up an affectionate correspondence.

In 1929, Franklin was governor of New York and assigned the 45-year-old Eleanor a bodyguard in the shape of 32-year-old bodybuilder and well-known womaniser Earl Miller*. He was totally devoted to her, checking her bills and squiring her round her public duties. They spent a great deal of time together, reading aloud, singing and playing the piano. He coached her at tennis and taught her how to shoot and dive. Some of her lesbian friends were distressed to see him "manhandle" her, especially when they were in bathing suits. They would walk hand in hand and he was seen to touch her knee. He claimed that she would have made a better president than her husband and called her not Mrs Roosevelt but "Lady" or "Dearest Lady". Nevertheless, a discreet veil is drawn over him in her autobiography.

When Roosevelt first ran for the presidency, Eleanor hated the thought of being closeted in the White House so much that she talked of running away with Miller. Their guns were spiked by Missy LeHand*. Miller said that, on a visit to Warm Springs, Missy had put him on night duty so that he could come to her bedroom. There has been speculation that Roosevelt put her up to it – to prevent Eleanor from running away with him – an action that would have destroyed Roosevelt's chances of becoming president.

Soon after, Miller said, Eleanor discovered that he was also "playing around with one of the girls in the Executive Office" and Eleanor took to her bed and cried for three days. She soon recovered, though. Once Franklin was safely installed in the White House, Eleanor rented an apartment above Esther Lape and Elizabeth Read's in Greenwich Village, where she entertained Miller. She managed to keep a hold over him during his three marriages, all of which ended in divorce. After Roosevelt's death, the protracted affair almost hit the headlines. On January 13, 1947, the then New York *Daily News* columnist – later the celebrated TV show host – Ed Sullivan wrote: "Navy Commander's wife will rock the country if she names the co-respondent in her divorce action." The Navy Commander concerned was Earl Miller.

When Roosevelt was elected president, Missy LeHand moved into the White House with her beloved "F.D.". They would dine together and she was often seen disappearing into the president's room in her nightdress. Not to be outdone, Eleanor moved in a lover of her own. This was cigar-smoking Associated Press reporter Lorena Hickok*, a well-known lesbian who had openly lived with other women before.

They had met in 1928, when "Hick" had come to visit the

First Lady of the Empire State. In her report, she had eulogised about Eleanor's "long, slender hands" and her "laced-trimmed hostess gown".

In 1932, she joined her on the presidential campaign trail. The two of them became inseparable and Hickok's flattering columns – cooked up with Eleanor herself – were syndicated throughout the United States and helped build Eleanor's image. Hick may well have had a hand in Eleanor's own daily column "My Day" which was syndicated in newspapers from 1936, although she never got a mention. This might have been because her presence might have been more properly confined to a column called "My Night".

Other press syndicates soon realised that AP were getting all the exclusives and assigned women reporters of their own to cover – or uncover – Eleanor's image. They could not compete with Hick, however, who had a unique inside track.

It has to be said that Hick was singularly unattractive. She was five feet eight but weighed two hundred pounds, smoked cigars, cigarettes and pipes, drank Bourbon on the rocks and was very much "one of the boys".

She and Eleanor went to great lengths to hide their affair. Hick even edited and retyped Eleanor's letters – some three-and-a-half thousand in all – burning all of the originals in an attempt to cover their tracks. Even so, explicit expressions of their love slipped through. Eleanor wrote to Hick, saying: "I wish I could lie down beside you tonight and take you in my arms"; "I ache to hold you close" and "Most clearly I remember your eyes, with a kind of teasing smile in them, and the feeling of that soft spot just north-east of the corner of your mouth against my lips …"

They even exchanged rings and had jealous lovers' tiffs. When Roosevelt first entered the White House, they were seen walking across Lafayette Park together. They lived together in the north side of the White House, whose staff could not have failed to notice what was going on. White House maid Lillian Parks recalled Eleanor and Hick disappearing into Eleanor's bathroom for long periods, claiming that it was "the only place they could find the privacy for a press interview". Not a face-to-face, surely. The staff considered this "hardly the kind of thing one would do with an ordinary reporter, or even with an adult friend".

Even though Roosevelt had his hands full with Missy LeHand – and there was a war on – he was not happy with this bizarre domestic arrangement. He hated Hickok and was once heard to cry: "I want that woman out of this House." He was president, for God's sake, but even though he could kick Hitler out of occupied Europe, he could not evict one feisty dyke from his own home.

The atmosphere in the White House was not improved when Hickok, jealous of Eleanor's continuing relationship with Earl Miller, fell in love with a female tax-court judge. Eleanor got her own back by bedding the youthful Joseph P. Lash, who later wrote the 1971 dual biography *Eleanor and Franklin*. This further enraged the president as Lash was under surveillance at the time. Eleanor was not amused to discover that their room in the Blackstone Hotel in Chicago had been bugged by Army Intelligence. The tapes "indicated quite clearly that Mrs Roosevelt and Lash engaged in sexual intercourse", said an FBI report. Maybe, as her biographer, she was merely giving him a Hickok-style press interview. Later, Lash was refused a commission in the US Army. A number of indiscreet letters from Eleanor to Lash surfaced, which was all the more embarrassing as Lash was engaged to be married at the time.

In 1941, having had an affair with William Bullitt*, Roosevelt's pre-war ambassador to the Soviet Union, Miss LeHand suffered a brain haemorrhage, moved out of the White House and died three years later. Roosevelt was catered for by other "handmaidens". He had kept in touch with Lucy Mercer Rutherford*, who had secretly attended all four of his inaugurations. Even during the war, he would be driven out for a secret rendezvous with her by the Secret Service. On one occasion, the presidential Pullman car was shunted into a siding near the Rutherford estate at Allamuchy, New Jersey.

After Roosevelt died in the newly widowed Lucy's arms in the cottage at Warm Springs, Eleanor left the White House, telling reporters: "My story is over."

It wasn't, though. Long-time friend Bernard Baruch proposed. She refused, but continued an active sex life as the US delegate to the United Nations. After all, as she herself would have declared, it was her human right.

11 More Head

Some names have sexual connotations. If inappropriate this can be a blight. If it is apt, though, it can be a positive blessing. In the case of Agnes Moorehead, a leading character actress and a card-carrying lesbian, it was a delight.

Although she is best known as the mother-in-law and elderly witch in the 1960s TV sitcom *Bewitched* – which is still regular morning TV fodder around the world – her first two movies, Orson Welles's* *Citizen Kane* (1941) and *The Magnificent Ambersons* (1942), are among any cineast's top one hundred films.

When she first arrived in Hollywood as part of Welles's Mercury Theatre, Agnes was pretty easy going. She had a series of intimate lady friends who she would often be seen out with. According to veteran director Jerry Paris: "When one of her husbands was caught cheating, so the story goes, Agnes screamed at him that if he could have a mistress, so could she."

Agnes, however, had missed the free-and-easy Sapphic circles of the early Hollywood. In the post-war Eisenhower* era, everything was strait-laced. In show business circles, though, her preferences were well known.

"The whole world knows Agnes was a lesbian," said actor Paul Lynde. "I mean, as classy as hell, but one of the all-time Hollywood dykes."

Actress Elsa Lanchester*, wife of Charles Laughton*, who toured with Agnes in George Bernard Shaw's* *Don Juan* in Hell in the 1950s, said: "Miss Moorehead was the soul of discretion. More than she needed to be – secondary actresses don't dwell in the same goldfish bowls reserved for the stars ... Someone who knew her extremely well said that Agnes was no longer 'active' that way, but she always had romantic friendships with other women."

According to Lee Van Cleef*, who played alongside her in Howard Hughes's* Mongol epic *The Conqueror* (1956),

Moorehead had an ill-disguised crush on Susan Hayward★, who was also thought to swing that way.

"Agnes had it bad for Susan," said Van Cleef, "but she could always mask it as sisterly or motherly affection, and Susan didn't seem to mind. They went way back."

Agnes has a similarly enduring relationship with Debbie Reynolds★.

In 1956, she played a lesbian madam opposite Jane Russell★ in *The Revolt of Mamie Stover*, though her sexuality was toned down by the censors. In 1957, she played a lesbian in *Jeanne Eagels*, as coach and mentor to Kim Novak★. And on TV in the 1950s she did readings from the diaries of lesbian harpsichordist Wanda Landowska.

In 1970, Agnes was asked on a Los Angeles chat show why she had never won an Oscar. She snapped back: "Neither has Barbara Stanwyck★."

This may have been because Stanwyck got to play the lead in *Sorry Wrong Number* (1948), a part for which Agnes had received rave reviews when she had performed the role on the radio. Boze Hadleigh, author of *Hollywood Lesbians*, said that this led to "friction between the two strong actresses" – whether in a nice way or in a nasty one she did not make clear.

Changing her tone, Moorehead went on to say, "Greta Garbo★ never won the Academy Award either."

In 1964, she joined the cast of *Bewitched* which turned out to be a hotbed of gay and lesbian activity. The husband, Darren, was played after season six by Dick Sargent, who came out on National Coming Out Day in 1991. In 1992, he was co-Grand Marshal of the Los Angeles Gay Pride Day Parade with Elizabeth Montgomery, the series' Samantha. It almost makes you want to twitch your nose.

Endora's – Agnes's – warlock husband was played by the late Maurice Evans, a Shakespearean actor who was also thought to be gay. Mr Kravitz was played by lifelong bachelor George Tobias. Gay stand-up Paul Lynde played Sam's Uncle Arthur. And one of the twins who played Tabitha – Darren and Samantha's witchlet daughter – came out as a gay activist in 1992. You'll never look at the series the same way again.

In an interview in 1973, Moorehead admitted that she had "loved many women, of course", but when it came to sex, she said: "That's men's concern, or habit. They talk that way and want to drag women down to their level, to have no class. Young women are often very willing."

As far as Agnes Moorehead was concerned there were many lesbians living in Hollywood – "Everywhere. Most of them are nice people and not promiscuous – like the men."

But then Agnes Moorehead died in 1974 and did not live long enough to read the preceding chapters.

Another delightfully named Hollywood lesbian was Paramount wardrobe mistress Edith Head. Her name even prompted the popular graffito: "Edith Head gives good wardrobe." As the studio's foremost costumier, she had every reason to stay in the closet.

Born in 1897, she was 23 before women got the right to vote in the US. Actress Joan Hackett said: "Edith Head came from a generation that was so terrified, it was afraid to voice its support for its own rights, even the right to vote – never mind voicing support for fellow lesbians and gays, and forget about coming out of the closet. No way. Not in this life."

According to Elsa Lanchester*, Head was not even her real name.

"She wanted you to think she was born Edith Head," she said. "Her real surname was something like Poser."

In fact, her real name was Edith Claire Posener, though she hid her real sexuality behind two lavender marriages. The first was to Charles Head, who she never talked about. They divorced in 1938. By that time she was already head of Paramount's costume design department and it is thought that she felt she no longer needed to have a husband for career purposes. Rumours abounded. Some said that he was an alcoholic, others that he was gay, others still that he was just a friend. By 1945, she denied ever having been wed.

Her second marriage was to art director Wiard Boppo Ihnen, to whom she was married for 30 years. According to Barbara Stanwyck*, they were "close pals". Elsa Lanchester* said: "She and her husband led separate lives. He was usually at his ranch … He was over 50 when she married him."

They were good friends before they married and remained so.

For most of that time she was a close friend of Anne Baxter who, as a 19-year-old, played under Agnes Moorehead in *The Magnificent Ambersons* (1942).

According to Baxter, she kept her distance from the stars and rarely let her hair down, though they were at a screening of *Queen Bee* (1955), starring Joan Crawford*, when Edith turned to Anne during one of the more malignant scenes and said: "I wish I could do that."

Edith was particularly unimpressed by the male stars. She loved to tell a story about Marlon Brando* who, in his youthful prime, "walked into my office stark naked". Edith did not turn a hair.

"Of course, you must know that she doesn't like any men … that way," said Elsa Lanchester. "Edith did not like most women either. Not if they're not young and attractive."

The last of her eight Oscars was awarded for the costumes in *The Sting* (1973), so she got to see Paul Newman* and Robert Redford in their jockeys, or less.

"But it was the women stars, the beauties in their bras and panties, that turned her on," said Hollywood reporter Paul Rosenfield. "So she developed a poker face and an aloof attitude to mask her true feelings. When her work was over, Edith would climb into her monogrammed Jeep and go home alone."

Home was an adobe hacienda in Coldwater Canyon called Casa Ladera, which she had bought from Bette Davis*. One of her few guests was Elizabeth Taylor*, who came often. Edith had designed her a much-copied strapless evening gown for *A Place in the Sun* (1951). She also left her a Mexican coin necklace when she died.

The beauties in their bras and panties included Dorothy Lamour*, Claudette Colbert*, Paulette Goddard*, Hedy Lamarr* and Audrey Hepburn* – for the studio. Away from the set she looked after Marlene Dietrich*, Ginger Rogers* and

Ingrid Bergman*. Like Elizabeth Taylor*, Barbara Stanwyck* belonged in both categories and remained a close friend after other associates were gone.

Bra and panties were okay, but Edith found it disrespectful when actresses turned up for a fitting without any underwear – except if it was the notoriously pantiless Tallulah Bankhead* or Carmen Miranda* who "made up for it in other ways".

However, in an interview shortly before her death in 1981, Edith Head boasted: "I've seen most of the stars naked. Some are rather thrilling – beautiful breasts, bodies. There's no vulgarity in nudity."

Did this just apply to naked actresses? she was asked.

"Naturally," she said. "Who wants to see naked men?"

I'm with you all the way on that one, Edith.

12 Stand Wick? I Don't Think So

A list of Barbara Stanwyck's screen credits says it all: *The Locked Door* (1929), *Illicit* (1931), *Forbidden* (1932), *Ladies They Talk About* (1933), *The Secret Bride* (1935), *The Bride Walks Out* (1936), *This Is My Affair* (1937), *Stella [Does?] Dallas* (1937), *Always Goodbye* (1938), *The Mad Miss Manton* (1938), *Golden Boy* (1939), *Remember the Night* (1940), *The Lady Eve* (1941), *The Gay Sisters* (1942), *Flesh and Fantasy* (1943), *Double Indemnity* (1944), *The Bride Wore Boots* (1946), *The Strange Love of Martha Ivers* (1946), *Variety Girl* (1947), *The Other Love* (1947), *Sorry, Wrong Number* (1948), *The File on Thelma Jordon* (1949), *No Man of Her Own* (1950), *The Furies* (1950), *To Please a Lady* (1950), *Clash by Night* (1952), *Jeopardy* (1952), *All I Desire* (1953), *The Moonlighter* (1953), *Blowing Wild* (1953), *The Maverick Queen* (1955), *These Wilder Years* (1956), *Walk on the Wild Side* (1962) ... And a generation of TV audiences know her from her part in TV's *The Big Valley*. Was she trying to tell us something?

Born Ruby Stevens on July 16, 1907 in Brooklyn, New York, Barbara Stanwyck was known as "Missy" to film crews and friends. Two years after she was born, her mother was pushed off a moving trolley car by a drunk, hit her head on the pavement and died two weeks later. A few weeks after that, her father, another heavy drinker, deserted the family and went to work as a bricklayer on the Panama Canal. He was never heard of again.

Ruby and her younger brother, Byron Jr, were farmed out to foster homes and supported by older sister Mildred, who was a chorus girl. Ruby soon followed in her footsteps and joined the Keep Kool Cuties. According to *Variety*: "These 16 girls are pips, lookers and dancers. They kick like steers and look like why-men-leave-home in their many costume flashes."

"She told me after we got to know each other that being a chorus girl could be humiliating and dangerous," said co-star and fellow lesbian Marjorie Main. "The rich men who did not want to tangle with prostitutes would often hire showgirls instead."

Ex-showgirl Joan Crawford* said that many high kickers were bi or lesbian and that it was common for them to be propositioned by both sexes.

At the age of 17, Ruby joined the Ziegfeld* *Follies* and featured in the famous "Ziegfeld Shadowgraph", where she did a striptease back-lit behind a white screen.

"I tossed my clothes out into the audience," she said. "But if they did not wear three-dimensional glasses, they didn't get to see anything."

The only people to see everything were backstage.

She then moved into the legitimate theatre, acquiring the name Barbara Stanwyck on the way. At this time she was dating a young man named Edward Kennedy – no, not that Edward Kennedy* – and almost got married. However, she did the proper actressy thing and fell in love with her leading man, Rex Cherryman – a good name for an inveterate womaniser. Cherryman died on his way to a European tour aged 30. Another man had let her down; it only made her more determined to succeed on her own merit.

Typecast as the lead in *Burlesque*, she was introduced to rising star Frank Fay by pianist Oscar Levant*. After the loss of Cherryman, Fay offered her a shoulder to cry on. He had been divorced twice, was an alcoholic and was probably impotent, but when he proposed Stanwyck jumped at the chance.

Barbara was offered the chance to play the lead in the silent-movie version of *Burlesque* (made as *The Dance of Life* in 1929) after it had been a hit on Broadway, but Fay would not let her go to Hollywood until he got a movie deal, too. When he did, and the news spread that Barbara Stanwyck was moving to California, the head of United Artists, Joseph Schenck*, turned up in New York to make her an offer.

She started out with two flops. Then, after a misunderstanding with director Frank Capra* over the casting couch, Harry Cohn* signed her to Columbia for *Ladies of Leisure* (1930). She was soon wowing critics. The *Hollywood Reporter* said: "The best things about *Night Nurse* [1931] are its title and cast names plus Misses Stanwyck and Blondell* stripping two or three times during the picture."

By this time, Fay's movie career was all washed up. He began drinking heavily. There were fights, both at home and in public. In an apparent effort to save their marriage, they adopted a ten-month-old baby boy and christened him Dion Anthony Fay. The problem was that Barbara felt no maternal instincts whatsoever but, in publicity terms at least, it boosted her femininity. It did nothing to help the relationship. Fay continued drinking and brawling. After a fight around their swimming pool – after Barbara had gone to a girlie show – Frank hit her once more. She filed for divorce and a veil was drawn over the whole messy business.

"Two things Barbara doesn't address are her childhood and her first marriage," said co-star Clifton Webb*.

Her second marriage was to Robert Taylor*. According to George Cukor*, who was gay himself and who directed Taylor in his breakthrough movie *Camille* (1936) with Garbo*, Taylor was either gay or bisexual. His nickname was "Pretty Boy" and the rumours that he was gay threatened his career as a matinee idol.

MGM boss Louis B. Mayer* thought that Taylor was not manly enough to become a fully fledged star. What he needed was to stop being pretty and single. So he was aged and grew a moustache. The studios usually preferred their male leads to be unmarried – so that female fans would consider them available – so if Taylor wanted to ditch the fairy image, he had to get married.

In *This Is My Affair* (1937), the critics said that Taylor made love to Stanwyck "persuasively", so Taylor acquired a studio bride in the form of his co-star, who was four years his senior. She called him "Junior"; he called her "the Queen".

They were an odd couple. While she liked tailored clothes, suits, sport outfits and slacks made out of men's materials, he favoured a looser, softer, flouncier look. He put women on a pedestal and treated them like ladies. Barbara opened her own doors and lit her own cigarettes. Mayer*, though, figured that a strong woman was just what a mother's boy like Taylor needed. At it was, Robert Taylor spent his wedding night with his enormously possessive mother. There was no love lost between her and Stanwyck. Both of them wanted to be boss. Poor Bobby boy was caught in the middle.

There has been speculation that there might have been more to their marriage than lavender.

"Barbara loved Bob and it may have led to the bedroom," said director Mitchell Leison, but more than that "she wanted companionship and, as a star, she realised that there were off-screen rules one lived by".

The problem was there were always temptations in the movie business. Lana Turner* admitted to flirting with Robert Taylor during the filming of *Johnny Eager* (1942). Taylor expressed some disappointment that she was not as busty as her publicity shots. Her face was delicate and beautiful, though, and he said that he had never seen lips like hers.

"Though I was not one to run after blondes, Lana was the exception," he said. "I couldn't take my eyes off her, and there were times during *Johnny Eager* I thought I'd explode."

It was her voice that attracted him most. She sounded like a breathless child. She did not seem to know how to talk without being sexy, he complained. She only had to say "good morning" and Taylor melted.

"She was the kind of woman a guy would risk five years in jail for rape," he said.

Despite his natural proclivities, she turned him on and Taylor knew he had to have her, even if it was only for one night. He foolishly told Barbara of his desire for Lana and asked her for a divorce, but after a short separation they reconciled after a suicide attempt. Barbara ended up in the Cedars of Lebanon Hospital. She never spoke to Lana again.

After this brush – and what a brush – with the heterosexual world, Taylor realised that he had married the wrong woman. He wanted someone who was feminine, who wore frilly clothes in soft colours, who cooked and cleaned, who wanted children and who would let him be the boss. Someone like Lana, perhaps? However, he was willing to stick with Barbara out of an enduring respect for her.

"Besides," he said years later, "it's tough hurting someone you know loves you sincerely and would do anything for you."

During the Second World War, they were separated when he joined up. This experience got him away from women's apron strings and he began to mature. They tried to reconnect after the war and took a trip to Europe. They made a round of the sights in Paris, including the Folies Bergères, where Barbara was aghast at the sight of "thousands of girls running around with just a piece of chiffon on".

Back in Hollywood, Taylor began hanging out with the likes of Clark Gable★ and Errol Flynn★, and started to get involved in their drunken antics. John Wayne★ recalled a party at the Taylors' house where Barbara retired to bed early.

"The booze and beer flowed," he said. "Just a bunch of guys getting drunk and having a good time, until she appeared at the top of the stairs in her nightgown and yelled at Bob. 'Get up here now!' she shouted and told him to join her in bed. I can't repeat what else she said, but it had to do with sex and what she wanted him to do."

The problem was that he now needed a woman for physical purposes and Stanwyck could not make his wick stand. He claimed that it was because he was having prostate problems. She said it was because he was gay. He did not need other women and she sent him to a psychologist to prove it. Unfortunately, the doctors did not confirm her diagnosis.

During the shooting of *The Bribe* (1949), Taylor complained to his co-star Ava Gardner★ that his marriage was failing. The reason was, she said, he could not get it up for his wife. Ava decided she had a cure for that. She would be seen on the set massaging his crotch with her toe. He would take her back to his mother's house to make love to her. When his mother complained about this arrangement, he pointed out that he was merely safeguarding his career.

"Would you rather I went to a motel and got photographed?" he asked.

In *The Conspirator* (1949), Robert Taylor gave Elizabeth Taylor* her first screen kiss. It was a revelation for both of them.

"I've just been kissed by Robert Taylor," she told her hairdresser in ecstasy.

Fresh from *National Velvet* (1945), Robert considered Elizabeth a little girl. He was soon made to think differently, however.

"For God's sake, she was stacked," he said. "I didn't realise it until she appeared on the set in a negligée. She was just a child, but I could not help myself ... It wouldn't have been so bad if they shot the scene with me sitting down. Finally I spoke to the cameraman and he aimed the lens from my waist up."

Robert Taylor flew to Rome to shoot *Quo Vadis* (1951). He had a field day there playing around with female fans and actresses. Rumours reached the ears of Hollywood gossip columnists that he had been seen "swimming, dining and dancing with numerous Italian beauties". Eventually, the names of two women in particular emerged – the starlets Marina Berti and Lia De Leo. De Leo even told the Italian press that Taylor was tired of his wife and that he wanted a divorce "after meeting me".

Stanwyck hated flying, but she still got on the plane to Rome to confront Taylor. He played innocent, but she kept on and on about Lia De Leo, until he eventually said: "At least I can get it up with her."

The divorce proceedings took just three minutes.

When Taylor returned to Hollywood, they were often seen out together. On the quiet, though, he was seeing Virginia Grey*, who had just been dropped by Clark Gable* after seven years when he got drunk and eloped with Douglas Fairbanks Sr's* widow, Lady Sylvia Ashley*. Seven years later, Virginia appeared in a movie with Barbara.

"The first day on set, she let me have it with words I cannot repeat," recalled Virginia. "There was no mention of Bob, but she had no other reason to dislike me so intensely. I had done the unpardonable. I had gone out with Robert Taylor."

Barbara was a martinet. "If people can't be on time – on the dot! – I don't want them around," she told young actors.

When she appeared in *Clash by Night* (1952), she bent over backwards for the ingénue Marilyn Monroe*. Actor Paul Douglas recalled: "Barbara said Marilyn was carefree and, even when Marilyn blew her lines again and again, Barbara was patient and understanding. I like Barbara, but never thought of her as being quite so sympathetic."

She continued seeing Robert Taylor until he finally got hitched to the German actress Ursula Thiess. After that she was seen out with active young men, though it was assumed that this was simply a beard. The studio worked hard on her image. The rumour mill linked her name to grieving widower Jean-Pierre Aumont*, producer Norman Krasna and Sear Roebuck heir, Armand Deutsch. Pictures were cropped to make it appear that she having dinner alone with Robert Wagner*, though Clifton Webb was also in tow.

"It's all nonsense," said Wagner. "This silly gossip has certainly hurt my chance for a real friendship with a fine woman and great actress."

She usually spent her time at home drinking and relaxing with her loyal maid Hariett Coray. She was an intensely private person and her press agent, Helen Ferguson, said that her personal life was exactly that – personal.

Unfortunately there seems to have been a slip-up with someone who was not nearly so reticent. Tallulah Bankhead* claimed to have bedded her. According to the *Pink Panther* lesbian Capucine*, Barbara was "sapphically inclined". She had come across various women she had bedded, including some famous names. Capucine also claimed that this was why Barbara Stanwyck and Bette Davis hated each other.

"When Miss Davis was new to movies, she was in a picture with Miss Stanwyck," she said – it was *So Big!* (1932), adapted from the novel by the lesbian author Edna Ferber. "And Miss Stanwyck, she tried to approach Bette Davis, who screamed and said no, no, never. So Barbara Stanwyck was very hurt, especially after Bette Davis became the bigger star."

Capucine also heard that on *Clash by Night*, where Barbara was so kind to Marilyn Monroe*, "the two became good friends, but more than that ... This is what someone said who worked on their movie". Being a veteran of the Hollywood glamour-girl gay scene, Capucine thought this was "very possible". She herself had been approached by Joan Crawford*, who had been turned down by Marilyn.

In *Walk on the Wild Side* (1962), Capucine had played a lesbian opposite Barbara but, being Hollywood, there was no kissing.

"But I would not have minded," said Capucine. "Why should I?"

In 1981, the *Hollywood Star* gave Barbara Stanwyck headline billing in their list of Hollywood's top 70 bisexual actresses. Barbara speculated that they used the term "bisexual" rather than "lesbian" for legal reasons. She was very defensive in interviews after this exposure, particularly over the nature of her marriage to Robert Taylor*.

Asked to write her autobiography, she steadfastly refused, saying: "Unless I told the whole truth, it would be silly to write a book. Since I'm not going to let it all hang out, I'm not going to write a book."

Don't worry, dear. I'll do it for you.

* The Daisy Chain

A
sterisks in the text indicate that the person has appeared in another book in the *Sex Lives* ... series. Starred figures, plus those who appear for the first time elsewhere in this volume, appear in alphabetic order below. Now you too can start to play Truman Capote's* game "International Daisy Chain" at home – or, better, in bed. You could even play it for a forfeit, Strip Daisy Chain perhaps. Pick any two people from this list and see how many lovers you need to make a daisy chain between them. The player who can make the chain with the least lovers wins. According to Capote*, Mercedes de Acosta* – featured in this volume – is the wild card. With Mercedes, he said: "You could get to anyone – from Pope John XXIII* to John F. Kennedy* – in one move." Remember, though, there are plenty more links out there in the rest of my *Sex Lives* ... series.

Acosta, Mercedes de – *Sex Lives of the Hollywood Goddesses, Sex Lives of the Hollywood Idols, The Sex Lives of Famous Lesbians*
Agrippina – *Sex Lives of the Roman Emperors*
Apollinaire, Guillaume – *Sex Lives of the Great Artists*
Amherst, Lord Jeffery – *Sex Lives of the Famous Gays*
Anne, Queen – *Sex Lives of the Kings and Queens of England*
Anthony, Susan B. – *The Sex Lives of Famous Lesbians*
Ashley, Lady Sylvia – *Sex Lives of the Hollywood Idols, Sex Lives of the Hollywood Goddesses, Sex Lives of the Hollywood Goddesses 2*
Atthis – *The Sex Lives of Famous Lesbians*
Aumont, Jean-Pierre – *Sex Lives of the Hollywood Goddesses, Sex Lives of the Hollywood Goddesses 2*
Bankhead, Tallulah – *Sex Lives of the Hollywood Goddesses, Sex Lives of the Hollywood Idols, Sex Lives of the Hollywood Goddesses 2*
Barney, Natalie – *The Sex Lives of Famous Lesbians*
Barrymore, Ethel – *Sex Lives of the Hollywood Idols*
Bayreuth – *Sex Lives of the Great Dictators*

Beaton, Cecil – *Sex Lives of the Hollywood Goddesses*

Beery, Wallace – *Sex Lives of the Hollywood Idols, Sex Lives of the Hollywood Goddesses*

Benchley, Robert – *Sex Lives of the Hollywood Goddesses*

Bergman, Ingrid – *Sex Lives of the Hollywood Idols*

Bernhardt, Sarah – *Sex Lives of the Kings and Queens of England, Sex Lives of the Famous Gays*

Blondell, Joan – *Sex Lives of the Hollywood Idols*

Bogart, Humphrey – *Sex Lives of the Hollywood Idols, Sex Lives of the Hollywood Goddesses, Sex Lives of the Hollywood Goddesses 2*

Bonaparte, Napoleon – *Sex Lives of the Great Dictators, Sex Lives of the Kings and Queens of England, Sex Lives of the Popes, Sex Lives of the Famous Gays*

Bonheur, Rosa – *The Sex Lives of Famous Lesbians*

Bonmariage, Sylvain – *The Sex Lives of Famous Lesbians*

Botticelli, Sandro – *Sex Lives of the Great Artists*

Brando, Marlon – *Sex Lives of the Hollywood Idols, Sex Lives of the Hollywood Goddesses, Sex Lives of the Hollywood Goddesses 2*

Braques, Georges – *Sex Lives of the Hollywood Goddesses*

Brooks, Louise – *Sex Lives of the Hollywood Idols, Sex Lives of the Hollywood Goddesses*

Brooks, Romaine – *The Sex Lives of Famous Lesbians*

Bruce, Virginia – *Sex Lives of the Hollywood Goddesses 2*

Bullitt, William – *Sex Lives of the US Presidents (Sex Lives of the Presidents in the US)*

Burne-Jones, Edward – *Sex Lives of the Great Artists*

Buzzell, Eddie – *Sex Lives of the Hollywood Goddesses*

Campbell, Mrs Patrick – *The Sex Lives of Famous Lesbians*

Capote, Truman – *Sex Lives of the Hollywood Goddesses, Sex Lives of the Hollywood Goddesses 2, Sex Lives of the Famous Gays*

Capra, Frank – *Sex Lives of the Hollywood Idols*

Capucine – *Sex Lives of the Hollywood Goddesses 2*

Caron, Leslie – *Sex Lives of the Hollywood Goddesses 2*

Chaplin, Charlie – *Sex Lives of the Hollywood Idols, Sex Lives of the Hollywood Goddesses*

Chevalier, Maurice – *Sex Lives of the Hollywood Goddesses, Sex Lives of the Hollywood Goddesses 2*

Churchill, Winston – *Sex Lives of the Kings and Queens of England, Sex Lives of the Great Dictators, Sex Lives of the Famous Gays, Sex Lives of the Hollywood Idols, Sex Lives of the Hollywood Goddesses, Sex Lives of the Hollywood Goddesses 2*

Claire, Ina – *Sex Lives of the Hollywood Idols, Sex Lives of the Hollywood Goddesses*

Clermont-Tonnerre, Lily, duchesse de – *The Sex Lives of Famous Lesbians*

Clinton, Bill – *Sex Lives of the US Presidents* (*Sex Lives of the Presidents* in the US)

Clinton, Hillary – *Sex Lives of the US Presidents* (*Sex Lives of the Presidents* in the US)

Cocteau, Jean – *Sex Lives of the Famous Gays*

Cohn, Harry – *Sex Lives of the Hollywood Goddesses, Sex Lives of the Hollywood Goddesses 2*

Colbert, Claudette – *Sex Lives of the Hollywood Idols, Sex Lives of the Hollywood Goddesses*

Colette – *The Sex Lives of Famous Lesbians, Sex Lives of the Hollywood Goddess 2*

Connolly, Cyril – *Sex Lives of the Great Dictators*

Cooper, Gary – *Sex Lives of the Hollywood Idols, Sex Lives of the Hollywood Goddesses, Sex Lives of the Hollywood Goddesses 2*

Coward, Noël – *Sex Lives of the Hollywood Idols, Sex Lives of the Hollywood Goddesses, Sex Lives of the Hollywood Goddesses 2, Sex Lives of the Kings and Queens of England, Sex Lives of the Great Artists*

Crawford, Joan – *Sex Lives of the Hollywood Goddesses, Sex Lives of the Hollywood Idols, Sex Lives of the Hollywood Goddesses 2*

Cukor, George – *Sex Lives of the Hollywood Idols, Sex Lives of the Hollywood Goddesses, Sex Lives of the Hollywood Goddesses 2*

Curzon, Lord – *Sex Lives of the Famous Gays*

Damira, Lili – *Sex Lives of the Hollywood Idols, Sex Lives of the Hollywood Goddesses 2*

D'Annunzio, Gabriele – *Sex Lives of the Great Dictators, Sex Lives of the Great Artists, Sex Lives of the Famous Gays*

Davies, Marion – *Sex Lives of the Hollywood Idols, Sex Lives of the Hollywood Goddesses*

Davis, Bette – *Sex Lives of the Hollywood Goddesses*

Debussy, Claude – *Sex Lives of the Great Composers, Sex Lives of the Great Artists*

Delarue-Mardrus, Lucie – *The Sex Lives of Famous Lesbians*

Dietrich, Marlene – *Sex Lives of the Hollywood Goddesses, Sex Lives of the Hollywood Idols, Sex Lives of the Famous Gays*

D'Orsay, Fifi – *Sex Lives of the Hollywood Goddesses*

Douglas, Lord Alfred – *Sex Lives of the Famous Gays*

Duncan, Isadora – *Sex Lives of the Great Artists, The Sex Lives of Famous Lesbians*

Edward, Prince – *Sex Lives of the Kings and Queens of England*

Edward VII (Bertie, Prince of Wales) – *Sex Lives of the Kings and Queens of England*

Edward VIII – *Sex Lives of the Kings and Queens of England, Sex Lives of the Famous Gays*

Elgar, Edward – *Sex Lives of the Great Composers*

Eugénie, Empress – *Sex Lives of the Great Dictators*

Fairbanks Sr, Douglas – *Sex Lives of the Hollywood Idols, Sex Lives of the Hollywood Goddesses, Sex Lives of the Hollywood Goddesses 2*

Fairbanks Jr, Douglas – *Sex Lives of the Hollywood Idols, Sex Lives of the Hollywood Goddesses, Sex Lives of the Hollywood Goddesses 2*

Flynn, Errol – *Sex Lives of the Hollywood Idols, Sex Lives of the Hollywood Goddesses, Sex Lives of the Hollywood Goddesses 2*

Forst, Willi – *Sex Lives of the Hollywood Goddesses*

Forster, E.M. – *Sex Lives of the Famous Gays*

France, Anatole – *Sex Lives of the Famous Gays*

Frasso, Countess Dorothy di – *Sex Lives of the Hollywood Idols, Sex Lives of Hollywood Goddesses 2, Sex Lives of the Great Dictators*

Freud, Sigmund – *Sex Lives of the Great Artists, Sex Lives of the Great Composers*

Gabin, Jean – *Sex Lives of the Hollywood Goddesses*

Gable, Clark – *Sex Lives of the Hollywood Idols, Sex Lives of the Hollywood Goddesses, Sex Lives of the Hollywood Goddesses 2*

Garbo, Greta – *Sex Lives of the Hollywood Goddesses*

Gardner, Ava – *Sex Lives of the Hollywood Idols, Sex Lives of the Hollywood Goddesses, Sex Lives of the Hollywood Goddesses 2*

George V, King – *Sex Lives of the Kings and Queens of England*

Gert, Valeska – *Sex Lives of the Hollywood Goddesses*

Gide, André – *Sex Lives of the Famous Gays*

Gilbert, John – *Sex Lives of the Hollywood Idols, Sex Lives of the Hollywood Goddesses, Sex Lives of the Hollywood Goddesses 2*

Gill, Eric – *Sex Lives of the Great Artists*

Goddard, Paulette – *Sex Lives of the Hollywood Idols, Sex Lives of the Hollywood Goddesses 2*

Golightly, Holly – *Sex Lives of the Hollywood Goddesses, Sex Lives of the Hollywood Goddesses 2*

Goudeket, Maurice – *The Sex Lives of Famous Lesbians*

Grainger, Percy – *Sex Lives of the Great Artists*

Grant, Duncan – *Sex Lives of the Famous Gays*

Grey, Virginia – *Sex Lives of the Hollywood Idols*

Haines, Billy – *Sex Lives of the Hollywood Idols*

Hall, Radclyffe – *The Sex Lives of Famous Lesbians*

Hauser, Gaylord – *Sex Lives of the Hollywood Goddesses*

Hayward, Susan – *Sex Lives of the Hollywood Idols, Sex Lives of the Hollywood Goddesses*

Hearst, William Randolph – *Sex Lives of the Hollywood Idols, Sex Lives of the Hollywood Goddesses*

Hemingway, Ernest – *Sex Lives of the Hollywood Idols, Sex Lives of the Hollywood Goddesses*

Henry VIII – *Sex Lives of the Kings and Queens of England*

Hepburn, Audrey – *Sex Lives of the Hollywood Goddesses, Sex Lives of the Hollywood Goddesses 2*

Hepburn, Katharine – *Sex Lives of the Hollywood Goddesses, Sex Lives of the Hollywood Idols, Sex Lives of the Hollywood Goddesses 2*

Hickok, Lorena – *Sex Lives of the US Presidents (Sex Lives of the Presidents in the US)*

Hitler, Adolf – *Sex Lives of the Great Dictators, Sex Lives of the Famous Gays, Sex Lives of the Kings and Queens of England*

Hoang, Nadine – *The Sex Lives of Famous Lesbians*

Hopper, Hedda – *Sex Lives of the Hollywood Idols, Sex Lives of the Hollywood Goddesses, Sex Lives of the Hollywood Goddesses 2*

Howard, Hughes – *Sex Lives of the Hollywood Idols, Sex Lives of the Hollywood Goddesses, Sex Lives of the Hollywood Goddesses 2*

Isherwood, Christopher – *Sex Lives of the Famous Gays*

Jacob, Max – *Sex Lives of the Great Artists*

Jaray, Hans – *Sex Lives of the Hollywood Goddesses*

John, Augustus – *Sex Lives of the Great Artists*

John XXIII, Pope – *Sex Lives of the Popes*

Joséphine, de Beauharnais, Empress – *Sex Lives of the Great Dictators*

Juan, Don – *Sex Lives of the Great Composers*

Kennedy, Edward – *Sex Lives of the US Presidents (Sex Lives of the Presidents in the US)*

Kennedy, John F. – *Sex Lives of the US Presidents (Sex Lives of the Presidents in the US), Sex Lives of the Hollywood Goddesses, Sex Lives of the Hollywood Goddesses 2*

Keppel, Alice – *Sex Lives of the Kings and Queens of England*

Keynes, Maynard – *Sex Lives of the Famous Gays*

Kraly, Hans – *Sex Lives of the Hollywood Goddesses*

Lamarr, Hedy – *Sex Lives of the Hollywood Idols, Sex Lives of the Hollywood Goddesses 2*

Lamour, Dorothy – *Sex Lives of the Famous Gays*

Lanchester, Elsa – *Sex Lives of the Famous Gays*

Laughton, Charles – *Sex Lives of the Famous Gays, Sex Lives of the Hollywood Goddesses, Sex Lives of the Hollywood Goddesses 2*

LeHand, Marguerite "Missy" – *Sex Lives of the US Presidents (Sex Lives of the Presidents in the US)*

Levant, Oscar – *Sex Lives of the Hollywood Goddesses 2*

Liszt, Cosima – *Sex Lives of the Great Composers*

Loos, Anita – *Sex Lives of the Hollywood Goddesses, Sex Lives of the Hollywood Idols, Sex Lives of the Hollywood Goddesses 2*

Louÿs, Pierre – *Sex Lives of the Famous Gays*

Lubitsch, Ernst – *Sex Lives of the Hollywood Idols, Sex Lives of the Hollywood Goddesses, Sex Lives of the Hollywood Goddesses 2*

McCarthy, Senator Joe – *Sex Lives of the US Presidents (Sex Lives of the Presidents in the US), Sex Lives of the Famous Gays*

MacDonald, Jeanette – *Sex Lives of the Hollywood Idols*

Marx, Karl – *Sex Lives of the Great Dictators*

Mary, Queen – *Sex Lives of the Kings and Queens of England*

Mata Hari – *The Sex Lives of Famous Lesbians*

Matisse, Henri – *Sex Lives of the Great Artists*

Matul, Tamara "Tami" – *Sex Lives of the Hollywood Goddesses*

Maugham, W. Somerset – *Sex Lives of the Famous Gays*

Mayer, Louis B. – *Sex Lives of the Hollywood Idols, Sex Lives of the Hollywood Goddesses, Sex Lives of the Hollywood Goddesses 2*

Mendelssohn, Felix – *Sex Lives of the Great Composers*

Mercer Rutherford, Lucy Page – *Sex Lives of the US Presidents (Sex Lives of the Presidents in the US)*

Miller, Earl – *Sex Lives of the US Presidents (Sex Lives of the Presidents in the US)*

Monroe, Marilyn – *Sex Lives of the Hollywood Idols, Sex Lives of the Hollywood Goddesses, Sex Lives of the Hollywood Goddesses 2*

Morrell, Lady Ottoline – *Sex Lives of the Great Artists, Sex Lives of the Famous Gays*

Mozart, Wolfgang Amadeus – *Sex Lives of the Great Composers*

Mussolini, Benito – *Sex Lives of the Great Dictators, Sex Lives of the Famous Gays*

Navarro, Ramon – *Sex Lives of the Hollywood Goddesses*

Nazimova, Alla – *Sex Lives of the Hollywood Goddesses, Sex Lives of the Hollywood Idols*

Newman, Paul – *Sex Lives of the Hollywood Idols*

Nijinsky, Vaslav – *Sex Lives of the Famous Gays, Sex Lives of the Great Artists, Sex Lives of the Great Composers*

Novak, Kim – *Sex Lives of the Hollywood Idols, Sex Lives of the Hollywood*

Goddesses, *Sex Lives of the Hollywood Goddesses 2*

Novello, Ivor – *Sex Lives of the Hollywood Goddesses 2*

Onassis, Aristotle – *Sex Lives of the US Presidents* (*Sex Lives of the Presidents in the US*), *Sex Lives of the Great Dictators*, *Sex Lives of the Hollywood Goddesses*

Palmer, Evalina – *The Sex Lives of Famous Lesbians*

Parker-Bowles, Camilla – *Sex Lives of the Kings and Queens of England*

Philip II of Spain – *Sex Lives of the Kings and Queens of England*

Picasso, Pablo – *Sex Lives of the Great Artists*

Pickford, Mary – *Sex Lives of the Hollywood Idols*, *Sex Lives of the Hollywood Goddesses*

Polignac, princesse Edmond de – *The Sex Lives of Famous Lesbians*

Pougy, Liane de – *The Sex Lives of Famous Lesbians*

Powell, Eleanor – *Sex Lives of the Hollywood Goddesses 2*

Proust, Marcel – *Sex Lives of the Famous Gays*

Puccini, Giacomo – *Sex Lives of the Great Composers*

Queensberry, Marquis of – *Sex Lives of the Famous Gays*

Rambova, Natacha (Winifred Hudnut) – *Sex Lives of the Hollywood Goddesses*, *Sex Lives of the Hollywood Idols*

Reinhardt, Max – *Sex Lives of the Hollywood Goddesses*

Reynolds, Debbie – *Sex Lives of the Hollywood Goddesses 2*

Rio, Dolores del – *Sex Lives of the Hollywood Goddesses*, *Sex Lives of the Hollywood Idols*

Rodin, Auguste – *Sex Lives of the Great Artists*, *Sex Lives of the Great Composers*

Rogers, Ginger – *Sex Lives of the Hollywood Goddesses*, *Sex Lives of the Hollywood Goddesses 2*, *Sex Lives of the Famous Gays*

Roosevelt, Eleanor – *Sex Lives of the US Presidents* (*Sex Lives of the Presidents in the US*), *Sex Lives of the Hollywood Goddesses*, *The Sex Lives of Famous Lesbians*

Roosevelt, Franklin Delano – *Sex Lives of the US Presidents* (*Sex Lives of the Presidents in the US*), *Sex Lives of the Great Dictators*, *Sex Lives of the Famous Gays*

Roosevelt, Theodore – *Sex Lives of the US Presidents* (*Sex Lives of the Presidents in the US*)

Rossetti, Dante Gabriel – *Sex Lives of the Great Artists*

Russell, Jane – *Sex Lives of the Hollywood Idols*, *Sex Lives of the Hollywood Goddesses*, *Sex Lives of the Hollywood Goddesses 2*

Sackville-West, Vita – *Sex Lives of the Famous Gays*

Saint-Saëns, Camille – *Sex Lives of the Great Composers*

Sand, Georges – *Sex Lives of the Great Composers*

Sartre, Jean-Paul – *Sex Lives of the Famous Gays*

Sappho of Lesbos – *The Sex Lives of Famous Lesbians*

Schenck, Joseph M. – *Sex Lives of the Hollywood Idols, Sex Lives of the Hollywood Goddesses, Sex Lives of the Hollywood Goddesses 2*

Schiaparelli, Elsa – *Sex Lives of the Great Artists*

Schlee, George – *Sex Lives of the Hollywood Goddesses*

Schlee, Valentina – *Sex Lives of the Hollywood Goddesses*

Schulberg – *Sex Lives of the Hollywood Idols, Sex Lives of the Hollywood Goddesses*

Schumann, Robert – *Sex Lives of the Famous Gays*

Shaw, George Bernard – *Sex Lives of the Famous Gays, Sex Lives of the Hollywood Goddesses, Sex Lives of the Hollywood Goddesses 2*

Sieber, Rudi – *Sex Lives of the Hollywood Goddesses*

Simpson, Wallace – *Sex Lives of the Kings and Queens of England, Sex Lives of the Great Dictators, Sex Lives of the Famous Gays*

Smyth, Ethel – *The Sex Lives of Famous Lesbians*

Spellman, Cardinal – *Sex Lives of the Famous Gays*

Stanwyck, Barbara – *The Sex Lives of Famous Lesbians, Sex Lives of the Hollywood Idols, Sex Lives of the Hollywood Goddesses*

Stein, Gertrude – *The Sex Lives of Famous Lesbians, Sex Lives of the Great Artists, Sex Lives of the Hollywood Goddesses*

Sternberg, Josef von – *Sex Lives of the Hollywood Idols, Sex Lives of the Hollywood Goddesses, Sex Lives of the Hollywood Goddesses 2*

Stolowski, Leopold – *Sex Lives of the Hollywood Goddesses*

Strachey, Lytton – *Sex Lives of the Famous Gays*

Stravinsky, Igor – *Sex Lives of the Great Composers, Sex Lives of the Great Artists, Sex Lives of the Famous Gays*

Sullivan, Arthur – *Sex Lives of the Great Composers*

Taylor, Elizabeth – *Sex Lives of the Hollywood Idols, Sex Lives of the Hollywood Goddesses, Sex Lives of the Hollywood Goddesses 2*

Taylor, Robert – *Sex Lives of the Hollywood Idols, Sex Lives of the Hollywood Goddesses, Sex Lives of the Hollywood Goddesses 2*

Tchaikovsky, Pyotr Ilyich – *Sex Lives of the Great Composers*

Temple, Shirley – *Sex Lives of the Hollywood Goddesses*

Thalberg, Irving – *Sex Lives of the Hollywood Idols, Sex Lives of the Hollywood Goddesses, Sex Lives of the Hollywood Goddesses 2*

Toklas, Alice B. – *Sex Lives of the Hollywood Goddesses, Sex Lives of the Great Artists, The Sex Lives of Famous Lesbians*

Troubridge, Lady Una – *The Sex Lives of Famous Lesbians*
Turner, Lana – *Sex Lives of the Hollywood Idols, Sex Lives of the Hollywood Goddesses, Sex Lives of the Hollywood Goddesses 2*
Valentino, Rudolph – *Sex Lives of the Hollywood Idols*
Valéry, Paul – *Sex Lives of the Famous Gays*
Vanderbilt, Gloria – *Sex Lives of the Hollywood Goddesses*
Verdi, Giuseppe – *Sex Lives of the Great Composers*
Victor Emanuel II, King of Italy – *Sex Lives of the Great Composers*
Victoria, Queen – *Sex Lives of the Kings and Queens of England, Sex Lives of the Famous Gays*
Vinci, Leonardo da – *Sex Lives of the Great Artists*
Virgin Mary – *Sex Lives of the Popes*
Vivien, Renée (Pauline M. Tarn) – *The Sex Lives of Famous Lesbians*
Wagner, Richard – *Sex Lives of the Great Composers*
Walewska, Marie – *Sex Lives of the Great Dictators*
Warhol, Andy – *Sex Lives of the Great Artists*
Warner, Jack – *Sex Lives of the Hollywood Idols, Sex Lives of the Hollywood Goddesses 2*
Wayne, John – *Sex Lives of the Hollywood Goddesses*
Webb, Clifton – *Sex Lives of the Hollywood Idols*
Welles, Orson – *Sex Lives of the Hollywood Idols, Sex Lives of the Hollywood Goddesses, Sex Lives of the Hollywood Goddesses 2*
West, Mae – *Sex Lives of the Hollywood Goddesses 2, Sex Lives of the Hollywood Idols, Sex Lives of the Great Artists*
Wilde, Dolly – *The Sex Lives of Famous Lesbians*
Wilde, Oscar – *Sex Lives of the Famous Gays*
Wilde, Willie – *Sex Lives of the Famous Gays*
William II, Kaiser – *Sex Lives of the Kings and Queens of England*
William of Orange – *Sex Lives of the Kings and Queens of England*
Windsor, Duchess of – *Sex Lives of the Kings and Queens of England, Sex Lives of the Great Dictators, Sex Lives of the Famous Gays*
Windsor, Sophie – *Sex Lives of the Kings and Queens of England*
Woolf, Virginia – *The Sex Lives of Famous Lesbians, Sex Lives of the Famous Gays*
Ziegfeld, Florenz – *Sex Lives of the Hollywood Idols, Sex Lives of the Hollywood Goddesses, Sex Lives of the Hollywood Goddesses 2*

Bibiliography

Adventures of the Mind by Natalie Clifford Barney, New York University Press, New York, 1992

Agnes Moorehead – A Bio-Bibliography by Lynn Kear, Greenwood Press, Westport, Connecticut, 1992

Agnes Moorehead – A Very Private Person by Dr Warren Sherk, Dorrance and Company, Philadelphia, 1976

Album Secret by Natalie Barney, Eva Palmer and Renée Vivien, Éditions à L'Ecart, Muizon, 1984

The Angel and the Perverts by Lucie Delarue-Mardrus, New York University Press, New York, 1995

Barbara Stanwyck by Al DiOrio, Coward-McCann, Inc, New York, 1983

Before Sexuality – The Construction of Erotic Experience in the Ancient Greek World by John J. Winkler *et al*, Princeton University Press, Princeton, New Jersey, 1990

Bessie – Empress of the Blues by Chris Albertson, Abacus, London, 1972

Bessie Smith by Jackie Kay, Absolute Press, New York, 1997

The Bessie Smith Companion by Edward Brooks, Bayou Press, Oxford, 1989

Bessie Smith – Empress of the Blues by Elaine Feinstein, Penguin, Harmondsworth, Middlesex, 1985

Beyond the Well of Loneliness – The Fiction of Radclyffe Hall by Claudia Stillman Franks, Avebury, London, 1982

The Biography of Alice B. Toklas by Linda Simon, Bison Books, New York, 1991

Biography of Mademoiselle Rosa Bonheur by F. Lepelle de Bois-Gallais, E. Gambery and Co, London, 1856

Blues Legacies and Black Feminism by Angela V. Davis, Pantheon Books, New York, 1998

Colette – A Life by Herbert Lottman, Minerva, London, 1991

Colette – A Taste for Life by Yvonne Mitchell, Weidenfeld and Nicolson, London, 1975

Colette – Free and Fettered by Michèle Sarde, Michael Joseph, London, 1978

Creating Colette: Volume One – From Ingenue to Libertine by Claude

Francis and Fernande Gontier, Steerforth Press, South Royalton, Vermont, 1998

The Constraints of Desire – The Anthropology of Sex and Gender in Ancient Greece by John J. Winkler, Routledge, New York, 1990

Eleanor Roosevelt by Blanche Wiesen Cook, Bloomsbury, London, 1997

The Eleanor Roosevelt Encyclopedia edited by Maurine H. Beasley, Holly C. Schulman and Henry R. Beasley, Greenwood Press, Westport, Connecticut, 2001

Eros – The Myth of Ancient Greek Sexuality by Bruce S. Thornton, Westview Press, Boulder, Colorado, 1997

Everybody Who Was Anybody – A Biography of Gertrude Stein by Janet Hobhouse, Weidenfeld and Nicolson, London, 1975

From Sappho to De Sade – Moments in the History of Sexuality by Jan Bremmer, Routledge, London, 1989

Games of Venus – An Anthology of Greek and Roman Erotic Verse from Sappho to Ovid, Routledge, New York, 1991

The Gay 100 by Paul Russell, Kensington Books, New York, 1995

Gertrude and Alice by Diana Souhami, Weidenfeld and Nicolson, London, 1991

Gertrude Stein by Jane Palatini Bowers, Macmillan, London, 1993

Gertrude Stein Remembered by Linda Simon, University of Nebraska Press, Lincoln, 1994

The Girls – Sappho Goes to Hollywood by Diana McLellan, Robson Books, London, 2000

Here Lies the Heart by Mercedes de Acosta, Andre Deutsch, London, 1960

Hollywood Lesbians by Boze Hadleigh, Barricade Books, New York, 1994

Idylle Saphique by Liane de Pougy, Jean-Claude Lattès, Paris, 1979

Leonard and Virginia Woolf by Peter F. Alexander, Harvester Wheatsheaf, Hemel Hempstead, 1992

Liane de Pougy – Courtisane, princesse et sainte by Jean Chalon, Flammarion, Paris, 1994

The Life and Death of Radclyffe Hall by Lady Una Troubridge, Hammond Hammond, London, 1961

The Life and Work of Eleanor Roosevelt by Sarah J. Purcell and L. Edward Purcell, Alpha Books, Indianapolis, 2002

Looking Back – Recollections by Colette, The Women's Press, London, 1987

Love as War: Homeric Allusion in the Poetry of Sappho by Leah Rissman, Verlag Anton Hain, Königstein, 1983

Love, Sex and Marriage in Ancient Greece – A guide to the private life of the

Ancient Greeks by Nikos A. Vrissimtizis, private printing, Paraskevi, Greece, 1997

Loving Garbo by Hugo Vickers, Jonathan Cape, London, 1994

Mother of the Blues – A Study of Ma Rainey by Sandra R. Lieb, The University of Massachusetts Press, Boston, 1981

My Apprenticeships – Music-Hall Sidelights by Colette, Penguin Books, London, 1967

My Blue Notebooks by Liane de Pougy, Andre Deutsch, London, 1979

Noël Coward and Radclyffe Hall – Kindred Spirits by Terry Castle, Columbia University Press, New York, 1996

No Ordinary Time – Franklin and Eleanor Roosevelt: The Home Front in World War II by Doris Kearns Goodwin, Simon and Schuster, New York, 1994

Not a Passing Phase – Reclaiming Lesbians in History 1840–1985 by the Lesbian History Group, The Women's Press, London, 1989

The One Who is Legion or A.D. After-Life by Natalie Clifford Barney, Eric Partridge Ltd, London, 1930

Our Three Selves – The Life of Radclyffe Hall by Michael Baker, Hamish Hamilton, London, 1985

Portrait of a Marriage by Nigel Nicolson, Weidenfeld and Nicolson, London, 1973

Portraits to the Wall – Historic Lesbian Lives Unveiled by Rose Collis, Cassell, London, 1994

Radclyffe Hall at the Well of Loneliness – A Sapphic Chronicle by Lovat Dickson, Collins, London, 1975

Radclyffe Hall – A Woman Called John by Sally Cline, John Murray, London, 1997

Reflecting on The Well of Loneliness by Rebecca O'Rourke, Routledge, London, 1989

Rosa Bonheur – The Artist's (Auto) Biography by Anna Klumpke, University of Michigan Press, Ann Arbor, 1997

Rosa Bonheur – A Life and Legend by Dore Ashton, Secker and Warburg, London, 1981

Rosa Bonheur – Reminiscences by Theodore Stanton, Andrew Melrose, London, 1910

The Sappho Companion by Margaret Reynolds, Chatto and Windus, London, 2000

The Sappho History by Margaret Reynolds, Palgrave, New York, 2003

Sappho's Sweetbitter Songs – Configuration of Female and Male in Ancient Greek Lyric by Lyn Hatherly Wilson, Routledge, London 1996

Secrets of the Flesh – A Life of Colette by Judith Thurman, Bloomsbury, London. 1999

Sexual Life in Ancient Greece by Hans Licht, Constable, London, 1994

Stanwyck by Jane Ellen Wayne, Robson Books, London, 1986

Souvenirs indiscrets by Natalie Clifford Barney, Flammarion, Paris, 1960

Three Roosevelts – Patrician Leaders Who Transformed America by James MacGregor Burns and Susan Dunn, Atlantic Monthly Press, New York, 2001

The Trials of Radclyffe Hall by Diana Souhami, Virago Press, London, 1999

Until the Break of Day by Mercedes de Acosta, Longmans, New York, 1929

A Very Close Conspiracy – Vanessa Bell and Virginia Woolf by Jane Dunn, Jonathan Cape, London, 1990

Virginia Woolf by Clare Hanson, Macmillan, London, 1994

Virginia Woolf – A Biography by Quentin Bell, The Hogarth Press, London, 1990

Virginia Woolf – Lesbian Readings edited by Eileen Barrett and Patricia Cramer, New York University Press, New York, 1997

Virginia Woolf's Women by Vanessa Curtis, Robert Hale, London, 2002

Virginia Woolf – A Writer's Life by Lyndall Gordon, Oxford University Press, Oxford, 1986

Vita – The Life of Vita Sackville-West by Victoria Glendinning, Penguin, London, 1984

Who's Who in Gay and Lesbian History, edited by Robert Aldrich and Gary Witherspoon, Routledge, London, 2001

Without Precedent – The Life and Career of Eleanor Roosevelt edited by Joan Hoff-Wilson and Marjorie Lightman, Indiana University Press, Bloomington, 1984

Women and Slaves in Greco-Roman Culture edited by Sandra R. Joshel and Sheila Murnaghan, Routledge, London,1998

Women in Ancient Greece by Sue Blundell, British Museum Press, London, 1995

Women of Bloomsbury – Virginia, Vanessa and Carrington by Mary Ann Caws, Routledge, New York, 1990

Your John – The Love Letters of Radclyffe Hall edited by Joanne Glasgow, New York University Press, New York, 1997

Index